"Because evil is a term fraught with religious overtones, it tends to be under-theorized in our largely secular contemporary culture. Yet something like evil continues to exist, arguably more forcefully today than ever, so the authors of this timely and important book assert. They argue boldly that understanding the continued presence of evil in the modern world requires reconceiving evil through the mythical figure of the trickster, a cross-cultural symbol that represents the perennial temptation to ignore the inherent limits of human thought and action. A wide ranging study that draws on multiple disciplinary sources, Horvath and Szakolczai illustrate forcefully how contemporary efforts to maximize productivity across all sectors of our social order violates the ethos of limits, and only liberates further the forces of destruction. In an age of increasingly mindless (and therefore runaway) processes, we would do well to heed the message of this significant study."
– *Gilbert Germain, Professor of Political Thought at the University of Prince Edward Island, Canada*

"A complex and timely meditation on the nature of evil in human societies, reaching back into the distant past – while not all will agree with its methods or conclusions, this book offers provocative ideas for consideration by anthropologists, philosophers, and culture historians."
– *David Wengrow, Professor of Comparative Archaeology, University College London, UK*

"This book offers an original and thought-provoking engagement with a problem for which we still lack adequate perspectives: the disastrous experience of advanced modernity with what we can provisionally call demonic power."
– *Johann Arnason, Emeritus Professor of Sociology, La Trobe University, Australia*

"Horvath and Szakolczai provide a remarkable service in bringing the neglected figure of the trickster into the spotlight. This is a book to be recommended and savoured as a fillip to the sociological imagination today."
– *Chris Rojek, Professor of Sociology, City University of London, UK*

The Political Sociology and Anthropology of Evil: Tricksterology

This book offers a new approach to the problem of evil through an examination of the anthropological figure of the 'trickster'. A lesser known and much more recent term than evil, the authors use the trickster to facilitate a greater understanding of the return of evil in the modern era. Instead of simply opposing 'good' and 'evil', the figure of the trickster is used to pursue the trajectories of similarities and quasi-similarities through imitation.

After engaging with the trickster as presented in comparative anthropology and mythology, where it appears in tales and legends as a strange, erratic outsider, the authors seek to gain an inside perspective of trickster knowledge through an examination of mythology and the classical world, including both philosophers and poets. The book then goes on to trace the trickster through prehistory, using archaeological evidence to complement the diverse narratives. In this way, and by investigating the knowledge and customs surrounding evil, the authors use the figure of the trickster to provide an unprecedented diagnosis of the contemporary world, where external, mechanical rationality has become taken for granted and even considered as foundational in politics, economics, and technologised science. The authors advance the idea that the modern world, with its global free markets, mass mediatic democracy and technologised science, represents a universalisation of trickster logic. *The Political Sociology and Anthropology of Evil: Tricksterology* will be of interest to scholars working in the fields of social theory, political anthropology and political sociology, as well as those interested in the ways in which evil can infiltrate reality.

Agnes Horvath is a founding and chief editor of *International Political Anthropology*. She taught in Hungary, Ireland and Italy, and was affiliate visiting scholar and supervisor at Cambridge University. She is the author of *Modernism and Charisma*, the co-author of *The Dissolution of Communist Power: The Case of Hungary* and *Walking into the Void: A Historical Sociology and Political Anthropology of Walking*, and the co-editor of *Breaking Boundaries: Varieties of Liminality*, *Walling, Boundaries and Liminality,* and *Divinization and Technology: The Political Anthropology of Subversion*.

Arpad Szakolczai is professor of sociology at University College Cork, Ireland and previously taught social theory at the European University Institute in Florence. He is the author of *Max Weber and Michel Foucault: Parallel Life-Works*, *Reflexive Historical Sociology, Sociology, Religion and Grace: A Quest for the Renaissance, The Genesis of Modernity, Comedy and the Public Sphere, Novels and the Sociology of the Contemporary,* and *Permanent Liminality and Modernity*, and the co-author of *Walking into the Void: A Historical Sociology and Political Anthropology of Walking* and *From Anthropology to Social Theory: Rethinking the Social Sciences*.

Contemporary Liminality

Series editors:
Arpad Szakolczai, University College Cork, Ireland

Series advisory board:
Agnes Horvath, University College Cork, Ireland
Bjørn Thomassen, Roskilde University, Denmark
Harald Wydra, University of Cambridge, UK

This series constitutes a forum for works that make use of concepts such as 'imitation', 'trickster' or 'schismogenesis', but which chiefly deploy the notion of 'liminality', as the basis of a new, anthropologically-focused paradigm in social theory. With its versatility and range of possible uses rivalling and even going beyond mainstream concepts such as 'system' 'structure' or 'institution', liminality is increasingly considered a new master concept that promises to spark a renewal in social thought.

In spite of the fact that charges of Eurocentrism or even 'moderno-centrism' are widely discussed in sociology and anthropology, it remains the case that most theoretical tools in the social sciences continue to rely on taken-for-granted approaches developed from within the modern Western intellectual tradition, whilst concepts developed on the basis of extensive anthropological evidence and which challenged commonplaces of modernist thinking, have been either marginalised and ignored, or trivialised. By challenging the assumed neo-Kantian and neo-Hegelian foundations of modern social theory, and by helping to shed new light on the fundamental ideas of major figures in social theory, such as Nietzsche, Dilthey, Weber, Elias, Voegelin, Foucault and Koselleck, whilst also establishing connections between the perspectives gained through modern social and cultural anthropology and the central concerns of classical philosophical anthropology *Contemporary Liminality* offers a new direction in social thought.

Titles in this series

8. The Spectacle of Critique
From Philosophy to Cacophony
Tom Boland

9. Divinization and Technology
The Political Anthropology of Subversion
Edited by Agnes Horvath, Camil Roman and Gilbert Germain

10. The Political Sociology and Anthropology of Evil: Tricksterology
Agnes Horvath and Arpad Szakolczai

For more information about this series, please visit: https://www.routledge.com/sociology/series/ASHSER1435

The Political Sociology and Anthropology of Evil: Tricksterology

Agnes Horvath and Arpad Szakolczai

LONDON AND NEW YORK

First published 2020
by Routledge
2 Park Square, Milton Park, Abingdon, Oxon OX14 4RN

and by Routledge
52 Vanderbilt Avenue, New York, NY 10017

Routledge is an imprint of the Taylor & Francis Group, an informa business

© 2020 Agnes Horvath and Arpad Szakolczai

The right of Agnes Horvath and Arpad Szakolczai to be identified as authors of this work has been asserted by them in accordance with sections 77 and 78 of the Copyright, Designs and Patents Act 1988.

All rights reserved. No part of this book may be reprinted or reproduced or utilised in any form or by any electronic, mechanical, or other means, now known or hereafter invented, including photocopying and recording, or in any information storage or retrieval system, without permission in writing from the publishers.

Trademark notice: Product or corporate names may be trademarks or registered trademarks, and are used only for identification and explanation without intent to infringe.

Every effort has been made to contact copyright-holders. Please advise the publisher of any errors or omissions, and these will be corrected in subsequent editions.

British Library Cataloguing-in-Publication Data
A catalogue record for this book is available from the British Library

Library of Congress Cataloging-in-Publication Data
Names: Horvath, Agnes, 1957- author. | Szakolczai, Arpad, author.
Title: The political sociology and anthropology of evil : tricksterology / Agnes Horvath and Arpad Szakolczai.
Description: First Edition. | New York : Routledge, [2019] |
Includes bibliographical references and index.
Identifiers: LCCN 2019025306 (print) | LCCN 2019025307 (ebook) |
ISBN 9781138312142 Hardback
Subjects: LCSH: Political sociology. | Tricksters.
Classification: LCC JA76 .H675 2019 (print) | LCC JA76 (ebook) |
DDC 306.2--dc23
LC record available at https://lccn.loc.gov/2019025306
LC ebook record available at https://lccn.loc.gov/2019025307

ISBN: 978-1-138-31214-2 (hbk)
ISBN: 978-0-429-45841-5 (ebk)

Typeset in Times New Roman
by Taylor & Francis Books

**In memory of Alessandro Pizzorno
unforgettable teacher and colleague**

Contents

List of figures   x
Preface   xi
Acknowledgements   xiv

Introduction   1

PART I
Presenting the trickster   13

1. The trickster in anthropology: The figure as seen from the outside   15
2. Techniques of trickster entrapment: The nets of spiders and magicians   24
3. Hermes the trickster and the Kabeiroi: Moving towards evil   43
4. Plato's *Theaetetus*: The Sophists and secret trickster knowledge   65
5. Vedic tricksterology   79

PART II
Tracking trickster traces: evil machinations   103

6. Prehistoric trickster: Archaic outlines of evil   105
7. The troglodytes: Evil proto-scientific methods for transformation   119
8. Monsters: Creatures of the flux   142
9. Evil alchemy: The incommensurable   159

Concluding comments: On methodology in tricksterology   180

Bibliography   186
Name index   193
Subject index   196

Figures

6.1 Phallic Isturitz trickster. 108
6.2 Big-bellied trickster at Tassili, with tail and hanging phallus; Neolithic mural painting. 109
6.3 Mime trickster in the La Marche cave: the animal profile. 112
6.4 The Dog–Man hybrid trickster, Gourdan cave, Dordogne, bone incision. 113
6.5 Phallic Mesolithic figurine, Lepinski Vir, Serbia, *c*.6000 BC. 114
7.1 Cross view of several floors together and the millstone gate in the right middle. Kaymakli, Cappadocia. 128
7.2 Kaymakli underground passages. 132
7.3 Kaymakli's andesite floor stone, with the 57 soul hollows. 133
8.1 The entrance to the Choir of the Monastery in Najera. 153

Preface

This book is written and organised around two key title words, 'evil' and 'trickster', in order to address a mindlessness that, in our understanding, lies at the heart of the contemporary. It might not sound evident why this is so, and understanding the book without some familiarity with the political anthropology and the connected, genealogically oriented historical sociology that we have been doing for several years might not be easy. Yet, the problem that we address is easy enough to understand, and also quite evidently central.

Evil is a well-known term and a very old concern, at the centre of most if not all religions and spiritualities, even magic and sorcery, and thus basically a concern at the heart of all culture. However, it has gone out of fashion, in a way, with the Enlightenment and its rationalism, based on and furthered by the scientific vision of the world, which suggested that it knows everything universally. However, actually, this world vision only undermined any knowledge about our concrete surroundings, so while it pretended that its universal knowledge ended all ignorance, thus eliminated the possibility of evil, it actually escalated the problem of evil by its own ignorance of the problematic character of its universalistic perspective. Such pretence to do away with evil, in another, quite different terminology can be called exorcism. The act, however, evidently failed to succeed, as the past centuries of modernity, while repeatedly promising to end evil forever, rather led to the proliferation of evidently evil deeds on a scale that was hardly known before. This, in fact, is not even an isolated event in world history, rather returns repeatedly: periods that seems to promise a return to the legendary Golden Age, with a sudden flourishing of the arts and the sciences, have a pattern-like tendency to lead to wars, conquests and empire-building, infesting the world at an astonishing speed with all kind of evils, thus proliferating suffering on an unprecedented scale. Thus, the problem of evil needs to be posed again: not by repeating worn-out slogans, but by taking it seriously.

So what is our intention, through studying, jointly, evil and the trickster? We suggest taking seriously the problem of evil by considering it as a genuine issue for thinking. Instead of reducing evil to phenomena that are evidently so, like committing violent, indecent or otherwise unlawful acts that are the contrary of the good ways, our ways, we will attempt to understand evil in the etymological sense, as an arrogant ignoring of our limits. In particular, we'll investigate how the trespassing of the limits of life and death generates cumulative developments that lead to a sudden pullulating of evil, together with some apparent processes of growth and development that, however, soon reveal themselves as largely illusionary, even monstrous.

In terms of our way of proceeding, we suggest that we give up the notion of opposites (originated in the ideas of Protagoras, and becoming central in rationalistic logics) and replace it with an analysis of similarities and quasi-similarities: imitations, as well as attraction and dissemination, de-ordering and re-ordering, and especially subversion as relatively independent processes. Their mechanism is to be investigated in order to explore how they might bring wealth and growth together. For example, instead of arguing that individual oppositions and differentiation causes changes, whether mechanically or dialectically, one could argue with a better justification that blankness and mimicry are preconditions for changes as alterations in the very order of things. Each such change needs to be indeterminate at the beginning and independent from others, thus historically contingent rather than caused by opposing forces.

Imitation and mimicry have a tight connection with zero, or nothingness. This starts with the fake character or non-reality of mechanical imitation, but goes further. The zero is associated with emptiness and the void, as the 'new' usually emerges not through the fight of opposites, but on an empty place, or a place that has become vacated, so requires filling, and is always immediately filled by the flux. It is in this sense that every new creation is supposed to be preceded by destruction. We can thus introduce the idea of creative destruction, so central for anthropological trickster figures, but also modern economics and politics, based on Locke's *tabula rasa*, but even before the architecture of Alberti and Leonardo da Vinci, the building of forts not on naturally favourable sites, likes rocks on mountaintops, but on razing everything to ground level so that the perfectly shaped universal fortress could be built. The meaning of the zero is none, its reason is unknown, as nobody is able to follow its relations, through zero everything becomes tapered into confusion, a smeared mirror of the meaningful world and so perfectly mimetic for its effects, as if a virtual existence was invocating the forms of the real. This demonic growth through the zero, through multiplication by division, through creative destruction is specific, like a disease, and just as every disease it has its own pattern of growth, multiplication, development and decline, without any change of its own, as it is paralytic and sterile concerning any ability for mindful concern and action. One could say it is mechanistic, if it were not a human decision that started the whole trickster move, as we will show later on.

Evil is not the opposite of good, but is part of it, as the indeterminate is part of the determinate, a zero point of accumulation, a premature formlessness, which does not have a definite character of its own, so it is open and extended into every possibly man-made connection or relation for their digestion and dissolution. It offers peace for those challenged only at the price of a complete subversion, a price implying that all those who possessed forms before its annihilating invasion must have forgotten their meaning and altered their own reason. In order to lure people into such subversion the evil trickster takes up the most various shapes, adjusting itself to any circumstance, and even there changing its appearance continuously.

However, the trickster in any form is still a trickster, never able to grow into meaning, remaining just a grim, mechanical substitute. It is only capable of stealing souls, not able to become a soul itself, as emptiness is an unchangeable constant. There is nothing to do with an empty heart. Smiling in perplexity, in vacuous smoothness and seductive translucency that hides their hard, alert eyes for every misfortune and weakness in the others, evil tricksters are ever in readiness to take and possess the properties of anybody. Their shallow and sleek figures never cease to follow our world, so we can also trace their various appearances.

This book is an essay, in the original sense of a tentative, concerning how to discover and follow the trickster's ways of infiltration into our reality.

Agnes Horvath and Arpad Szakolczai
Florence, 19 April 2019

Acknowledgements

Our deepest gratitude is to the large and growing group of students and academics around the journal *International Political Anthropology*, without whose continuing support a project like this book could not have been brought to conclusion, even conceived. This includes, in particular, our fellow editors and authors, but also our current and former colleagues, associates, friends, and students, who not only contributed to the success of the journal, but also the organisation and running of the various conferences, symposia, workshops and summer schools associated with it. Without pretending completeness, we'd like to mention those who were our closest associates over the years: Harald Wydra, Bjørn Thomassen, Kieran Keohane, Tom Boland, and John O'Brien, and also Zoltán Balázs, Kieran Bonner, Glenn Bowman, Manos Marangudakis, Peter McMylor, Gianfranco Poggi, Richard Sakwa, Iván Szelényi, Stephen Turner, Marius Benţa, Sam Boland, Paolo Bonari, Brian Finucane, Daniel Gati, Arvydas Grišinas, József Lőrincz, Federica Montagni, Egor Novikov, Camil Francesc Roman, János Márk Szakolczai, Jesenko Tešan and Diletta Tonatto. While certainly not everyone associated with *IPA* would agree with every one of our claims in this book – far from it – this is certainly a recognised and flourishing academic community, without which we could not have even imagined this project.

In the early stages of our respective careers we had the great luck of being helped by exceptional academic mentors. They were Elemér Hankiss, Alessandro Pizzorno and Philippe Schmitter. We will always be grateful for them.

Political anthropology, while falling outside standard disciplinary canons, does generate an area, perhaps a field, which has its own coherence, based on but moving beyond social and cultural anthropology, incorporating classical political philosophy and philosophical anthropology. It is kept together by the classical concern with the concrete person, which is in a specific and direct sense foundational, as shown in the Greek origins of philosophy, including the Presocratics and Aristotle, but especially and primarily Plato.

This book is dedicated to the memory of Alessandro Pizzorno (1924–2019). He was teacher to one of us, and colleague to the other. He still had classical education, judgment and character. His master ideas were recognition, reputation and respect, in acknowledgment of the validity of an existence in reputation. These are not universalistic values, but deeply rooted in familiarity with the good, derived from and applied in concrete contexts.

Introduction

> ... flux. Fear, hideousness, vampires, dragons, the multiple, at first, inspire fear. It comes from the calumny or the foul demons of the night. What terrifies is not the meaning of the noise – the thing spoken, forspoken – but the increasing multiplicity that says it. Fear comes from the swarming, the tide ... Rationality was born of this terror.
>
> Michel Serres, *Genesis* (Serres 1995b: 66–67)

In this book we suggest that the figure of the trickster, as it was developed in comparative anthropology and mythology, offers a priceless, at once new and ages-old approach to the problem of evil. However, before we introduce the figure, it is worthwhile to explore a little, in the spirit of Nietzsche's *Beyond Good and Evil*, and also of the passage by Serres cited above, what lies behind the seemingly trivial problem of evil as well, starting in the simplest possible way by the meaning and origin of the related words.

The etymology of the English evil offers the surprising insight that evil originally was not connected to hostile spirits, and not even to malevolent acts, rather to acts that are 'exceeding due limits' (Onions 1966: 332), or that fail to take into account certain limits that are commonly acknowledged and respected. Evil in that sense is thus closely connected to the Greek word *hubris*, which plays quite a central role both in Greek mythology – the Titans who were sent as a punishment to the Tartarus due to their hubris – and especially the arch-titan Prometheus; but also in Greek law, being – according to Louis Gernet (2001) – the source of Greek penal law. The other key European root, present in French *mal* and Italian *male*, both descending from Latin *malus*, are connected to illness, thus in the limit case to mortality. As a final preliminary example, we mention Hungarian, where – according to the 1825 Czuczor-Fogarasi Dictionary – the word for evil, *gonosz* is linked to the word used both for care and thinking, *gond*, arguing that both represent an act of twisting and turning – in the case of thinking, due to the problems pressing on one's mind. Thus, evil is always associated with some or other developments which involves the leaving of the accepted ways of doing, thus, of going beyond, in one way or another, of the limits, in the most extreme case from life to death and then back to life; or from mindfulness to consciousness.

Compared to the word evil, the word trickster, especially as a technical term of the social sciences, is much less known, and more recent. Of course, the expression confidence trickster is well known in English, as given a crucial and manifold characterisation in Dickens – and the great novelist is indeed still a prime source to understand its nature; but it is not considered as an important word. As a simple indication, the Online Etymological Dictionary (www.etymonline.com) only gives one line about this word: '1711, from trick (n.) + -ster'. It cannot possibly be shorter. Similarly, the attention of social scientists is rather limited, and the history of the term in anthropology is particularly strange. It appeared in nineteenth American anthropology, and central attention to it was given by Paul Radin, one of the first PhD students of the re-founder of American anthropology, Franz Boas, but Radin failed to published his milestone work until his 70s.[1] Even later the impact of the term was rather limited, restricted to comparative mythology and literature, with a strong resistance against its application to contemporary political, social and economic reality. In fact, the original title of this book was 'Tricksterology', but – due to problems of market recognition – title and subtitle had to trade places. Thus, in fact, we will approach the problem of evil through the trickster – they are both enmeshed in ignorance over due measure for our world. This is the central, announced novelty of this book – and thus trickster is indeed evil, mindlessness itself.

Before we become completely perplexed, we must clear up the question of what we intend to signify when we use the word trickster. Obviously we, the authors must be quite familiar with what we mean, whereas readers are now at a loss. The trickster, to begin with, as a figure, and any knowledge transmitted about him in local traditions, whether direct and changeable folktales or more established mythologies, is a twice external figure; or a figure in which exteriority is raised as if on a second power. The trickster is not only outside any stable, concrete, living human community, but any knowledge about it only comes from the outside. In anthropological accounts the trickster comes through as a distant, impenetrable, at once strange and menacing but also vague and not really serious, even not really real figure – a kind of pipe dream-cum-nightmare that can be disturbing, but that should not really be taken seriously. But if such vagueness, on one hand, can lead to a slackening of attention, it might also involve a different problem: the scarcity of proper knowledge itself can be the result of a trick, only increasing the perplexity generated by the figure.

Thus, as most if not all knowledge about the trickster comes from external sources, and external perspective, what could be the internal knowledge about the trickster? How does the trickster see itself? What are the trickster stories told by tricksters themselves, especially about themselves? What is the source of their persuading power? Where to situate the trickster at all? Any answer to such questions is rendered difficult, if not impossible, due to two reasons that seem to reassert themselves, in an obvious manner. First, if the trickster is a lonely outsider, not belonging to any communities, then obviously there can be no tradition in which such self-knowledge is transmitted. Once the concrete, lonely figure passes away, any knowledge it possessed is lost. However, such a perspective ignores the fact that the trickster is only an outsider to a given community. As evidently every community knows them, there must have existed many tricksters, who among themselves were connected by invisible but very real ties. Still, and beyond the self-view of tricksters, such figures are also considered as possessors of knowledge, and of a secret knowledge, but how did this knowledge emerge, and how was it accumulated? And with what kind of result? All this creates a further problem, rendering any effort to know who or what tricksters really were again impossible, as the character of a secret is that it is a secret; thus, it is not divulged.

However, it is right here that a possible way to the answer can be found – and it is even necessary that this be so. Secret knowledge must find a way to be transmitted; otherwise, it would simply be lost. The mode of transmitting such knowledge is well-known: these are secret rituals, or mysteries, at the heart of which are the initiation rites, or the introduction of new candidates into the ways, and in particular the secret knowledge, of the closed brotherhood, while at the same time being transformative in the sense of transforming a mere candidate, or a person external to the group, to becoming one of them.

According to this perspective the account given by testimonies, or in any stable local tradition about the trickster is not the full truth – rather, it is exactly half of the truth, as if one part of a *symbolon* that must be fitted together with the other part. The trickster, on the one hand, from the perspective of witnesses, is indeed a lonely outsider, who does not belong to them – in fact, who does not belong to any of the communities around; not even to any normal human community, with its human, social and cultural lineages. Yet, on the other hand, it only appears as a complete outsider, as it does have a kind of community on its own: a closed group of fellow tricksters or initiates. Thus, traces of tricksters, and especially of trickster knowledge, must be searched for in those traditions that focus on the transmission of secret knowledge to a group of initiates. So we should search for remote places, abandoned, inaccessible or deserted, for possible dwelling places of the trickster. Such places, as we'll see, include the Tassili Desert Mountains, the Kaymakli underground structures in Cappadocia, the Grime Graves flint mine, or some Palaeolithic caves.

Still, the presence of the trickster is felt everywhere, in the entire cultural tradition of mankind. Even more, this presence is felt so strongly that it gained a transcendental character, though the trickster is rarely ever a full, proper deity, just as it is hardly ever a proper human being. Almost always, it is in-between – a bit divine, a bit human, and fully in-between: living between the sky and the earth, not belonging fully either to the sky or to the earth, rather moving between the two, communicating between the two realms, bringing news, or bits of information. Also, it often has an animal face and shape, and thus is not just situated between, but is itself an in-between being, a hybrid, composite, sometimes a monster. It is thus not real, not even super-real, in the sense in which the god(s), while they do not exist in the sense of humans, animals and objects, being visible and touchable, but are arguably

4 Introduction

more real than the real. The trickster is not like that, as its unreality belongs to the in-between, neither here, nor there. It is thus rather super unreal.

Of its manifold unrealities there is one particularly unreal in-betweenness that has special importance for the storyline of this book, which is the borderline between the living and the dead; another way to pose the limits between mortals and the immortals or the divine.[2] We are mortals, cannot aspire to live like immortals – behaving so is the greatest possible act of hubris, reason even for the cruel punishment of the Titans however immortals. Death is therefore part of our fate, our nature, and we should not be so terribly preoccupied with it, also because death is not a complete annihilation. A belief in immortal beings implies also that there is something after death, but this will not be the same kind of existence as before. In fact, the modern obsession with death is already an indication of very deep-seated problems with modern secularism. Nevertheless, just as dying is a crucial passage, connected with various rites of passage, it also involves an in-between sphere, between the living and the dead, and – even more perplexingly, problematically – the possibility of some interference or intrusion between these realms. It might happen, through some chance event, that the borderline separating the realm of the living and the dead breaks down, and this is the kind of in-betweenness that generates the greatest possible drama, the drawing of the afterlife into this life – and which is thus the source of the greatest possible evil, a substitute replacing the real.

Therefore the trickster does have an enormous impact on reality, as its deadly mindlessness is the core, the non-essential essence of the trickster. Endlessness, unfinalisability, a kind of permanent liminality, another modality of death can become the driving force of an unreal existence – thus, we can start to behave as tricksters, as if we became trickster – and not just some of us, but entire human cultures. This is when we start to live like dead, in the in-between – whatever is not solid, a substance, a real one, but an in-between irresponsibility. Two key modern words capture the irresponsible in-between, interest and media, as they literally mean 'in-between'.

Thus, as our readers perhaps start to perceive, certainly to their great astonishment, our claim is not simply that the trickster, this hardly known figure of comparative anthropology and mythology can be quite relevant for understanding our interest-driven and media-governed world. The presence of tricksters, or of trickster knowledge, presents a permanent threat to any human community – and of the greatest threat, the threat of unreality. This is because tricksters do not simply trick or lie in a purely gratuitous manner, rather take up and exaggerate, slowly push beyond any limits, the most natural and important aspects of life – the individual body and the borders between bodies: time, space, surface, by using Eros to liberate the flux. They use any disturbance as an occasion for generating and magnifying the flux, accumulating fluxes into the generation of new creatures: unlimited times, spaces, surfaces.

This is why a central concern for any community is how to handle tricksters. This has no clear and easy solution, as pushing them outside only renders their eventual return more threatening, while any integration and assimilation into the society is partly impossible, and partly only feeds the seeds of its own destruction. Tricksters, or rather a trickster logic can easily gain the upper hand, transforming and taking the place of entire communities, even regions and cultures. This is what evidently happened, as Gregory Bateson realised, in Papua New Guinea; this is the kind of history that is contained in Livy's *History of Rome*, and thus what is taken by Serres and Girard, among others in the footsteps of Hobbes and Nietzsche, as the normal course of human history. This is also what is happening to us, now. Our aim is to render visible the trickster logic animating some of the most self-evidently taken for granted features of our own reality, like the market or exchange economy, the democratic public sphere, and especially technologised science, which can only be done through detailed long-term historical inquiry.

Plato and other guides

For such an adventurous undertaking one needs good guides, and this book will indeed rely on some special guides. At a first level this will be offered by the ideas of Plato. While it may sound strange that a book addressing and belonging to sociology and anthropology would rely first of all on Plato, we have a very good reason for doing so, as we consider Plato as indeed our contemporary. Plato was not the remote founder of modern philosophical idealism, to be relegated to the dusty shelves of background readings for introductory courses in philosophy, rather a vital thinker whose work was animated by the problems of his age and – as our problems are quite similar – is of crucial use for us.

Apart from Plato, we will also rely upon antique philosophy, including prominently the Presocratics, but also Aristotle and Cicero, as well as classical poets like Homer, Hesiod, or Virgil. Furthermore, among contemporary perspectives, we will draw on Nietzschean genealogy, as continued by Max Weber, Eric Voegelin (especially his ideas about Gnosticism, central for the book), Reinhart Koselleck (with his classic work connecting secret societies and the Enlightenment) and Michel Foucault, among others; and also a series of political anthropologists. As we have discussed these figures amply in previous publications,[3] we do not feel the need to repeat this here. Furthermore, concerning oriental trickster influences and the question of modernity as trickster destiny, we also rely on a series of guides like Michel Serres, Roberto Calasso, Károly Kerényi, or Lewis Hyde – philosophers, mythologists, essayists who were outside post-Newtonian mainstream academic social science, without feeling the urge to coerce interpretation into an absolute and universalistic perspective, thus have much more to offer for understanding our own times and place. Particularly important for our book is the work of a series of thinkers who seriously questioned long-standing dogmas identifying the progress of modern technologised science with the general benefit of mankind. They prominently include Michel Serres, Bruno Latour, Stephen Toulmin and Frances Yates. Finally, we will also use as guides writers like

Milton (*Paradise Lost*), and Goethe (*Faust*), but also Dante and Shakespeare – also because all of them have undergone very unique travels.

Such guides are all the more necessary as the question of evil, for obvious reasons, was much neglected in modern thinking, and when it was taken up, the discussion had grave limitations, as it was imprisoned in Gnostic-Manichean dualisms of good and evil. While Nietzsche's call for moving beyond such dualism is well known, it has not managed to alter the situation. Our hopes therefore are understandably very limited; yet, it is our aim to suggest a political sociology and anthropology of evil by presenting the anthropologically based figure of the trickster. This figure, derived from the experience of the most varied cultures, in our view can be helpful to overcome the impasse into which thinking about evil arrived by our days, through a long and winding road. As we cannot enter this theme in detail, must limit ourselves to sketching the bare outlines.

Thinking about evil

In our civilisation evil came to be conceptualised in the Middle Ages through the idea of the original sin and the figure of the devil. According to the former, due to distant events evil became rooted deeply inside every human being, corrupting it. This view has evident Gnostic and Manichean origins and affinities. The latter figure over the times gained increasingly unrealistic, caricature-like features in the imagination, rendering it easy to recognise in principle, but increasingly more elusive in reality. This view on evil became both radicalised and challenged in the late Renaissance and the Reformation, as part of the deep schism undergone by Europe. On one side, through Luther and especially Calvin, there was a reassertion of original sin, radicalising the ideas by St Paul and Augustine on divine grace, culminating in the claim that human nature is so radically corrupt that man is incapable of any good by itself. On the other the idea emerged, in late Renaissance Humanism, radicalised by the Enlightenment in early modernity, that evil is due to a lack of education, so it can be eliminated by a progress of learning which became increasingly reduced to formal skills. This position became a cornerstone of philosophical rationalism whose founder, René Descartes was himself immersed in a Gnostic imagery (Neiman 2002: 10). According to rationalism evil, in particular the devil, simply did not exist – which, as many came to argue, is nothing but one of its greatest tricks.

During the *Sattelzeit* of modernity, or on its liminal threshold, at the height of Jacobin terror, in 1793 Kant came to argue the position, from inside the Enlightenment and philosophical rationalism that evil, even radical evil does exist and is seated deep inside all of us: 'there is a radical innate evil in human nature' (Kant 2018: 65).[4] This is a Gnostic position, and Kant's thinking was furthermore imprisoned in the alchemy-based Enlightenment idea of a purely cognitive education. He only made a further step on this road by claiming that even if knowing the good, man is ready to commit evil acts, due to rational self-interest, or even sheer malice. Kant situated and justified his argument in manners typical of Sophistic and Enlightenment perspectives that do not take history seriously. Vaguely evoking the omnipresence of evil in human history (53), he ignored the dynamics of history, in particular the presence or absence of liminal instances where certain modes of behaving can suddenly appear and spread through imitation, rather supporting his points through an eclectic collection of anecdotes (65–71) which, in the still ruling academic tradition of modern philosophical rationalism is supposed to make the argument self-evident for every isolated thinking mind. The solution, for Kant, was the pursuit of universal 'maxims', or sheer consciousness, as evil simply cannot be 'extirpated [*vertilgen*]' (69), reducing the right measure to discursively fixed and universalistic rules, a legacy of ascetic Protestant obsession with written texts and exact words. This idea, as Kierkegaard – and later Unamuno (1968) or Camus (1956) – argued, was similarly untenable, as '[w]hatever is to be good must come at once; for "at once" is the divinest of all categories and deserves to be honoured ... so much so that what is not done at once is of evil' (Kierkegaard 1988). From this non-Kantian perspective every human being is guided by a pre-conscious inner force to do the good, otherwise one would fail to have the right reaction in the right moment, and instead would justify one's actions by various ratiocinations justifying oneself as always being the 'good', being entrapped in normative discourse, so taking up a rhetorical and not Platonic-philosophical position.

As Jeffrey Alexander (2003) argues in his insightful chapter 'A Cultural Sociology of Evil', in an evident effort to lay the foundations for the sociology of evil, this Kantian position is caught in the worst kind of dualism between good and evil, where the idea is to set up a table of values, Kant's 'maxims', that is universally 'good', arguing that whoever lacks such values is simply evil. Taking into account Nietzsche's ideas, more through Bataille than Foucault, Alexander makes important steps towards overcoming such dualism by arguing, against followers of Kant like Habermas and Honneth, that evil can be promoted, 'ironically, in pursuit of the good' (110). He rather sees some points in the ideas of Bauman, according to which the escalation of evil in the 20th century was due to certain aspects of modernity itself, or even of Foucault (109, 114–115). He also recognises that the problem of evil is much more serious than rationalistic accounts presume: it has its own vitality, even desire (115), and is not just the absence of the good values.

However, probably due to his overwhelming reliance on Durkheim, Alexander's views are still deeply rooted in rationalistic dualism. He claims that 'for every value there is an equal and opposite antivalue, for every norm an antinorm' (Alexander 2003: 110), which also implies the untenable Durkheimian position about the 'functionality' of crime and the reduction of pathology to matters of statistics. Even more problematically, Alexander assumes a dualism even more radical than Kantianism, with evil having not just its own dynamics, but its 'cultural and institutional "autonomy"' (117), even its own 'evil values' (114). The result is a double impasse, which furthermore is internally inconsistent. Alexander on the one hand accepts the need to fight and combat evil (109, here mistakenly locating it at the heart of Foucault's work), understandable once one attributes evil its own independent existence and values; though in other places implies that such ideas about 'epochal struggles ... between evil and the good', with the final triumph of the good over evil are deeply problematic (116), even accusing – quite rightly – Amnesty International with 'an obsessive concern with defining, exploring, and graphically presenting evil' (119), which thus in the name of eliminating evil forever rather contributes to spread it. On the other hand, and in line with his constructivist, thus fundamentally Kantian position he insists that we should recognise the 'social construction of evil', and even that it has been 'empirically and symbolically necessary for the social construction of good' (112), implying a resignation to the inevitability, even functionality of evil. This is clearly insufficient.

An important further step in the sociology of evil was made by Baudrillard (1990, 2013; see Germain 2019), in books that furthermore directly recognise the complicity of not just the market economy but technology and even the idea of public transparency in promoting evil, while purportedly set to eliminate it forever. Baudrillard fully recognises that evil is not substantial or essential but imitative, and that the basis of such imitativity is not the absence of values, not even certain specifically evil values, rather the void itself (Baudrillard 1990: 11–12). This void is propagated by a flux, fluid circulation, excess liquidity (17–18), or a continuous 'metamorphosis', a change of form generating intoxication (*ivresse*) (76–77). As a result, evil not simply changed its location, but such permanent transformation led to the escalation of evil, as it is evil itself: 'the anamorphosis of contemporary forms of Evil is infinite' (88). Mere energy, sheer violence of movements, disequilibrium, vertigo, is itself the principle of evil (111–112).

This helps to understand the utter vainness of liberation movements, as every liberating the good also liberates evil (Baudrillard 1990: 113). Liberation in the sense of setting free from previous stability by eliminating limits only leads to an acceleration in the void (11), in the incommensurable – as there are no equivalences, only an 'epidemics of values' (13), a prime example being 'sexual liberation', which as a 'right' is ridiculous (93). Thus, and quite rightly, Baudrillard argues that the current 'human rights' narrative, at least in the context of the advanced countries, became deprived of any sense and meaning, rendering the recognition of evil impossible, and leading to the 'irresistible ascent of stupidity [*bêtise*]' (94). Such purported defence of people, focusing on prevention and searching for possible security hazards anywhere, only helps to further 'endemic terror' (109).

Promoting liberation by purely technical means, 'the perpetrating on the world an unlimited operational project' have the further effect of only ending up destroying reality itself. By now the 'the real ceased to be real', and the concrete fabric of human existence, the context of the concrete being or 'objective reality' was replaced by an indestructible machinery, an 'integral reality', or 'a reality without limits', recalling Orwellian total control (2013:

13–4, 125; see Boland 2008). Thus, the rule of reversibility became irreversible, rendering the machination practically indestructible (Baudrillard 1990: 71–3), and setting up an 'irreversible movement towards the totalization of the world' (Baudrillard 2013: 16). Our destiny became to have no 'principle or final purpose [*destination*] whatever (14). The revolution that some are still projecting into the future has already happened: we live in its aftermath, or 'after the orgy' (Baudrillard 1990: 11), but the outcome is not what one was hoping for. The overall result is rather 'pure circulation', spun by the economy and magnified by public transparency, as the end-product of all liberation – which, we have seen, in such limitless and crusading format is just the liberation of the void – is 'to foment and aliment the net [*réseau*]' (12). Any thinking that tries to separate, as if clinically, good from evil by such universalistic means is naïve, as it ignores and even promotes the occult presence of evil (Baudrillard 2013: 109–110). However, the ultimate position of Baudrillard strikingly recalls that of Alexander, perhaps due to the omnipresence of Durkheimian ideas in sociology, as it appears that for him evil is not simply promoted by a mistaken, Gnostic-puritan vision of 'pure' good, but is truly intertwined with it: 'It is only through the distorted, disseminated figures of evil that one can reconstitute, in perspective, the figure of the good' (110). This mode of thinking is incompatible with the ideas of Plato, whom Baudrillard, just as other moderns or postmoderns, though for opposite reasons, misread as distant precursor to modern philosophical rationalism.

So, as much as he is fighting modernity, Baudrillard's position is still deeply rooted on its horizon, imbibed with Marx and Freud, even if arguing against them, offering only a perceptive commentary from inside; a kind of transcendental journalism, in the terminology of Foucault. The problem is that, in the absence of proper attention to history and context, such work is bound to reproduce what has been known long before. Giving only one example, about the vanity of the revolution Baudrillard might have incorporated Girard's (1961) work on Stendhal, all the more so as the novelists of the 19th century, as Pietro Citati (2000) argues magnificently, knew much more about evil in modernity than social scientists and philosophers ever imagined.

In order to move beyond the horizon of modernity, we need to start from anthropology (including mythology), and history (including ancient history and archaeology).

Yet, first of all, we must take seriously Plato, a starting and endpoint of thinking. Alfred Whitehead famously argued that the European philosophical tradition is a series of footnotes to Plato, and this applies also for political anthropology. Concerning Plato, the central focus in this book will be on *Theaetetus*, a dialogue much devoted to the flux and the question of secret knowledge, or the efforts of Socrates to render evident the vacuity of the claims of those who create credit and power for themselves by attracting the flux, thus becoming exclusive and heedlessness possessors of hidden, secret knowledge. It takes us back to Pergouset and Tassili, the guardians of memory of Çatalhöyük, or Nietzsche's ascetic priests,[5] possessors of the flux

10 *Introduction*

as noncorporeal but sensual flow, but even more to troglodyte settlements, the uterine darkness of begetting.

The flux and the void

When Plato in the *Theaetetus* examined the problem of the flux, or how can one eliminate the careful solidity of the individual by the accumulation of fluxes, he was faced with the total dissolution of carefulness. When the flux is accumulated in the transformation process, it promotes the fluidity necessary to remove the borders of self-care and self-protection and creates new entities. For the proper functioning of the flux a space is needed, the *khóra* (*Timaeus*), and Plato was never in friendly terms with its double nature of birth and death. Further on, flux may be in an encircled or encysted empty space,[6] evoked by the sign of the nil, 0, but also as a walled gap or matrix, with the hook symbol of the Greek upsilon (Y), best shown by the shafts in underground settings. These are places for alternating substances, bracketing the hooked one inside, like a receptor of effluences, while also evoking the pit or shaft with their closely curved cone shape, or in the form of a circle, where every perspective is joined to the fixed point of its vortex, lying outside of its solid base.

The living dead

We cannot offer a detailed view of the trickster until we know more of the particulars connected with its extraordinary involvement with death, resulting in the living dead. As a first approximation, the flux generates annihilation processes, which lead to a rapid development of anxiety, even heedlessness, and ends up in death. Or – and this is the alternating way of the trickster – the flux induced by combinations of desires and fears leads not to death, but incites a new course of action, by a procedure of the trickster, so into the creation of a new circle. The trickster brings about or stimulates the occurrence of fluxes into a circular continuum. The trickster procedure brings the fluxes into the body, producing their entrapment inside. Consequently it causes the flux used to induce artificial existence by liminalising the body with fluxes, initiating or accelerating its multiplication. Instead of death, the living entity experiences an infinite, sequential dynamics of decomposition, the increase of its body mass in continuous schism, as if in an eternal recurrence.

The living dead are the accumulation of fluxes, based on a repetitive operation for creating new versions, deployed by unscrupulous minds, cutting short reality. This creates a void for the easier accumulation of fluxes inside, a process that allows evil to grow, till it is pressed upon mortals with exasperating force.

Chapter structure

The book consists of two main parts. Part I, 'Presenting the Trickster', serves as a general introduction to the figure of the trickster, also offering some ideas why this anthropological figure offers a new perspective on the old problem of evil. The central organising idea is that while the trickster of anthropological stories and folktales is always presented from a distance, from the outside, we explore the possibility of finding narratives and perspectives which gain insights about the figure from the inside. Our main focus, in order to best deal with the problem of evil through the trickster, will be on the special characteristics of 'trickster knowledge'. Part II, 'Tracking Trickster Traces: Evil Machinations', continues this investigation on an archaeological and historical scale, searching for traces of the trickster back in prehistoric times. Its focus is the idea that the evil trickster is not by nature part of our world, but the outcome of certain machinations by which the flux is released from its bounds, and this is why this evil is the operation of men.

Part I consists of five chapters. Chapter 1 presents the figure as discussed in the anthropological literature, extending the investigation to comparative mythology. It recaps how the trickster was seen, over the centuries and the millennia, from the outside. Chapter 2 uses two books by E. E. Evans-Pritchard, one of the classics of anthropology, in order to gain a more 'internal' perspective about the trickster figure, focusing on witchcraft, sorcery, magic, especially witch doctors or magicians. Chapters 3–4 are devoted to Greek examples. As Greek culture is one of our oldest systematic written sources, it is particularly helpful for contrasting the way the trickster is seen from the outside and how some trickster figures operated inside society; and as it is one of the sources of our civilisation, it is particularly helpful in our quest for understanding how our world could have become dominated by trickster logic. The link between these two chapters is similar to the links between chapters one and two. Chapter 3 presents some trickster figures in Greek mythology, focusing on Hermes, but also discussing some murky figures of Greek mythology, the various *daimones*, much connected to metallurgy, in particular the Kabeiroi. The connection between Hermes and the Kabeiroi is shown to be homologous to that of the Zande trickster and the magicians. Chapter 4 takes a closer look on one particular work of Greek thinking, Plato's *Theaetetus*, as this dialogue contains a series of special hints about a trickster knowledge that is both secret and unspeakable, due to its destructive, incommensurable character. Chapter 5 then pursues the problem of trickster knowledge inside Vedic Hinduism, focusing on the theoretical justification of sacrificial rituals.

The four chapters of Part II trace the track of the trickster in the broad historical, mythological and archaeological record, back to prehistoric caves. Chapter 6 starts by taking seriously one of the commonplaces of the literature on the trickster that the figure is very old, a probable survival of prehistoric times, and analyses a series of prehistoric trickster images. Such images, from Palaeolithic caves, the Tassili Desert Mountains, from the Grimes cave in Suffolk, or Lepenski Vir in Serbia, show trickster figures that are strikingly similar to more recent impersonations, like the Phlyakes actors of Greek mime plays, or Pulcinella of early modern Commedia dell'Arte, impersonating a certain aspect of Eros. Chapter 7 probes into the difficult question of identifying the real-life operators behind trickster images. Following hints from classical mythology, literature and philosophy, it argues that these were troglodytes. Through their activities the perplexing, enormous and deep, manmade underground structures in Cappadocia, Central Turkey, were used to incite deeply buried forces in order to use their fluxes in their transformative machinations. Chapter 8 returns to images, of monsters and demons, interpreted as creatures of the flux, filling emptiness. After a short review of the literature on monster or composite beings, the chapter discusses a poem by Emily Dickinson on emptiness, and then some strange images in the choir of a monastery in Najera, Northern Spain, designed under the support of the Borgia pope Alexander VI. Chapter 9 focuses on the proliferation of the incommensurable by secret and occult practices for new creation through transformation, especially alchemy.

Following the two parts we present some 'Concluding Comments', which aim to assess the significance and meaning of the findings contained in the book regarding the pervasiveness of trickster logic.

Notes

1 For further details, see Szakolczai and Thomassen (2019, ch. 5).
2 God or gods, the difference is not important for our concerns here.
3 See Horvath, Thomassen and Wydra (2015), Horvath and Szakolczai (2018b), Szakolczai and Thomassen (2019).
4 For a good summary of the conventional perspective, see Dews (2008).
5 For more details, see Horvath and Szakolczai (2018a).
6 See Bowman (2019) on encystation.

Part I
Presenting the trickster

1 The trickster in anthropology
The figure as seen from the outside

Anthropological and ethnological accounts about the beliefs of archaic people since the beginnings abound in stories about a most particular figure. This figure, on the one hand, is a marginal outcast, derided as a good-for-nothing and an ignorant fool, but on the other hand is most respected and feared, considered as a culture hero, even a second founder of the world. Such stories were particularly widespread in North America, West Africa and South-east Asia, but are present all around the planet, playing a major role even in various European mythologies and folktales, as Loki in Scandinavia, the leprechaun in Ireland or Hermes in Greece. The figure, technically called a 'trickster', therefore embodies paradox and ambivalence.[1]

However, as if raising ambivalence to another level, such stories were often played down, ignored, or even outright hidden by the rising anthropological discipline itself. Thus, while the discussion of the trickster was present in the American anthropology in the 19th century, when Boas decided to re-found anthropology this discussion became all but lost. Even more strikingly, Paul Radin, who came to write the classic work on the trickster as an agent of transformation, was Boas's student and defended his PhD thesis before the First World War, but did not gain a position in anthropology. We do even know the exact theme of his thesis, and he did not publish his book on the trickster until the age of 73. Similarly, in English anthropology, the figure of the trickster was propagated by John W. Layard,[2] who did his studies in Cambridge, but for a set of not fully clear reasons became marginalised in anthropology, never having a proper position, and his work on the trickster only reached a limited audience. The outcome of all this is that even now the figure is hardly known in the social sciences, though we argue in this book that it is most helpful to make sense of our world – particularly in capturing the ambivalence of modernity, that the price of progress is destruction. It is as if destined to open the doors to the secrets of modernity, concerning the false promises of an infinite growth brought about by technological change, for which one only has to give up mindfulness and believe blindly in progress. Apparently, it was due to this character that it became ignored, as if a hidden knowledge not to be divulged, together with similar key concepts like liminality, rites of passage and imitation, by some of the founding fathers of the social sciences, like Boas and Durkheim, and their main students, like Radcliffe-Brown, Malinowski, Kroeber, Lévi-Strauss or Bourdieu.

According to Radin (1972: xxiv), the trickster is one of the oldest and most universal figures of human culture, even a kind of *speculum mentis*.[3] The figure can perhaps be best introduced through the highly unique way in which it is situated, in-between the human, the animal, and the divine (Bright 1993: 174–176; Horvath 2008; Radin 1972); at any rate, hybrid and unreal, though effective in promoting transformation.

In most folktales, all around the world, the trickster is represented in an animal form. Such animals prominently include the snake, the spider and the fox, but also the monkey, coyote, hare, and many others. These animals are proverbially associated with a cunning and sly attitude, always ready to attack by deploying some ruse, jumping out of the dark or stealing from behind, setting up traps for the unwary; but also with a kind of lonely outsider status, being always alone, without companions, and also far from the general scenery of life where other animals are supposed to share a common living space. Thus, the specific type of knowledge characteristic of the trickster – cunning, deceit or ruse, in contrast to more direct (whether pacific or violent) means – is evident. The trickster is never straight, neither friend nor a specific foe, always hidden and crooked, and rather intent on first confusing any such distinction, questioning the very meaning of straightness itself, then projecting its own crookedness as equal in rights, eventually even as a model. Furthermore, if the trickster is directly represented in a human form, it always evokes very ancient times, often even directly called as 'the old man' (Bright 1993: xi, 20; Guenther 1999: 7–8; Stephenson 2000: 195; Layard 1930: 59–60). Tricksters are unsettled wonderers, appearing out of nowhere and again disappearing into nothingness, being closely associated with storytelling and hunting, in particular the invention of fishing nets, thus the kind of activities dominating human lives before settlement and the invention of agriculture. The close association with wild animals also points to distant origins. Finally, and at the same time, the trickster also has links to the other realm, the supernatural, though he is hardly ever described as a deity proper, and his associations are almost always connected not to the realm of the divine proper, rather to obscure areas of the underworld, the world of the living dead. The living dead is just an automatism, lacking a proper soul and the ordering power of the mind, like a Golem, while also serving as model for the first machine, a substitute for man's power.

While such an in-between position, extending at the same time to the human, the animal and the divine, is already quite unique, even more specific is the trickster's ability of shifting shapes between different corresponding forms. The ability of metamorphosis, or of taking up different forms, is a characteristic of gods in many traditions – though in our reading this fact itself indicates some kind of trickster interference. Yet, for gods this is rather a minor attribute, and never questions their fundamental character. Specific to the trickster is a certain – again paradoxical, ambivalent, even absurd – essential hybridity: the trickster is not a divinity that occasionally might don an animal shape, rather it as if hovers between these different shapes, leaving normal humans at a loss in guessing whether the being they encounter is a human in a fox shape, an inferior – and easily infernal – deity masked as an old man, or a spider that can transmogrify itself into a demon at any moment. The most paradoxical hybridity of the trickster, however, is that it comes from nothing and itself is nothing, a living dead, with multiple, undefined souls.

A further, crucial feature of the trickster, if we combine the various traditions, is that while it is a kind of divinity, it is in permanent conflict with the gods, especially the main, creator deity, and even more so with the main female deity, the Great Goddess. Behind various trickster stories we not only get a glimpse of very ancient times, which in contemporary terminology we can easily associate with the Neolithic, even the Palaeolithic, but of a very ancient conflict between the gods and the kind of obscure semi-divinities or rather in-between beings that are the tricksters. The outcome of such struggles, almost always and quite inevitably, is that the trickster loses; however, a good indication that this is not the full story is contained in the fact that it is also considered, in many traditions, as – using a problematic term – the second founder of the world.

Such figures, and events, could easily be translated into the Biblical language of the original sin and the devil, or the conflict between Zeus and the Titans, in the terminology of Greek mythology. Alternatively, one could opt for the opposite solution and make use solely of the anthropological and mythological tradition outside our own culture. We decided upon an approach that perhaps is more difficult at the start, but promises to be more rewarding, and which is to argue that the trickster belongs to a single tradition, that can be traced to the Palaeolithic, using archaeological facts, and should be approached genealogically, starting from the most remote past, and not projecting backwards our own worldview, following evolutionist schemas. Thus, from this perspective, let us try to make sense of this strange being, the trickster, which came to challenge the divine given order.

To start with, in the various traditions, taken together, the trickster is described through practically any possible negative human characteristics. The trickster is a liar and a thief, a glutton and a lecher, a cheat, deceiver, outlaw, outcast, fool and clown, a street robber and brigand, an intriguer but also using insolent language, an impudent immoral braggart; cold, impotent, never to be satisfied, full of resentment. In order to make sense out of such a seemingly infinite list we can start by noting that the trickster can be characterised not simply by a series of negative features, but first of all by a number of lacks, gaps, and absences. We can start by one of the most evident and striking characteristics of the trickster, its lack of any cooperation. The trickster is not only lonely, but simply fails to belong anywhere. Solitude even in our days is a taxing condition, but in prehistoric times it was almost unthinkable and unliveable – except, evidently, for the trickster. In fact, the ultimate punishment in those days, as evidenced by the term '*homo sacer*', was banning (see Agamben 1998) – and the trickster indeed shows many similarities to the *homo sacer*.

Being alone means not simply being outside the community, but having no family; in fact, being outside the lines of descent or filiation characteristic of family-based communities, thus human life. The trickster is not only impotent, its offspring being artificially produced hybrids (Horvath 2019c), but does not seem to have parents either, in most accounts. However, just as it is true for most of his other features, this can suffer a radical reversal: suddenly, strikingly, the trickster settles down and has a family, even a multiplicity of children, where – as a further reversal of the standard storyline – it can even change gender, giving birth to numerous offspring (Radin 1972: 137–140). Still further, in just as sudden and striking manner, the trickster might leave his family and return to his aimless wandering ways. In several accounts this aspect of the trickster has a further variation: while he is impotent, unable to generate normal offspring, it succeeds in bringing into the world a new breed of monsters, or hybridity (Dumézil 1986).

The trickster stories, as they survived into our present, remain at the phenomenological level: they tell us how these figures were perceived and experienced over the long centuries and millennia, but can hardly offer proper reasons and explanations about how tricksters had become what they were, and what they were set to do. They tell us how the trickster appears, always out of the blue, and often with surprising suddenness (in fact, such sudden appearance belongs to one of its central features, or key tricks), but cannot relay why the trickster is man-made, as it was conjured up by man himself – by some foolish minds, the kind which was incapable for goodness, for good dispositions. It is here that more reflexive, philosophically based accounts help move further. Such a point was advanced by Leon Battista Alberti in his *Momus* (see Horvath 2013: 65–74), suggesting that central for the trickster is the incapacity to trust and to give, thus ordinary sociability and filiation.

Closely connected to his lack of sociability is the absence of any authentic emotions of cooperativity. The trickster not only cannot love anybody else, but is incapable of friendship as well. In many stories the trickster figure is presented as a friend of the gods, and they even need him, due to his keen cunning intelligence (Détienne and Vernant 1978); but even the gods cannot trust him (Dumézil 1986: 10; Turville-Petre 1964: 128, 131–136). In fact, the trickster simply does not feel anything, one of the main reasons why it is able to suggest solutions to problems, with its ruse, in situations where others are overcome by their emotions.

But the trickster not only lacks a number of basic characteristics, fundamental for human and social life, but simply *is* absence, almost nothingness itself. This is captured in a particularly telling etymology of the name of a demon that in some accounts is identified with the Winnebago trickster: 'he-of-whose-existence-one-is-doubtful' (Radin 1972: 150).

However, as if to compensate for such absences, the trickster also has a series of features that indicates the opposite of absence: excess, plenty, multitude, the key for its human usage and exploit – though never fullness, contentment, satisfaction. This is most evidently related to his performance of basic bodily functions. The trickster has an excessive appetite, a yearning for forms: it eats and drinks enormous amounts and – a logical consequence – it also evacuates its body very frequently, and in enormous quantities. Still, the act most characteristic of the trickster, which for him becomes indeed nothing else but a bodily function, is sexuality. He takes up every possible sexual shape and position, using indiscriminately any possible entry to the body (Blakely 2006: 3; Radin 1924: 18–19; Radin 1972: 137–138, 165–168; Layard 1930: 524–525; Dumézil 1986: 217–218; Horvath 2008; Turville-Petre 1964: 129, 131, 144), as inventive ploys for corruption.

These features culminate in a particularly important feature: the trickster embodies excess itself, or hubris. Here again the figure of Prometheus is particularly helpful, even the Titans in general, through their hubris, or outrageous arrogance. This term plays a particularly important role in Greek thought, as hubris captures a kind of personality trait that is different both from a deed that can be punished by law, but also from the idea of evil (Gernet 2001: preliminary chapter). Yet, hubris has vital, even foundational connections to the law, and also to evil. On the one hand, acts of hubris were not punishable by law (Gernet 2001: ch. 1). On the other, the etymological origin of the word 'evil' is the same as that of hubris, the idea of failing to give respect to due limits (Onions 1966: 332). Thus, even if we moderns might not associate hubris with evil or the diabolical, a main reason why it is often claimed that the idea of evil is foreign to Greek thinking, they knew it better and considered hubris as the very source of evil.[4]

By now, another turn has been completed. We started from the trickster's fundamental deficiencies; then moved to the opposite features, its excesses; and now we discovered that the source of its excesses, or its plenty, is another shortcoming: the failure to keep order and respect limits. The situation, actually, is even more perplexing, as the trickster essentially belongs to the limit, being nothing but a figure of the threshold, a boundary marker, even a mediator.[5]

Here we reach something in between a great wisdom and a mind-boggling paradox. A figure of the threshold, or the limit, just because it stands in between two realms, or modes of being, cannot belong exclusively to any of the two, thus must be literally in-between – a hybrid, demonstrating features of both. Yet, at the same time, a limit also means measure, thus has a certain model value, which cannot be taken up by an insignificant, weightless figure, being prone to any excess. How could someone destined to mark the measure become transformed into a figure of excess? This might well be the greatest mystery around this strange figure that is the trickster.

We need to investigate further, in particular concerning the specific type of knowledge attributed to the trickster, and the manner in which the in-betweenness, or ambivalence, of the figure has been thematised.

Ambivalence or ambiguity is a central feature of the trickster in every tradition (Détienne and Vernant 1978: 3–4; Guenther 1999: 4–6, 95–115). Such ambivalence includes elusiveness: when encountering a trickster, one can hardly even recognise whether this brings fortune or disaster (Radin 1972:

147–150); furthermore, one hardly knows whether one meets a trickster or not, given that the trickster is difficult to pin down, as it manages to change shape. Even further, the trickster is at home in confused and inchoate situations, thus purposefully attempts to proliferate them; can only live and thrive in situations which others find intolerable. Finally, the most important and also most lethal ambivalence of the trickster concerns its attitude with respect to knowledge – at any rate, one of its most characteristic and important features.

Very often the trickster appears, in the full ambivalent meaning of the term, as a witless idiot. Not being part of the community, of any community, he does not know how to behave, ignoring customs and all those aspects of a culture that can only be known through long-term personal belongingness. Yet, at the same time the trickster also knows many things, even things that are not known at all, or distinctly feared, by all members of the community. Thus, at the same time of being an idiot, the trickster also appears as a particularly knowledgeable man – even in the guise of a sage. However, this knowledge, even if often working, or functional, has a great limitation, in that the trickster's knowledge, everywhere and always, is imitative, driven by resentment for the knowledge of others. The trickster can only ever imitate things, never doing anything with full participation and inner conviction, as the trickster is only a mime, impersonification of the flux, incapable of participation, belongingness, genuine emotions that come from the heart. Thus, the more a trickster knows, or seems to know, the more dangerous it is, as it only exchanges, transforms, metamorphoses real knowledge, gained through experience and the heart, into tricks that can be imitated and that can lead astray the naïve – at least, for a time, in line with the old saying that it is possible to fool all people some time, some people even all the time, but it is not possible to fool all people all the time.

Recognising the bipolar ambivalence of not only the trickster, but also of its knowledge, is not the solution, only a step towards posing the problem. We now have to ask the right questions concerning the conditions of possibility of such knowledge. This again means to proceed genealogically, and trying to intuit, following the way Gregory Bateson (1958) discovered the quite closely related term schismogenesis, the sequential structure by which the trickster gained these features, building layers upon layers, in its relationship to knowledge, a central aspect of its being, which then created, in various traditions, the kind of phenomenological awareness about the activities of the trickster. In other words, what anthropologists and mythologists recorded is only a summary, or a factorial outcome, in forms systematised to various degrees, of the ways tricksters acted over long millennia. Here we should recall that the trickster is only considered as second founder of the world. This means that it is incapable for anything genuine and original, only ever imitating what has already been done before; however, at the same time, it is indeed something like a matrix, a perverted constructor, imitating the real world, thus playing a fundamental role in altering the order of reality.

The trickster as a second creator can be illustrated by some quite extraordinary aspects of Bushman/ San/ Khoisan mythology.[6] The trickster has a pervasive importance for Bushman mythology, just as Bushman rituals are dominated by trance (Guenther 1999: 4). This mythology makes a clear-cut distinction between the first and second creation. The first world of chaos was dominated by flux and fluidity (4–5). This was an inchoate world where '[b]eings and states were in flux and boundaries were fluid' (66). It was therefore an ambivalent world where the trickster was the primary protagonist, 'perfectly at home in this inchoate world' (96), where through its moral transgressions 'ambiguity reigned supreme' (66). The creator god was also present there, but this figure was 'clouded in vagueness', as he was an 'enigmatic divinity', who somehow became 'remote from the affairs of people' (63). As a result of this there was need for a second creation, this time by the trickster, and the 'improved' (as Guenther put it, 'altered' or 'less flawed'; 68) world in which we now live, and where the trickster is an undisputed ruler, even a god (97–98), is a consequence of this. The Bushmen offer the clearest case for a trickster god: 'nowhere does the figure's status as divinity appear to be defined as clearly as in Khoisan religion', not even in Greek Hermes or West African Eshu (6). The Bushman trickster has several names and several animals forms, thus cannot even be pinned down to a particular form or name (95–99). As a particularly intriguing point, names given to tricksters include names used for the spirits of the dead, or to children born to gods (98). Tricksters in human form are either giants or dwarfs, like 'the Nharo trickster Pate, a short manikin, resembling a cock-grouse in size and bearing' (98). Not surprisingly, as a result of all this not only Bushman cosmology and mythology, but also society is penetrated by ambivalence (4), while Bushman religion became 'infused with ambiguity' (5) – one of the most important of which is the '[m]oral ambivalence about killing and eating animals' (75). Such Bushman views are particularly amazing as they show a close correspondence to the central principles of ancient Eastern Gnosticism, distant thousands of years and miles away. The idea of the trickster as a second creator and its metamorphosis are tightly connected: the trickster alters the world order by imitating it, taking it apart, and putting it together differently, merely miming the original.

A skill generally attributed to the trickster, and central for its ambiguity, is the ability to take up various forms, to change shape, or metamorphosis (Burkert 1984: 841, in connection with sacrifice; Détienne and Vernant 1978: 20; Dieterlen 1989: 39; Guenther 1999: 70, 99–101; Radin 1937: 177–183, in connection with sacrifice; Radin 1972: 78–103, in the context of a thorough analysis of van Gennep's work of rites of passage), leading to his widely used designation as a 'transformer' (Bright 1993: 21; Radin 1924: 22; Radin 1927: 347; Ricketts 1965). This has three basic forms. The first, most common and evident is the assumption of animal forms (Dumézil 1986: 128; Guenther 1999: 98–99; Kerényi 1980: 159; Layard 1930; Radin 1972: xxiii–iv). In fact, the trickster is often presented, in folktales and ethnographic accounts, in the shape of animals, the most common being the snake, the fox, the coyote, the

22 *Presenting the trickster*

spider, the hare, or the monkey.[7] However, the power/ knowledge of metamorphosis implies something different, the actual ability of the trickster to transform itself into the shape of any body, even animal. Here the connections with imitation, or miming, are again tight. Imitating the sound or gestures of animals is a central skill of various jokers and pranksters in all cultures. However, still an enormous gulf separates the imitation of certain animals from the idea of actually *becoming*, at least for a time, such an animal itself. We either assume an archaic mind unable to make such distinctions – but the enormous mental skills required by cave art, or the creation of a language, go against such an idea – or we have to be able to account for the specific reasons why such a confusion could have become credible.

The second major modality of metamorphosis brings out such a difficulty particularly clearly. Tricksters quite often are not simply able to take up the shape of various animals, but can outright fly – which has a close affinity with the flux (Dumézil 1986: 230–231; Guenther 1999: 98–99; Layard 1930; Radin 1937: 117). This may or may not be combined with the taking up of a birdlike shape, and such capability is also closely associated with the mastery of fire. On the opposite end, tricksters are also associated with crawling, which is closely connected to the snake, the ancient symbol of Eros – with the link between snakes and birds assured by their hatching eggs.

The third major type of metamorphosis is gender or sex change, already alluded to (Radin 1972: 137; Turville-Petre 1964: 131). While tricksters are male, often characterised by an enormous penis, in search for any opening, they can also take up female form, a metamorphosis also associated with the most various kinds of sex acts.

As this brings out with particular clarity, though already present not only in the very idea of metamorphosis, but even in the stories about stealing fire, the trickster does, and represents in its being, a violation to the very order of nature, embodied in its hubris, one of its most important characteristics. The trickster has a variety of skills, knows many things that others do not even imagine, but such knowledge is never connected to awareness about the basic, underlying, graceful order of the world; it is from somewhere else. If the trickster ever touches upon the question of order, it is only to consider this order as something external and oppressive, a mere rigidity, thus justifying his restless, unceasing efforts to upset this order, to create a world turned upside down. This can even be seen in the relationship, or rather non-relation and non-knowledge, of the trickster concerning all the basic, ordinary human activities, as embodied in the tri-partite model discovered by Dumézil. The trickster is a clear antagonist of the sovereign power contained in the first function,[8] but is also the radical antithesis of the warrior ethic characteristic of the second function. The trickster is never a model of courage, rather often a coward, never engaging in open combats, relying rather on his wily intelligence. It is quite revealing that the trickster is never credited with the discovery of weapons, even those used against animals, like the bow or the spear, rather with entrapping animals in holes or nets. Finally, the trickster is not even associated with most of the ordinary skills and occupations characteristic of the third state, except for those connected with metallurgy, thus transformative and involving the fire, in particular the blacksmith, to be discussed soon in more detail. The trickster is not only an outlaw and an outcast, even an 'out-caste', recalling Dumézil, but is literally outside the ordinary everyday life of human beings.

Conclusion

Until now, our approach has been limited to reviewing the anthropological and mythological literature on the trickster, based on the perspective of trying to make sense of the way the trickster appeared from the outside. In the following chapters will take on the all but impossible task of glimpsing into the other side, the way tricksters looked for themselves, or the way they were. As a first step, we'll discuss two classic studies by Evans-Pritchard.

Notes

1 This chapter much draws on our earlier work, in particular Horvath (1998, 2008, 2019a), Szakolczai (2007b), and Szakolczai and Thomassen (2019, ch. 5).
2 It reached though W. H. Auden, for whom Layard, together with Tolkien, was a major source of inspiration.
3 This is somewhat problematic to use for the trickster, as the expression can be traced back to St Bonaventure (*Itinerary*, Prologue 4), the second founder of the Franciscan order, a Platonic-Christian theologian and philosopher, referring to the powers of the human mind or soul.
4 For an excellent anthropological study connecting evil and the trickster, see Overing (1985).
5 Greek *herma* 'border marking stone', etymological root of the word Hermes, name of another major trickster quasi-deity, and one which will have a fundamental importance for this book.
6 This has its own significance, as the Bushmen are one of the last archaic hunter-gatherer communities, with a language that shows similarities with the Afroasiatic family.
7 It should be noted that the three most common animals depicted in the megalithic sanctuary of Göbekli Tepe (10,000–8,000 BC) are the fox, the snake, and the spider; thus, this sanctuary can be considered as a 'trickster bestiary'. For further details, see Horvath and Szakolczai (2018a: 102–113).
8 Here the split between the kingly and the priestly represents the successful split of this first function, and the infiltration of the trickster-shaman-artist-priest into sovereignty, particularly characteristic of Vedic India.

2 Techniques of trickster entrapment
The nets of spiders and magicians

The previous chapter offered an introduction into the figure of the trickster, using a wide set of readings. This chapter will focus on two works by E. E. Evans-Pritchard. The reason is that these, with their contrasts, offer a perfect illustration for the problem the figure represented for modern anthropology, while also an introduction into the question of how – if at all possible – to move behind the merely external perspective of a social science. Thus, we'll argue that Evans-Pritchard's admitted blunder of not extending the original investigation to the figure of the trickster can be turned into an asset, as a joint reading of his two books can offer us a glimpse into a from inside perspective of the knowledge and world, especially world view, of tricksters. The unique value contained in and revealed by the two works is due to two factors, beyond their evident qualities. First, Evans-Pritchard stumbled upon a particularly significant, as revealing, trickster figure, the spider; and second, the two parts of his analysis, written and published 3–4 decades apart, fit perfectly together, as two parts of a *symbolon*, thus giving, in a snapshot, an almost complete analysis of the trickster, from outside (as seen by the people and contained in folktales) and from inside (as the knowledge is operated and transmitted by the real-world trickster figures). As the first study ignored the figure of the trickster, it could not be considered as being influenced or stimulated by the effort to understand the trickster, thus the two together offer a truly independent and thus revealingly confirming piece of evidence.

Evans-Pritchard is an undisputed classic of anthropology, one of the first professors of the discipline in Oxford, where he hold the chair from 1946 to 1970. His fame was much based on his classic work on magic, witchcraft and sorcery among the Azande (Evans-Pritchard 1976), based on his 1927 dissertation. In this work, there is no mention of the trickster. His collection about Ture, the Zande trickster, was only published decades later, as an explicit act of penance, as he recognised that he himself 'erred in this respect' (Evans-Pritchard 1967: 15): previously he failed to pay any attention to the figure of the trickster, or to folktales in general, given that his teachers, Seligman and Malinowski were simply not interested in such presumed trivialities.[1]

The Zande trickster, and what might it mean that a trickster is a spider

The Zande trickster is called Ture, a name that means spider. Ture is both a spider, and is a man – the difference creating no problem for the Azande. Ture is simply *the* central figure of Zande folktales; and as practically there is no difference there between mythology and tales, the only two stories that could be classified as myths telling the origins of the royal clan and the – quite fantastic, though considered as true – exploits of two archetypal witch doctors,[2] Ture the spider has an unchallenged centrality for Zande imagination.

What might it mean that the Zande trickster is a spider? On a first look, it is by no means obvious that this has any significance. Ture is just another typical trickster, manifesting the standard repertoire: he is 'a monster of depravity: liar, cheat, lecher, murderer; vain, greedy, treacherous, ungrateful, a poltroon, a braggart', being an 'utterly selfish person', everything against which Zande morality stands; yet, who nevertheless has another character, showing 'whimsical fooling, recklessness, impetuosity', even 'puckish irresponsibility', thus having 'an endearing innocence' (Evans-Pritchard 1967: 28). Moving to the level of interpretation, and still closely following Evans-Pritchard, such stories are seemingly universal and timeless, capturing – allegedly – some inevitable dark features of human nature, according which we all would like to kill our neighbours and take their wives, but even to kill our fathers and sons, and furthermore to make love to our mother-in-laws (30–32, 43, 93, 103, 139, 144–146, among many other stories – at the end of which Ture usually 'fled' and 'wandered off to a different country', 155). Such stories are fascinating, as they play out our deepest wishes and desires – the full truth. We are thus safely led back to a combination of neoclassical economics, neo-Kantian legalism, Marx and Freud: the dialectic of object and subject, consciousness and the unconscious, facts and norms.

However, in this way, we not only reduce the trickster to a simple reverse side of our own rationality, but, even more importantly, the possible significance of a spider trickster is lost. We thus suggest two different paths. One is through a particularly perceptive re-analysis of the Zande trickster by André Singer, in a Festschrift to Evans-Pritchard. The other, closely connected path concerns paying close attention to one of the most important, though strangely underplayed, insights of Radin: that the trickster, in so far as a culture hero, is also a transformer and a fixer; and that these two features, central and puzzling as they are, are also connected, in their substituting role.

Trickster formulas and short cuts

The work of Singer, just as that of Evans-Pritchard, was much inspired by and embedded in the spirit of its times. For Evans-Pritchard, it originally meant the Durkheimian functionalism of Radcliffe-Brown and Malinowski; for Singer, the Freudo-Marxism that came to dominate academia by the 1970s. Thus, Singer (Singer and Street 1972: xiii) makes much out of the

26 Presenting the trickster

trickster figure as a would-be 'rebel'; and tends to agree, following the late work of Evans-Pritchard, that even the most atrocious behaviour of the trickster can be accepted as a kind of playing out our own 'darkest desires' (Singer 1972: 86). Still, perhaps because Singer explicitly roots his re-analysis of Ture in a confrontation with the work of Radin, it brings to the surface a number of crucial features of the spider trickster.

His analysis starts with the recognition that central to the behaviour of Ture is a series of fatal confusions around ends and means. In reality, the ends and means of human life cannot be separated: we do not do things, like growing up, or have children, because we decide about some special ends, and then chose the best means to achieve them, but because we are born into a particular community (in fact, a series of concentric communities), and culture, and follow our ancestors and peers in the most rightful way can – until and unless something extraordinary happens, shaking things up. The absurdity of the ends-means separation, which neo-Kantianism elevated into the unquestionable height of rational thinking, is that the end of human life, in terms its ultimate act, is most evidently death; however, nobody could possibly suggest that this is the end of our life in the sense of an objective or aim. The trickster logic starts spinning itself by first separating ends and means, and then escalating problems – as such separation was already a serious problem – by putting them together in the wrong manner. Thus, the trickster has ends in the sense of fixations, or persistent aims (Singer 1972: 82–83), meaning that for him the most natural aspects of human life, like eating, drinking, or sex, become automatisms which it tries to pursue at any price, and of which he can never have enough. Such obsession with ends directly leads to a similar obsession with means: the life of the trickster is spent with machinations (an absolutely central word, for the purposes of this book, meaning an automatised plot against any order of life) in order to fulfil his insatiable ends (83).

Such machinations are characterised by three further crucial terms: imitation, formulas, and shortcut. As the trickster is an outsider and outcast to real life, because it just cannot do things right, it lacks the solid inner determination every being has in living life a principled kind of way, so has to imitate everybody in everything; it even takes delight in such imitations. Second, and for the same reasons, its concrete acts mean the application of rigid and simplistic formulas. Instead of doing things, the trickster behaves as if following an algorithm – as a feeling automaton, an *ante verbum* artificial intelligence. Singer characterises such formulas by three crucial terms: magic, ritual, and tricks, each having the character of being outside the normal everyday logic of human life. With an eye on modernity, we could add the term policy, especially those that follow the best practice, a central method by which our life is transformed by various fixations – as such best practices imply a universalistic rule, a presumed magic wand (bringing in at once another key word of Singer, and an allusion to alchemy, this time) that manages to dislocate the concrete practices that took into account time and place, serving a kind of generalised logic which can be called neoliberalism, but just as well bureaucratisation. Finally, instead of taking up the usual way, with its necessary hardships, the trickster always looks for shortcuts and bypasses. The example Singer gives is having sex without marrying, or taking up the enjoyment but escaping the consequences and responsibilities.

The question of shortcuts is a point that has much relevance for the book; for the moment, we only need to add two comments. First, this logic of the short cut also has its schismogenic counter-pair, as it is true for everything the trickster, this schismatic and bipolar creature does: this is the logic of asceticism, or the opposite idea that everything that involves excessive, almost unbearable hardship must by necessity be good, and hardship as such in itself is the best way to properly reach ends.[3] The trickster as a figure of shortcut can help us understand the astonishing aspect of the incommensurability (or irrationality) of the diagonal of the square, or of surd numbers. This is a phenomenon we all know from mathematics; in fact, the idea of irrational numbers is introduced in elementary school in this way; but we pay no attention to the meaning of the term irrational here, and are mystified by the problem this represented for the Greeks, primarily including Plato and even Aristotle. This can be understood, first, by realising that an irrational number is one that cannot be paired in a harmonious relation (the original meaning of ratio) with any other integer number; and second, that the diagonal of a square represents a shortcut in the sense of not following the path alongside the two sides of the square (or the square deal), rather taking a short cut – where the violence involved in the word 'cut' underlines the affront done to the square deal. The lesson is the standard Greek wisdom that everything must be done rationally, meaning following the right measure, the *metros* or *logos*, two central terms of the philosophy of Heraclitus, instead of trying to obtain unreasonable personal gain by taking a short *cut*. Thus, we have a proper definition concerning the irrationality of trickster rationality, based on shortcuts and end-means separation, or the fundamental principles of neoclassical economics, solving the problem of the irrational rationality of capitalism that preoccupied since such a long time Max Weber and his best followers like Karl Löwith.

Returning to Ture, the formulas of the trickster – magic, rituals and tricks – surprisingly often work, and bring quick success to the trickster. However, the folktale wisdom is – and the survival of any village community is a proof that the trickster failed to gain the upper hand – this only happens in larger entities, especially empires, which by definition can only be the result of trickster machinations – that the failure of the trickster is inevitable, and when he fails, he loses everything (89). In fact, this is the only reason, according to Singer, why the trickster is depicted, in spite of all the atrocities he committed, topped with his arrogance, as an endearing character.

Through the contrast with Radin's work Singer emphasises three central features of the trickster, confirming the analysis of the previous chapter, and carrying a crucial message for the book: that the trickster is less of a creator deity – this is only a late, priestly manipulation – rather is fundamentally intrusive (96); that the creative role identified with the trickster is due to its specific combination of creation and destruction, or of only creating out of destroying;[4] and that the trickster figure is fundamentally concerned with boundaries.

The trickster as transformer-fixer

The trickster is capable of magic, even of the most stunning of magical acts, transformation, including self-transformation. It can change not only its gender, but change between an animal and human form – thus it can be taken for granted, by audiences all around the world, that the trickster is at the same time animal and human, or a hybrid. Still, most importantly, in the midst of all this flux, the trickster also fixates. This can be shown through the effect mechanism of trickster stories, as conveyed by Evans-Pritchard.

Such fixating is done not just in the stories but through the stories. The trickster fixates the audience into the forms of behaviour, but even more importantly the forms of imagination it conjures up; the stories are therefore performative speech acts. Finally, it is in this way that we can understand why the trickster is a spider: it is so by capturing, entrapping and fixating the audience by weaving its own stories. The trickster being a spider is thus at the same time a performative speech act and a revelation. The trickster, but also the storyteller, is a spider because it indeed spins a web through the stories, and captures the audience – everyone, an entire culture – in the stories thus told. But, in an astonishing way, it does something even more: by identifying the trickster with the spider, it somehow even reveals its own nature.

The spider, however, not only reveals itself indirectly, through its activity of entrapping – thus recalling the duplicated representation of Foucault's *Order of Things* – but at the same time presents another key feature of the trickster, the creation of the very space of its own activities, a special, liminal place, out of the ordinary, where such an entrapping becomes possible. The spider weaves its own web as a special kind of place in which the victims then become entrapped, suspended – this special place, the web, is itself suspended, as if it were a gigantic screen, or – ever better – a kind of parabolic antenna.[5] Furthermore, this space is circular, with the storyteller (or magician/ trickster/ wizard) in its centre, recalling the village circle (rarely a square), in which public rituals are performed. Such circularity also recalls another key trickster animal, the snake, which produces a circle on the legendary occasion when it bites its own tail – an act which again recalls the act of entrapment, but also and in particular its demonic modality of entrapping in a vicious circle, *circulus vitiosus*, or the devil's circle. This not simply ties a knot between two of the most important trickster animals, the spider and the serpent, but at the same time places the accent in this connection on the demonic or even outright diabolical aspects of the trickster. Even further, the space created by the spider has a very special pattern, recalling the human skin, another boundary (and by implication also the polygonal walls of archaic Greek and Latin cities), and even the skin of reptiles, in particular again the snake. In the middle of this web, there sits the spider – or the trickster story-teller, or the trickster sorcerer, the Sophist, the Gnostic, the alchemist, or any other of the manifold trickster masks and impersonations.[6]

Apart from needing, and creating, a special place, the telling of trickster tales also requires a similarly special and liminal time, the darkness of the night: 'Ture tales are told after sunset', usually by men, and all around Africa 'it is regarded as improper, and also liable to bring about misfortune, should the tales be told in daylight' (Evans-Pritchard 1967: 18). The liminal features of the night and its uncanniness (*Unheimlichkeit*) were specifically emphasised by Károly Kerényi – a central and classic figure in the literature about the trickster, author of an afterword to Radin's 1972 book – in his milestone study of Hermes (Kerényi 1986; for more discussion, see Chapter 3).

Such a special place and time are fundamental for fixating all members of the community, and for a lifetime. While one might suppose that such temporal and spatial coordinates exclude the participation of children in such sessions, the opposite is true. The technique is the same as for theatrical performances of sorcery: 'Ture stories are implanted at an early age in the minds of children, who do not keep fact and fancy apart', and so as an adult '[h]e cannot totally reject something out of which his imaginative life has been formed' (Evans-Pritchard 1967: 31). Even further, children are often told such stories while going to bed, thus on the one hand exciting their eagerness, on the other assuring that whatever they heard would stay with them during their sleep, in their dreams (19). The similarities, but also the differences, between such trickster stories and standard European folktales are evident. The heroes of European folktales are rarely tricksters; and when they are, they do not perform the kind of exploits characteristic of Ture. However, parallels are tight with the impact of watching television, both set on inserting the void into the body since early childhood so that it would stay with them forever, blackening the soul through the impossible idea that you could be anything, thus forming a tight web of perfect entrapment into eternal dissatisfaction.

Why these are the Zande whose trickster is a spider?

While we cannot explain why in some cultures the trickster, identified as spider, reveals its nature, we can approach the issue from the perspective of the parallels between the conditions of emergence of the modern trickster world and of the Zande (and not only). Such conditions include massive dislocations, wars and violence, or a series of major crises, where indeed the most atrocious acts imaginable were regularly performed, as a fact – though not as a regular and normal feature of human nature. Under normal conditions, nobody wants to kill one's neighbour, not to say one's father, and similarly, would not want to make love to one's mother in law – the very act of putting such atrocious behaviour into words is an offence, which means that we have to be aware of what we are doing right now – though cannot do otherwise, emulating Plato who in the *Sophist* agreed with Parmenides that in principle we should not talk about things that are unreal, but given that this is what the Sophists do, he is forced to do so. But things like that happened in the distant past solely under chaotic liminal conditions. The central issue then is how to overcome such conditions, and return to normality and decency. However, tricksters – real-world tricksters – can only thrive under such conditions of uncertainty and ambivalence. So they take such liminal events as the heart of reality, as reality itself, and cunningly manage to fixate people into them, making liminality permanent.

Once such a feat is accomplished, a proper return to normality becomes all but impossible, and the situation can be prolonged into infinity – unless an external, stable, normal reference point is found somewhere; or until some external force gracefully gifts again normality.

From this perspective, and without going into details, one should start by noting the extremely liminal situation of the Azande, living in between the Central African Republic, the Republic of the Congo, and the Sudan; in between traditional African culture, Christianisation and Islamisation; and even on a linguistic borderline between Nilo-Saharan, Afro-Asiatic and Niger-Congo languages – the latter linguistic difference evidently preserving some memory of the highly conflict-ridden spread of settlement and the Neolithic into Africa.[7] The figure thus certainly captures and preserves long-standing schismogenic processes, persisting until the present, as in the moment we live the area is part of one of the most conflict ridden regions in the world.

Other spider tricksters

The figure is by no means limited to the Zande. The perhaps best-known case is Anansi of the Ashanti, a people in Ghana (Pelton 1980: 25–70); a figure that became widely spread in West Africa, and even extended to the Caribbean, becoming a Jamaican folk hero (Marshall 2007). Spider tricksters are also present in North-America. Examples include the Cheyenne Veeho – a figure similarly all-encompassing as Zande Ture; and Iktomi in Lakota (Sioux) mythology – a figure strikingly associated with a prophecy according to which its power will be extended over the entire Land, that has come to be interpreted as a strange premonition of the telephone and the internet. Finally, even the Nordic trickster-god Loki has a spider aspect, as *locke* is spider in Swedish (Clover and Lindow 2005: 84–85).

Iktomi

At one level, Iktomi is a typical trickster figure. He is conceited and lazy, preferring a snore to a good hunt – thus is a parasite (Zitkala-Sa 1901: 2). Being full of tricks, tricking both men and beasts, and is even trying to destroy the entire people (Walker 1980: 128; see also Walker 2006: 227), it is no surprise that it is without friends: nobody helps it or loves it, everybody being sick and tired of its 'vain words' and 'heartless laughter' (Zitkala-Sa

1901: 2). Revealing the shared character or even identity of the trickster figure across the broad area, the story about the trickster teaching the ducks to sing with closed eyes so that he could wring their necks, one by one, selected as a most telling Winnebago trickster tale by Radin (1972: 15) is the number one Iktomi story in Zitkala-Sa's collection, and is also the main story in Walker (2006: 166). Yet, the Sioux spider demonstrates a series of special features. He is particularly small, thus dwarfish, with a body recalling a fat bug (Walker 1980: 128). He is not simply an old man, but can make itself appear as such; and even further, can make itself invisible. He is also a hybrid, a monster, with the legs of a spider and the hands of a man; and is also capable of metamorphosis, or of physical transformation (Walker 2006: 165–166), in particular capable of moving in any sphere: swim, walk under the ground or on water, and even fly (Powers 1986: 114–115, 155–156).

Its most particular feature is its chthonic character, the predilection with the underground, or the underworld (Powers 1986: 91, 152–153). He has particular affinity with animals that are able to live or move underground, or with those connected to water, like frogs, lizards or turtles; thus can easily either disappear under the water or the ground (160–162). Taking all such abilities and living spaces together, Iktomi can be considered as being ubiquitous, encompassing all the spheres (155–156). A crucial consequence is that he not only can be anywhere, but see anything: 'there is nowhere a person can go without being seen or heard by spiders' (156). Iktomi is not only a forerunning of the internet, but also of the Panopticon and CCTV.

Thus, it is not surprising that the key distinguishing feature of Iktomi is his knowledge. For the Lakota, the trickster is the most knowledgeable of all creatures (155). It is particularly knowledgeable about the sacred (156), but is also reputed as the being that gave names to various things, and even can change such names (113–114, 152, 156–157). Most importantly, he did not disclose his own name – people came to name him as spider, but this is only one of its shapes (154–155).

The most important knowledge possessed by Iktomi concerns the weaknesses of people, by which he is able to manipulate and capture them (Walker 2006: 198). Strikingly, the Lakota were clearly aware about the tight connections between liminal situations and the impact of the trickster: if certain events happen, the appearance of Iktomi is inevitable. Such situations can help the spider to entrap people – and are closely associated with the spider's web (Powers 1986: 156). However, the Lakota were also aware that, no matter how skilful the trickster is in manipulating through its vast knowledge, gained by his omnipresence and the ability to change shapes, its powers are still limited, and for a quite striking reason: the trickster is 'driven to manipulate the weaknesses of others because he has been trapped by his own schemes to escape his physical identity' (Walker 2006: 198). Thus, the scheming of the trickster is traced back not to its strengths, but its fundamental weaknesses – and weaknesses which the trickster himself is perfectly aware of, thus is desperate to change his own physical appearance. Needless to say, from this it is evident that the ultimate trick of the trickster is to convince others – who do not at all need this – to give up their own features and change willingly their own character.

The last crucial feature of the trickster revealed by the Lakota is the close similarity between tricksters and demons (Walker 2006: 199). The central Lakota demon is Gnas, a frog, who created the world in order to saw discord between the gods – a clearly Gnostic motive, with its hostility to the world as it is, while the conflict-mongering among the divine recalls Alberti's Momus – who shares with Iktomi the predilection with tricking people (227).

Zande witchcraft and sorcery

Moving to Evans-Prichard's second book, at a first, evident, surface level, life in Zande society is penetrated and dominated by witchcraft: '*Mangu*, witchcraft, was one of the first words I heard in Zandeland, and I heard it uttered day by day throughout the months' (Evans-Pritchard 1976: 1). This is because daily life there – and in the broad area which is thoroughly penetrated by witchcraft, of which the Zande constitute its north-eastern edge (e.g. see 120–121) – is lived literally under the spell of witchcraft:

> Witchcraft is ubiquitous. It plays its part in every activity of Zande life; in agricultural, fishing, and hunting pursuits; in domestic life of homesteads as well as in communal life of district and court; it is an important theme of mental life in which it forms the background of a vast panorama of oracles and magic; its influence is plainly stamped on law and morals, etiquette and religion; it is prominent in technology and language; there is no niche or corner of Zande culture into which it does not twist itself.
> (Evans-Pritchard 1976: 18)

The main reason is that Zande culture does not acknowledge the possibility of a simple and sheer event. Nothing that happens – draught, death, illness, but literally the most minor misfortune, and not even misfortune – is supposed to take place without the operation of purposeful, dark, even sinister forces in the background: 'Azande attribute nearly all sickness, whatever the nature, to witchcraft or sorcery' (195).[8] One would presume that this situation offers a simple task for the ethnographer: illuminate and enlighten the primitive natives, through concrete cases and examples, about the falsity of their presumptions. Except that Evans-Pritchard soon had to realise that this does not work, as whatever happened offered a clear-cut proof for the Azande that their belief in magic was justified. How could this be the case?

The central issue is that belief in witchcraft is animated by a certain vision of the world, or a worldview, that situates anything that happens within a particular whole, interpreting it and giving meaning to it, and the dislocation of that whole is particularly cumbersome, if not impossible. This worldview did not exist on its own, but was systematically maintained by a group of people, the witch doctors or magicians, whom we consider as part of the ideal-type *Magi*, and who evidently also helped it to come into being. We need to explain the nature of the forces that help to root it so deeply inside a certain culture – a perspective that will offer us, we believe, priceless, and perhaps even astonishing insights into the nature of our own present.

Central to this worldview is the Gnostic, hostile idea that the world outside is an uncertain, threatening place, full of aggressive but invisible forces. We can immediately perceive that it is very difficult to convince somebody who holds such an idea that it is not so, as of course there are all kinds of threats and misfortunes in the world outside – bad weather, acts of treachery, even violence, illnesses and deaths. If we become too fixated on such eventualities, it might become considered a case of paranoia as an individual psychopathology. But what if this turns out to be the world vision of an entire culture? How could such a situation come into being? Of course, this is where terms like liminality, imitation, trickster and schismogenesis are vital, even indispensable; but let's go one step at a time.

Any misfortune, or even its threat, tests us; is a trial of one's force. Most of us under normal conditions manage to cope with such eventualities, without searching for others to blame. Such blaming is not an outcome of a primitive mentality, rather a serious error, a dead end to which one – or any community – had to be induced and entrapped. Central for such entrapment is the prior undermining of individual strength – the inner force that is inherent in us (Horvath 2019b), even in any living being, but which is more than a simple struggle for survival: it is the determination, or perhaps even decision (Heidegger), to maintain oneself (Pizzorno). How can this be undermined? And why?

The answer has two different sides. The first concerns ideas about the nature of the hostile forces, while the second the parallel vision concerning the inner forces, or rather weaknesses, of the individual. The two features support each other, forming a circle central for the way magicians could legitimate themselves.

Concerning the nature of evil forces, mobilised or activated by witches, the Zande held views that are strikingly close to some oriental religions and spirituality, but even Greek mythology. The soul of witches can leave their body, as a kind of emanation, which even emits light,[9] usually during night, when the victims are sleeping, and thus the witch from a distance tries to remove the soul of the victim, 'the soul of [the victim's] flesh, which he and his fellow witches will devour' (Evans-Pritchard 1976: 11). In other words, and clearly echoing Hermes, the aim of witches is to steal souls. The emission of a bright light is a crucial aspect of such nocturnal travels by the souls of witches, and with some evident consternation Evans-Pritchard make us privy to the story that one night he himself saw such a light, which he could not identify. As by morning a person indeed died nearby, all this 'accorded well with Zande ideas' (11). The question of distance is quite important, as according to the Zande witchcraft could be exerted from a distance, but only from a relatively short one (12), which corresponds strikingly well with the working of waves.

Another specific and particularly interesting aspect of witchcraft is that witches combine 'their destructive activities [with] subsequent ghoulish feasts' (Evans-Pritchard 1976: 14). This, one might say, is the standard theme of witches Sabbath, except that Zande magicians of course did not read their *Faust*, not being even familiar with European folklore, so the two traditions rather evidently have some common roots – unless one presumes a logical connection between witches and feasting. Here Natufian culture, between its weird cult of the dead and predilection with feasting, connected to burials, certainly invokes some fascinating connections.[10]

When witches die, their power does not diminish, but only increase, as their souls become evil ghosts, in contrast to the souls of other dead; ghosts which 'show a venomous hatred of humanity' (Evans-Pritchard 1976: 15). These ghosts represent a permanent danger to everyone, causing all kinds of misfortune. Thus, as every single misfortune, but especially death, is presumably a product of witchcraft, this must be avenged, which generates a pervasive and infective culture of vengeance (5–7). In order to limit their activity, evil spirits must be continually fought against, or resisted (88–89, 199). Such fights again evil spirits is also a central aspect of the theatrical character of magical sceances, and help to justify a permanent need for those persons, the witch doctors, who are most suited to fight such evils, and who for this first of all need to maintain regular contacts with the forces of evil (65).

'An act of witchcraft', Evans Pritchard argues, with some evident apprehension, perhaps even a touch of despair, is just a 'psychic act' (Evans-Pritchard 1976: 1), meaning that it is only the work of the mind, it is not real. However, whether such hostile forces exist or not – and here we declare ourselves truly agnostic, in the sense that we do not know whether or not such forces really existed, or exist, instead of the dogmatic position categorically denying the existence of any such force – such beliefs not only have evident impact on reality (like resulting in societies dominated by the problem of witchcraft), but have a connection with the incommensurable, or the irrational – in the Greek and not the modern sense of the word. Irrational numbers are those that, like the square root of 2, are not possible to set in common *ratio*, or harmonious proportionality, with other numbers. Witchcraft is certainly a play with the irrational, as we simply do not have a common measure with, say, the spirits of the dead. So they are better left in peace – and here we should pay close attention to the fact that the central concern of Azande – or other – magicians is to establish contact with them, with the presumed intention of eliminating evil forever, leading to the opposite and rather certain effect of becoming entangled with evil, if not forever, certainly for a long time. Resisting evil is a main way to increase and multiply its force. Resistance is rather the characteristics of objects, a wisdom language teaches us;[11] but hostile spirits are certainly not objects, so resisting them is simply meaningless. The real impact of such resistance is paying attention to them, and this is the worst thing one can do with them – again, irrespectively whether they exist (whatever this might mean with spirits) or not.

Concerning the second side, fundamental for a normal, healthy, non-pathological living is a certain self-evident, taken for granted trust or confidence in oneself; the conviction that we know who we are, what we are doing, and why, even if occasionally – but always only occasionally, and under very special circumstances! – we might have a vague feeling of being as if driven by forces beyond our control. Not so for the Azande – and evidently not only for them, but in all areas and cultures where belief in witchcraft and sorcery is endemic. Their vision of the world has a correlate in their vision of the human being, or themselves, as possibly, and fundamentally, guided by the same hostile forces even from the inside. The hostile supernatural forces have human accomplices, or witches. Such a status has a hereditary component, so relatives of a proven witch have a greater likelihood to be witches themselves; but this is not certain, and at any rate nobody can be sure until one dies that one is a witch or not.[12]

Given that witchcraft is connected only to particular events of distress, or misfortune, any Zande is only interested in it 'on definite occasions and in relation to his own interests, and not as a permanent condition of individuals'; thus, 'Azande are interested solely in the dynamics of witchcraft in particular situations' (Evans-Pritchard 1976: 4). However, the overall effect for the entire society, or culture, as we have seen, becomes a wholesale invasion by witchcraft – or a clear situation of permanent liminality. This would have an impact both on the character of the culture, and on the very structure of the society.

Concerning the former, Evans-Pritchard remarks about the general predisposition of the Zande that they are 'cheerful people who are always laughing and joking' (Evans-Pritchard 1976: 65), not being afraid of witchcraft because of the power of their witch doctors. However, laughter can mean many things, and while the general, benevolent and cheerful predisposition of no people can be doubted, living together with the ideas about the ever-presence of witchcraft certainly must colour such predisposition, creating a kind of duplicity, doubleness or even bipolarity which Evans-Pritchard perhaps was not able to catch. Similar effect was produced by another spider trickster, Anansi in Ghana; the relevant chapter in Pelton (1980: 25–70) is outright entitled 'Ananse: Spinner of Ashanti Doubleness'. The nature of such doubleness is well illustrated by the motto of the chapter, selected from an Ashanti tale: 'If you kill Ananse, the tribe will come to ruin! If you pardon Ananse, the tribe will shake with voices!' A country or culture becomes invaded by trickster logic when suddenly problems cannot be resolved – there is simply no way out of double bind situations. This point can be further supported by the particular features of Zande social structure, as example for a society infested with witchcraft.

Witch doctors by no means constitute the elite of Zande society. Quite on the contrary, they are rather outsiders – a crucial point, which in itself establishes a close connection between them and folktale tricksters. The society, like many African societies, was quite unequal, with a small aristocracy,

36 *Presenting the trickster*

whose only work was occasional hunting and whose reputation was way above that of the magicians (Evans-Pritchard 1976: 114–115), and the commoners (Gillies 1976: xiv). In contrast to this, magicians belong to a 'professional' group cultivating its own vested interests (Evans-Pritchard 1976: 66), often a secret society. In her 'Introduction', Eva Gillies (1976: xviii) makes a rather important comment about the negligence of anthropologists to become interested in secret societies – an omission recalling the similar lack of interest in terms like liminality, imitation, trickster, or schismogenesis, inculcated by Durkheim and Boas and transmitted through their students, and which generates the increasingly troubling impression that the official bastions of anthropology, far from promoting understanding, rather acted – for whatever reasons – as a similar kind of secret professional group trying to cover up their tracks. This is further supported by the astonishing similarity between modern technology and ancient magic, though not as Lévi-Strauss would have it in *The Savage Mind*, rather the opposite way: not justifying the savage, as being almost modern, rather showing the modern as indeed genuinely savage. Membership to such groups was granted through initiation rites, and the *esprit de corps* was strongly enforced: 'witch-doctors never contradict one another at a public séance; they present a united front to the uninitiated' (Evans-Pritchard 1976: 79). A further crucial feature of the group was its use of a particular jargon, helping to accept their ideas: '[t]he witch-doctor also gets his listeners into a suitable frame of mind for receiving his revelations by lavish use of professional dogmatism' (83). Such societies are also characterised by thorough misogyny (130), also evident in the connection between secret societies and the use of masks, with the prohibition of women to use or even touch masks. Finally, and most importantly, the content of their knowledge was strictly secret (68, 105, 116, 208–209), especially concerning the plants used as medication (96–97).

Becoming a witch doctor, magician or sorcerer was not an easy process.[13] It required money and also the toleration of extra hardship, as initiation ceremonies were quite taxing, even humiliating (Evans-Pritchard 1976: 109–110). It also turned one into an outcast – reconfirming that sorcerers are tricksters of a kind. So it is a costly and paradoxical investment, requiring the trick of enchanting, even seducing young children – which of course is highly immoral, though not more so than the way modern societies deploy similar tricks through communication technology. Initiation rites centre on inculcating not so much professional knowledge, but first of all unconditional adherence to the group. The ceremony involves two of the most important features widely associated with tricksters: metamorphosis, or the change into animal shape – the initiand is supposed to redefine himself as an animal, even accept that this is his real being (92); and a new name (110) – naming, especially changing names, is a central trickster and Sophist feature. Finally, and most importantly, a crucial part of initiation concerns a trip to underground caves, important for the gathering of the roots of the plants (99–100)[14] – but certainly having much broader, at once symbolical and very real meaning. In this regard, Evans-Pritchard conveys two particularly noteworthy aspects of the ritual: the initiand entered the cave on the back of the master of ceremonies, who was on all fours, as if imitating a horse; and when they were thus walking inside, '[t]he whole floor of the cavern vibrated' (100); a revealing sign for flux accumulation.

Still, in contrast to the *Magi* of Persia, the Brahmans of Vedic India, and the Levites of Ancient Judaism, magicians did not gain a high status, in spite of rendering themselves necessary and needed.[15] This, we think, is survival of an old, hunter-gatherer tradition, to be traced back perhaps even to prehistory, which ritual magic did not manage to displace completely, as in India and Palestine, probably because of the stronger roots of settlement and agriculture there. One crucial indication in this regard is that the Zande word for the action of witchcraft, *no*, is the same as the word for shooting (an arrow or a gun) (Evans-Pritchard 1976: 13). Evans-Pritchard adds the perceptive point that the connection is provided by both acts being a particular kind of action – causing injury – from a distance. In our reading, this implies a parallel between the actions of hunters, or the old aristocracy, and the new professional group of magicians – a symbolic, and perhaps not just symbolic, sign of competition, which even might use the widespread guilt associated with any act of killing, even of an animal – especially an easy killing.

Initiands are entrapped in the professional group of magicians, which then, on their own, they turn into promoting an entrapment of the entire community in their own scheming, leading to the disempowerment of the entire community. The significance of this point cannot be exaggerated, as this implies a definite internal disempowerment at the heart of every member of the community; a certain schismatic self-ignorance at the deepest level of the personality. And in the Zande worldview this does not remain a simple assumption, but is a proven, objective fact: inside the body of a witch there is supposed to be a concrete object rendering evident that the person was a witch; this can be extracted from the corpse after one dies; and such vivisection is done publicly, where the object is to be found by experts and shown up. The case is thus proven, and concluded.

This idea is part of a number of tight circles, generating the kind of mental entrapment from which, according to Evans-Pritchard, it was absolutely impossible to dislocate the Azande: 'the Zande mind is logical and inquiring within the framework of its culture and insists on the coherence of its own idiom' (Evans-Pritchard 1976: 16); in it there is 'a mingling of common sense and mystical thought' (108). Yet, even if many know that most witch doctors are charlatans, and accept that some of their acts might be fake, they still believe that at least some such acts are genuine, and their general and basic faith in the acts of magicians could not be questioned (107–108, 112–113, 150). These circles form a tight net; any order of their discussion is arbitrary, just as it applies to the ordering of the Ture tales (Evans-Pritchard 1967: 20).

The first such circle concerns the validation of the objectivity of witchhood. This is the task of magicians, who are radically different from, though

38 *Presenting the trickster*

of course closely connected to, the witches (who can cast spells) or the sorcerers (who are using bad medicine through certain rites) (Evans-Pritchard 1976: 176, 226–228). This is done by producing, in the etymological sense of 'lead or bring forth',[16] an object from inside the body of the dead, whether it was actually there (as a kidney stone, for example – and kidneys are notoriously important for all kind of sorcery, extending to the Etruscans or the Minoans) or not (as pulling a rabbit out of the hat, whether concretely or metaphorically, is a stock trick for illusionists of all ages).

The central issue that matters for the confirmation – and with this, we enter another circle – is the public nature and spectacle-like character of the performance (Evans-Pritchard 1976: 69–89). We associate the public sphere with modernity and classical Antiquity, the agora and the Forum, safeguard of rational discourse, freedom and openness, but in fact the public sphere was almost always present in settled communities as place of rituals, which were mostly performed wearing masks, evoking secrecy. Divination, or the identification of witchcraft, was also a ritual, performed publicly, where the central issue was that the result, no matter how shaky it might have been in terms of truth, was immediately proclaimed in public and thus became binding for everyone – as nobody possibly could have questioned it immediately and publicly; also because the inner confidence of every member of the society was already sufficiently undermined – but this belongs to another circle, still to be clarified.

Central to public validation was the performative character of rituals. Theatricality is an inherent part of every public activity, emphasised by the wearing of masks, but particularly so for divinisation rituals, where it became intrinsically and inseparably intermingled with the production of truth. Such rituals were often ecstatic, involving self-mutilation in a state of fury, which reminded Evans-Pritchard outright of the priests of Baal (Evans-Pritchard 1976: 76).

Theatricality involves a further circle, central for both the legitimation of the practice and for providing new recruits. This concerns the use of theatrical performance to enchant children (Evans-Pritchard 1976: 90–91), making them want to become a sorcerer – just as all children in our days want to become actors or football players. The effects of such theatrical performances are way more important than the recruitment of future sorcerers. They are vital for ensuring that the entire community, generation after generation, accepts this sorcerer vision of the world.

These sorcerer magicians are not to be dismissed light-handedly, as they capture, as if in a nutshell, Nietzsche's ascetic priest, as well as the prehistoric magician-sorcerer artists. This can be perceived with particular clarity in the guardians of memory in Çatalhöyük, or the elusive and enigmatic makers of the Tassili desert mountain images in the Sahara, but even followed back as far as the Shaft Scene in Lascaux cave or the monsters of Pergouset cave, in Palaeolithic France (Horvath 2013: 21–38; Horvath and Szakolczai 2018a: 62–85, 99–100, 122–146). Their manipulation of those ignorant of such secrets, through the mediation of the alchemists and Sophists, Byzantine dotti, Weber's *literati*, can be traced up to the *existentiell literati* of Heidegger

(2017, XII: 23): exponents of a metaphysical rationalism as presumed possessors of knowledge, who rather only further 'machination' (53–54), achieving control through technology, unknowingly, without recognising their own dangerousness (34–35). They ignore the 'simplicity of the essence of all things' (29), promoting the 'devastat[ion of] everything into nothingness' (29), thus became 'the genuine bearers of destruction [*die eigentlichen Träger der Zerstörung*]' (55).[17]

The foregoing can be illustrated through Joseph Conrad's *Heart of Darkness*, tightly based on the author's personal experiences. At the end of his trip into the heart of Africa, made to reach his new place of work Marlow, the hero of the novel found the station near the port as a place of 'inhabited devastation', showing signs of 'imbecile rapacity', where the people bought by the company aimlessly wonder around, with enormous, vacant blind eyes, staring at the nothing – he has 'never seen anything so unreal in [his] life' (Conrad 1999: 42, 45, 51–52). In such environment, ignoring circumstances, worked the agents of the company – the word 'agent' being repeatedly used, thus gaining symbolic value – with the chief accountant keeping up appearances with his parasol and suit, making the reader wonder whether it demonstrates strength of character or raving lunacy. The height of madness, however, was only reached after a further boat trip, up the river, when Marlow met his would-be boss, Kurtz, who rather became one of the foremost devils of the land, engaged in 'unspeakable rites', which one with solid feet under one's ground cannot even understand, and being surrounded by people who were too dull even to understand what was going on, as 'no fool ever made a bargain for his soul with the devil' (77). Marlow did not succeed to work under Kurtz, who devastated the area, as he – another hero of the modern limitlessness – 'lacked restraint in the gratification of his various lusts' (86), but heard his last words, which were 'The horror! The horror!' (97). Coming out of Poland and transiting through London, Conrad came to experience, as a shock, the encounter between two unreal worlds.

The inculcation of a sorcerer world vision is done in both direct and indirect ways. Directly, the enchantment produced is effective for everyone, not just the would-be sorcerers: every child is spell-bound, growing into a world where such theatrical sorcery performances are the most precious moments of collective – and not only – life. But the indirect effect is even more important, as the empowering of sorcerers goes hand in hand, as a typical schismogenic process, with the thorough and from inside disempowering of everyone else. The more we are enchanted with what we see, publicly, the more we become convinced, from the bottom or our heart, that without the sorcerers, left on our own force, we would be nothing.

What does this exactly mean? Here we touch upon the absolute core of what the Zande vision of the nature of man is – which is not just a vision, but the way, evidently, every Azande behaves, in a taken for granted manner. If power, knowledge and truth are in the hand of sorcerers, then an ordinary human being is completely helpless without such assistance. In fact, as Evans-

Prichard discusses in great detail, such theatrical rituals are by no means the only form of divination. As they are quite costly, there are other similar methods, ranging from chicken poisoning to the cheapest one, the small handheld wooden rubbing-board oracle (Evans-Prichard 1976: 168–171).

The technique in each of these cases is identical. There are always only two possibilities, corresponding to the radically dualistic nature of the Zande worldview – recalling the quite similar Gnostic or Manichean ideas, perhaps their descendant, through some strange transmission channels. These alternatives are stated in advance, then the lot is cast and – through some confirmation mechanism, as after all no human being is that credible, and the Azande are both extremely doubting and credible – the result is obtained. The technique is very simple, identical to the technique of any competitive game: there will certainly be a winner and a loser, especially if the possibility of a draw is excluded in advance.

Thus, the method or technique is perfect, it cannot fail, proving again the truth of sorcery and divination; however, even more important is the impact made on every member of the community. Making the right decision in a difficult situation requires inner strength and confidence in one's own force. But, as we have seen, the Zande vision of the world, penetrated by the logic of sorcery, goes into the opposite direction. The result is that nobody really has any confidence in oneself, in one's own ability of making the right decision; thus, '[I]f time and opportunity permitted many Azande would wish to consult one or other of the oracles about every step in their lives' (Evans-Prichard 1976: 123). This is obviously impossible, also would be very costly – so we basically arrive, again, to our own modern rational economic worldview, where everything we do, and want, depends just about costs, predicated on a presumed universal law of scarcity, and not on our own confidence in our own uniqueness, and the uniqueness of the human and non-human beings and objects around us, rendering the very principles of economic reasoning irrelevant for any normal, everyday human and social situation, as such reasoning is based on the idea of substitutability and exchange, but nothing that is truly meaningful and valuable in our life can be exchanged.

Let us resume the kind of trickster logic set in motion by Zande witchcraft and divination rituals, in order to help bringing out the parallels with our best practice policies.

To begin with, while one might fancy that the Azande simply look for reasons behind sheer luck, actually the way we and they deal with misfortunes is not that different in principle: '[t]hey and we use rational means for controlling the conditions that produce misfortune' (Evans-Prichard 1976: 65). We certainly conceive of what these conditions are in a different manner – though our ways of proceeding show further and quite striking similarities. This starts with an obsession with causality: it both cases it is assumed that there must be a particular chain of causation that is capable of explaining every single event (21).[18] Here we touch upon the peculiar omission in the scientific vision of the world that was codified in 1928 by the foundational manifesto of the Vienna school of philosophy: ignoring questions of contingency. According to this world-vision, there must be a reason or cause behind everything. If we are not able to explain a particular eventuality, this is because we are lazy in thinking, or our knowledge is still limited, which supposedly is an outrage. In sum, every particular event must have a general cause (22–23).[19] Anything that is not universal is limited, local, old-fashioned, obsolete, to be eliminated in the name of progress. Thus, proper knowledge about the cause of any concrete event can be gained if we follow a strict, rigorous procedure, and perform in this way the experiment, which gives the right result. Thus, if a sporting tournament is set up, with proper rules, at the end there will be a winning team and – by definition – this will be the best team. The procedure cannot and will not fail to deliver. But similar procedures can be set up, as it is now not just argued but acted upon, for universities, high schools, and practically for anything, leading to the right winners and losers. As we'll see, the same mode of action is followed in Vedic rituals, or any other sacrificial system, including the gladiators of the Roman Empire. With the feats of contemporary telecommunication technology, not only the best goals but the most clamorous errors are instantly accessible, and young people now cannot even understand while old people find videos about own goals, career-ending injuries or other casualties of the modern form of gladiatorship revolting. Just follow the procedures – and there will always be a winner, and enough fun to keep the spectacle running.

Back to the present: concluding parables

Witchcraft/exorcism and divination, like sacrifice, and just like certain kind of modern managerialism, rely on the scrupulous following of a set of rigid procedures.[20] One might say that one is rational, while the other not, but this is misleading, as there are no rational procedures, in the classical Greek sense of mindfulness (*phronesis*) – but perhaps in any proper sense of rationality – as rigid procedurality is irrationality itself, being automatic mechanisation. Such procedurality is based on the conviction, which is by definition false, though is also invariably self-justifying, that people in a concrete situation are constitutionally unable, whether because stupid or selfish, to find a proper way of behaving, thus they should be told from the outside, and in a pre-determined manner, what course of action to follow. But such a presumption only produces the result which is assumed: a set of weak, at once infantile and senile people, carried by the wind of their incommensurable desires, who cannot be trusted in anything, and thus must be explicitly and exactly told what to do.

Notes

1 The parallels with the way Malinowski and Radcliffe-Brown did not appreciate Bateson at the same moment, or how Turner was directed away from the study of rituals by his own teachers a couple of decades later, are tight. For details, see Szakolczai and Thomassen (2019).

42 *Presenting the trickster*

2 This story not only illuminates the centrality of witchcraft among the Zande, but further underlines the identity between folktale tricksters and real-life *Magi*.
3 Please, note that this helps to connect tightly asceticism and rationality, a connection whose centrality for the modern economy was perceived by Max Weber.
4 It should be noted that, while for us the adjective 'creative' gained a central positive meaning, the use of this sense only emerges in the 1670s (Online Etymological Dictionary), as until then creation was an exclusion prerogative of the deity. So our current, escalating use of the term is just another evident sign of the divinisation of man that is the driving force of modernity. We should add that our modern, mostly technological and economic creativity always assumed prior destruction, often ideologised as the 'necessary' destruction of 'outdated' traditions, this is just another indication of the trickster character of modernity.
5 In fact, 'weave' is also etymologically connected to 'wave', thus tying further the knots between the spider web and the modalities of entrapment characteristic of modern telecommunication techniques.
6 The snake Ouroboros motif will be discussed in detail in Chapter 9.
7 For details, see Horvath and Szakolczai (2018a).
8 About the distinction between 'evil' and 'misfortune', see also Baudrillard (2013).
9 This also recalls the ideas of Presocratics about the nature of the soul.
10 For details, see again Horvath and Szakolczai (2018a).
11 See German *Gegenstand*, or Latin *ob-jectum*.
12 We'll see that the same inner uncertainty is present concerning the perceived Zande need to consult an oracle possibly before any action.
13 Evans-Pritchard makes a distinction between witch doctors and sorcerers, but this is not relevant from our perspective, and could be misleading, as the term 'sorcerer' is widely used in a general sense for prehistory.
14 According to Pliny (30.19), the mole was held in particular awe in magic, connected to the medical value of certain plants.
15 As a general point, we are not making a claim about any concern with the divine being a priestly lie, as we do not question that something like the divine exist, if not as a 'reality', than as a 'super-reality'. We do not even question the possibility that hostile but invisible forces might exist. Our point only concerns the problem of the presence, and even unity, or a professional group who gains and maintains power by the performance of specific rituals by which it purports to gain access to such spirits.
16 The word was much used in this sense by Dickens, in this sense, and became central for Baudrillard's discussion of advertising.
17 The last expression is strikingly Weberian.
18 Here again Nietzsche's ideas, in the *Genealogy of Morals*, but also in *Twilight of the Idols*, are particularly relevant. This is because causation is fundamentally a legalistic term. As such, it certainly has its importance. But life cannot be reduced to laws, and so a search for a cause behind every happening necessarily inculcates a guilt culture. A better mode of living implies preparing people to be strong enough to recognise situations and react to the events happening to them, instead of knowing the procedures and always looking for a real or imaginary tribunal to prove them right.
19 For a good account on this problem, see Jonsen and Toulmin (1988).
20 Note that 'follow' means the same as 'imitate'; even the words are often identical. Thus, in Hungarian 'imitate' is *utánoz*, literally 'do something after', which is identical to 'follow'. But with this, the difference between imitation and rationality (in the modern, not classical sense) disappears, as 'rational' management and economics assume nothing else but the mechanical and mindless following, or imitating, of 'best practices'.

3 Hermes the trickster and the Kabeiroi
Moving towards evil

With this chapter we continue to move close to an inside perspective on the trickster, while also posing the question how our world could have become a trickster destiny. For this, we turn to the central Greek trickster figure, Hermes.

Hermes, the enchanting Greek trickster

The role played by the trickster in Greek mythology, and culture in general, takes up an absolutely central, hinge-like place in the architecture of this book. Such trickster figures, especially Hermes, fit in seamlessly with the general image gained through a comparative anthropological and mythological study. Thus, while the anthropological material contains huge gaps and was written down only recently, knowledge about the Greek figures goes back way before our age, and can rely upon long centuries, even millennia of extensive commentary, so offer a uniquely helpful perspective on the trickster. Furthermore, Greek culture is a main source of our civilisation, and its trickster figures, again first of all Hermes, show features that are close to some flagship values of modernity. As our aim is to capture the features of trickster destiny in modernity, a close reading of these figures is vital.

Due to evident limitations, this chapter will focus on Hermes, with some discussion of Prometheus and Dionysus, but leaving out, among others, such key figures as Momus or Heracles. We'll start unravelling the complex mysteries around Hermes by aiming right at the core, offering a close reading of the Homeric hymn 'To Hermes'.

The Homeric hymn to Hermes

The *Homeric Hymns* are central and also 'most delightful' works of Greek poetry (Rayor 2004: 2). They had long been assumed to have been composed by Homer, hence their name. Their archaic segments belong to the period just after Homer and Hesiod. The particularly moving hymn 'To Demeter' is the earliest testimony of the Eleusian mysteries.

Like all tricksters, Hermes makes his entry as a sudden apparition in the hymn that bears his name. The hymn not only starts by relating us the conditions of his birth, but conveys its striking character, given that Maia the nymph hid her pregnancy – and even offers a further reason, given that the character of the newborn, as it would be made soon apparent, was well worth hiding. Finally, and further underlining the apparition-like character of his emergence, immediately after being born the infant would perform a particularly revealing deed.

However, and even before this first exploit – as his first act is indeed an exploit, in all senses of the term – the hymn offers an overall characterisation. This is the first of seven such descriptions, and by far the longest. It has three main features: it offers a par excellence, textbook description of the trickster; it is extremely negative; and yet, it contains some redeeming features. These features are repeated throughout the seven characterisations, so we analyse them together.

These characterisations first of all make it evident that Hermes belongs to the quasi-universal anthropological category of the trickster. Hermes has unusual intellectual skills, resumed in the fortunate expression 'cunning intelligence' (Détienne and Vernant 1978): he is cunning (*polutropos*, an adjective only used for Hermes, Ulysses and the octopus), crafty, his schemes are always winning, and – in case this were not evident – he always uses his mental capacities in a deceitful way, being wily at heart. Beyond just deceiving, his deeds not only play with the rule and norms of human coexistence, but explicitly break them, as he is a robber and a thief, though more a thief than a robber, using more mental cunning than sheer force (see also Brown 1969: 7–8), in particular a thief and killer of cattle, an animal held in particularly high esteem in pre-modern settled societies. The success of his plots is assured by his familiarity with liminal situations, whether in time or space. Hermes has an intimate connection with the night, which is his comrade and accomplice; he is also a 'watcher by night'. It is here that another central feature can be located, his ability to induce or manipulate dreams, as he is a 'dream-leader'.[1] Concerning space, he shows the same sneaking feature with gates, a central spatial liminal device, as with spotting things at night, or during liminal times.

Hermes is a trickster, there can be no doubt about this; but it is just as clear that his acts cannot be taken lightly, as emphasised by the extremely negative way the figure is presented. This can be best shown by reviewing sequentially the various characterisations of Hermes, paying due attention to the persons formulating them.

The first two is offered by the narrator, starting with a thorough, comprehensive, and mostly negative description of the figure, though ending with a cryptic allusion to eventual great deeds. The second is interjected at a crucial instance: after the first deed of Hermes (yet to be presented), when in a nick of time his attention switches from his first victim to the next exploit. It is this moment when, as if the narrator was particularly struck by the viciousness of the figure, the mode of action by Hermes is described as being characteristic of 'knavish folk' (lines 66–67), when during night-time they are set to go for robbery.

The next description is particularly significant, as this – the first given by a concrete figure of the story – is offered by his mother (a nymph, thus not immortal), right after he returned home after having committed his first evil deeds. It starts by naming him as a rogue, full of wily lies, or one who is so shameless that as if wears shamelessness as a garment – a description particularly significant in the archaic Mediterranean world, where shame was one of the most abhorred thing in social life; hoping that Apollo would properly tie him down with unbreakable chains (a treatment recalling Prometheus – one of the key instances establishing parallels between Hermes and Prometheus, a Titan and not a god), and finally, and most damningly, stating that his father (Zeus) created him for the worry of both men and gods – a quite striking description, by a mother, of her just born son, almost amounting to a curse. Thus, for his mother, and talking here evidently in the name of mankind, the birth, or rather apparition, of the trickster is an unmitigated disaster.

Now come the series of three characterisations by Apollo, already evoked by the mother. The context, or the person of the characteriser, is particularly significant, as Apollo is not only a half-brother of Hermes, but the only other male deity to whom a long, narrative Homeric Hymn was devoted, starting similarly by telling his birth (the two other deities to whom such hymn was devoted are females, Aphrodite and Demeter, and their births are not described). Apollo indeed starts on the note as the mother, Maia was hoping, describing Hermes as a wily rogue and trickster, all the more so as Hermes slighted him by stealing his cattle. They even litigate, and Apollo takes his plight to their father, Zeus. There, in front of the supreme god, he offers a couple of descriptions: Hermes is a particularly vicious ('piercing') thief, who is so pert (mocking, delusive) that has no equals among men or gods. However, while Hermes denies, now for the third time, that he did anything wrong, rendering his lie worse by another false oath,[2] he also produces a couple of striking, even miraculous deeds, in particular by playing on the lyre, that softens the heart of Apollo. This leads to the third characterisation by Apollo, where the unreserved condemnation and the search for the right punishment are as if transmuted into a friendly recognition. While the main characterisation of Hermes as a wily and dangerous rogue is not changed – quite on the contrary, it is here that Apollo uses the trademark term *mékhaniótés* 'trickster' (line 436, a *hapax*) – but still, the ire of Apollo becomes softened, and Hermes now is even described as a 'comrade of the feast'. The reason is simple, and Apollo names it precisely: the lyre gifted by Hermes is well worth 50 cows.

The situation and the terminology used here are extremely significant, and needs to be unpacked. A comrade of the feast is a very particular title, one that has been used by Hermes for the turtle before killing him – a designation which has become true after the killing, and which was thus in a way justified or forgiven by Apollo. Even further, the expression is almost identical with the term parasite, as *parasitos* means a '(person) eating at another's table'. The parasite is another crucial trickster figure, and the knots between Hermes as trickster and the parasite are tied further by playing music being one of the key features of the parasite, his service offered for the free meal (see Serres 2014). However, the contrast with the Hermes kind trickster figure is also covered in the same line, as Apollo deploys a singular expression to characterise Hermes: he is a busy hardworking trickster, while the parasite is figure of laziness. Apollo thus betrays the expectation of Maia, as he makes peace with Hermes, even offers gifts.

This, however, is not the last word of the Hymn, as just before the closing invocation the narrator offers a final, seventh characterisation of Hermes. The rogue is left in peace, keeps interacting with both mortals and gods. His task even became such inter-action, or communication. Yet, the fundamental features of the trickster didn't change: he would mostly keep deceiving humans.

The way in which this is phrased again requires minute attention. To begin with, the both spatially and temporally liminal nature of the trickster is again emphasised: the trickster acts between mortals and immortals, and especially during the liminal time of the night. Second, he indeed offers a bit of help to humans, especially those in need of defence – thus, and again similarly to Prometheus, he pretends to be a kind of saviour of the downtrodden; he acts up as the enlightener, bringing benefits to mankind. However, and finally, one should be wary of much believing in his pretences: the trickster, after all, is only interested in his own benefits, and so will continue to only deceive, cheat or cajole humans.

The lesson is very clear: Greek culture somehow managed to pacify the trickster, admitting him into the pantheon of gods. But any such coexistence with the trickster remains labile, and it is only the divine gods that can keep the trickster in check. Humans will remain completely at the mercy of the trickster – the most so when they believe to strike up an alliance with him. We Europeans, encoded at the centre of our culture, inherited in some way this Greek domestication of the trickster, in Hermes, but this delicate balance is always threatening to collapse.

In order to better understand what all this might mean, we need to review now, still following the word and spirit of the Homeric Hymn, Hermes in act, complementing points made previously.

Hermes in action

The first act of Hermes, the making of the lyre out of the shell of a turtle, is so well known that it seems almost a waste of time and space to discuss it. Yet, it offers such a crucial introduction to the trickster, and the details are so important and significant, that some attention must be devoted it.

The story, in a nutshell, is that Hermes perceives a turtle, immediately realises that its shell can be made into a musical instrument, so kills it, prepares the lyre, and starts to play.

The first thing to notice about Hermes the trickster is the speed of his mind: the instant he perceives the tortoise, the musical instrument appears in his mind. This might seem the same thing as cunningness, or cunning intelligence, but there is a considerable difference: speed of mind is merely an objective feature of certain people, while the adjective cunning indicates some kind of devious use. Thus, a quick mind only becomes a trickster if something – some lack – pushes it into the direction of deviousness.

The next element in the story offers some hints in this direction, though in a puzzling and paradoxical way. This is the epithet used here for Hermes, 'luck-bringer' or 'benefit-bringer' (the term used is *eriounious*, a *hapax* with an uncertain meaning). Benefit-bringing implies a particular modality of action: an alteration of the world, and its order, by somebody who has a particularly quick mind, in order to promote his going concerns (interests). This implies a paradox at the heart of a quick mind: on the one hand, the perception of a connection – say, between the shell of the tortoise and a lyre; on the other, a separation – between the quick-witted and everybody else who become as if downgraded by the quick-witted. Having a quick mind is thus a gift, but a poisonous gift: it can be a way to conceptualise (conceive and make) others into mere instruments serving one's own interests or pleasures. The issue at stake is how to avoid the short-circuiting of the quick-witted into the service of his own self-interest. Or, we return to the ambivalence of the *hapax*: Hermes is a benefit-bringer – but to whom?!

The storyline, telling the first act of Hermes the trickster, only continues with whatever happens if the naïve, innocent trickster acts without any limits or boundaries. To start with, a quick wit objectifies other beings: they become mere instrument to serve his benefits, pawn in his game. But they should not be aware of this. Thus, the first step is to divert their attention, turning off their suspicion. So, instead of hostility, or even neutrality, the tortoise is addressed with great respect, as a friend, even – and this is a particularly significant detail – Hermes asks his help. However, before the tortoise would offer any response, Hermes's quick thinking is transformed into speedy action, with a number of things being done and said at the same time: he promises the tortoise of not doing him any harm – which is a sheer lie; states that he however must profit of the tortoise – which is a thinly veiled menace; deceives him further by pretending to offer him a safe haven inside against the threats of outdoors – a central domesticating trick. He then took up, brought inside and swiftly killed the animal, transforming its shell into the lyre – just as he conceived it first in his mind.

Kerényi's Hermes

Even a casual familiarisation with the hymn 'To Hermes' makes it evident that we are not facing an ordinary trickster figure – if there ever was one. Rather, in the figure of Hermes the ambivalence usually surrounding the trickster is raised as if on a second, or even third, power. We must start with

48 *Presenting the trickster*

the question of what possibly this could mean – and here we need a really good guide. This will be Kerényi.

Kerényi (1980) starts by posing just the questions that are central for this book as well: how could that be considered as a deity? And what was the significance of all this for the Greeks?

Kerényi here has a guide on his own, Rudolph Otto, a crucial figure in the understanding of the sacred, and in particular Otto's claim that Hermes was not simply a Greek pantheon, but had a world of his own. But how could possibly Hermes have a world on its own, when this world is not identical simply with the realm of gods, outside human existence? This must needs be some kind of trick, ruse, deceit – so entering the world of Hermes necessarily implies a resignation to a second reality, thus to accept being deceived; but, on the other hand, this world also must have very close and vital links to the real world, both the world as it is experienced ordinarily by humans, and the super-real of the gods, otherwise Hermes could not gain the significance it did for Greek culture – and there is no need to argue about the significance of Greek culture itself.

Investigating the nature of this world of Hermes, it not only implies a special sphere – and, given that we know that Hermes is first of all a mediator between the humans and the divine, thus his sphere must also be somewhere in between these realms – but also following a particular logic (Kerényi 1980: 59). Given that, in the terminology of our book, our interest is not in identifying certain persons or occupations as tricksters, rather to identify a certain trickster logic, or the incommensurable, at the heart of modernity, the relevance of these ideas for our book are evident. The first element in this logic is that whatever happens, it 'as if falls from the sky' (59). This means not only that Hermes the trickster always appears suddenly, and with great speed, as if out of the blue – though this is indeed a central feature of Hermes, and we need to give good further attention to it; but that Hermes manages to conjure up an entire world in which whatever happens does not follow the normal sequentiality of everyday life, but has an unpredictable and unintelligible character, in which we become at the mercy of forces external to and way above us. By this, we of course do not solicit belief in Hermes as a deity, rather argue – and no doubt following the Greeks who did not believe in the existence of Hermes in the manner a faithful is supposed to believe in its God – that the world of any human being might quite suddenly be transformed or transfigured in this way; and connected this experience, certainly a real possibility, to the conjuring up of the figure of Hermes. Second, if we enter such a world, or if our world suddenly becomes transfigured in this way, the character of our own actions also change: whatever we do will look as a piece of bravery; or, our own mental disempowerment transforms us into actual, acting heroes. Third, a central feature of this modern or transformed modality of living our lives implies a sudden valorisation of pleasure, a kind of transformation not only of our perceptions and actions, but even our values: our search for pleasure is no longer subject to responsibility. Finally, living in this world implies being subsumed to or penetrated by a certain exchange mentality: we have to accept that every gain implies a loss, not only in the standard, general sense that things have their resistance and acts have their consequences, but that this new, hermetic world is penetrated by a kind of hedonistic calculus in which we have to resign ourselves to trying to maximise our pleasures, but at the same time accept that we have to pay, beyond morality and responsibility, for every pleasure gained.

Kerényi identifies two concrete situations as possible worlds of Hermes, one temporal, the other spatial: the night, and the road. The night directly involves a special place, the bed, the place where humans sleep and dream, make love, and also die; while the road is associated with a particular time, when we travel. Common to all is liminality, and the temptation of extending such moments forever. This is best seen through Ulysses, the hero most connected to Hermes, who is always on the road in the *Odyssey*, but never arrives. Such permanence extends the state of being suspended into a limitless condition, creating a reality in which 'everything becomes spectrally unreal' (Kerényi 1980: 68–69).

Hermes can be rightfully considered as the deity of liminality as such – different from, and in a way stronger, than those deities who are only connected to one such aspect, whether that is sexuality, birth-giving, marriage, dreaming, or death. Thus, the world of Hermes, identified by Otto and Kerényi, is nothing else but permanent liminality; it is as if suspended between life and death (68). Being connected to all the major, indeed crucial, transitional phases of life means that in a way Hermes is the deity most connected to human reality, the reality of life, the appearance, intensification and disappearance of life – and yet, is at the same time the most fleeting, threatening and unreal, as – whether considering this realm as the night-time, or as the artificial summary of all the liminal moments of life – the overwhelming majority of normal, waking human life is not spent on such liminal activities. Entering the realm of Hermes thus always involves the risk of not coming back sanely to our ordinary life. Yet, this is a risk we cannot avoid – and which even brings its own pleasures, unless we lost our measure, or sense of limit.

We need to ponder here a bit on this claim concerning Hermes as being a god of liminality as such, as this is one of the central findings of the book. Two points must be made. The first concerns the significance of the claim: what does it mean that there is a god of liminality? And the second concerns its modality: in what exact way did Hermes become the god of liminality for the Greeks?

Concerning the first, we assert that the figure of Hermes demonstrates that, at the time to which awareness about the figure can be dated, the Archaic period, considered as central in the milestone work of Anthony Snodgrass (1980), Greek culture gained an awareness about liminality, much as the concept has been acquired in our cultural anthropology. The Greeks were not simply aware that transitory periods in life, like birth and death, adolescence and illness, or the passage of seasons are important, but they assigned a deity

50 *Presenting the trickster*

to this transitoriness. The Homeric Hymn tells about the birth and growing up of Hermes at the same time as inserting the figure into the canonical list of Olympic deities – a stunning feat of poetic power. If we can rightfully consider Greek culture as the stunning inventor of abstract thinking – a position recently reasserted with striking force and clarity by Michel Serres – then our further claim is, in line with the similarly innovative work of Anthony Snodgrass, that the source and condition of possibility of this discovery can be traced further back, from the classical to the archaic period of Greek culture, and its basic source is the recognition of incommensurable liminality as a paradoxical arche-type of abstraction. It is paradoxical, as the rise of abstract thinking, through geometry, in Greece coincided in the discovery of liminality, through Hermes, through the role played by the irrational (*alogos*) and thus inexpressible (*arrheton*) character of the diagonal of the square. Such a connection between rational thinking and the discovery of liminality is also shown in particular clarity with the 'first word' of Greek philosophy (Patočka 1983), contained in the first (and only) fragment of Anaximander, also the founder of geography, and discussed amply, and at crucial places, both by the Pythagoreans and Plato, central figures in the history of geometry, and of the Forms as such, is *apeiron*, which is verbatim identical with liminality. It also has to do with the two poems of Homer, foundations and unsurpassable masterpieces of world literature.[3] The *Iliad* and the *Odyssey* are both about the transformation of a temporary event, a war or a travel, into a permanent condition. Hermes as the god of permanent liminality conjures up a new world, outside the transitory, liminal moments of life.

This is itself is a quite incredible achievement, confirming from contemporary cultural anthropology the classical perspective on Greek exceptionality. Yet, there is a second point, concerning the modality of this Greek vision of liminality. The Greeks, already through their major mythological poems offered a unique vision of liminality, thus raising exceptionality to a second power. Knowledge about liminal events always involves possible manipulation. This is why liminal deities are tricksters. It is to such trickster liminal deities that the most revolting sacrifices are revolved. Hermes incorporates the ambivalence, even the manipulative or destructive aspects of liminality. Hermes steals, robs, cunningly misleads people, and even steals their soul. Concerning sexuality, he goes way beyond the limits of decency (Kerényi 1980: 82). He is thus a typical trickster figure. Yet, he is also showing features that nowhere are associated with tricksters: a kind of naïve innocence, even a degree of gracefulness. Hermes is not just a trickster who acts without scruples, but also a god of gracefulness and glory (71), who even has a spirit and art of life (79).

Thus, through this unique, exceptional figure of Hermes, we can understand that the while Greeks pioneered abstract thinking, they also – and inseparably from this – were masters of grace and beauty. The genuine feat of the Greeks was to combine unprecedented innovativeness with abstract, rational thinking, while recognising the grace and beauty of life, nature, and the world – and still not ignoring or playing down the inevitable tragic aspects of existence. A central aim of the book will be to explore how such Greek and Hermetic origins could eventually give rise to the modern trickster land – where the adjective Hermetic, through alchemy, neo-Platonism and Gnosticism, gained a quite different meaning and became the foundation, through a series of twists, of the modern scientific world view.

For the moment, we need to compare here Hermes to other, similar deities.

Dionysus the ecstatic trickster

Dionysus as a deity has a number of common features with Hermes, touching the core of both figures. Dionysus also has a world of its own, a world outside normal ordinary events, the realm of self-forgetful intoxication, also associated with the night. Even further, Dionysus is also associated with travel, and in several senses: he transports human beings to his realm by techniques of intoxication like wine, music or dancing. He is also a mobile, unsettled god, even associated with omnipresence (Kerényi 1976: xxiv), who – in a typical trickster manner – always comes from the outside, an 'arriving god', who then causes a sudden, escalating, spiralling whirlwind, a tempest, associated with epidemics in both senses of the word, then leaving everything behind, looking for new victims. They both have epiphanies, appearing suddenly out of the blue, and similar visionary powers. Yet, this world of Dionysus is by no means identical to that of Hermes, as Hermes is not associated with wine, and does not use artificial stimulants. Still, their mode of action is quite similar. Dionysus has another feature not shared by Hermes, a kind of internal force and power, beyond the mere use and abuse of circumstances (Détienne 1989: 61). This is close to Nietzsche's will to power, and is placed at the centre of Kerényi's (1976) work as the indestructible force of life.

Prometheus the titan trickster

The parallels between Hermes and Prometheus are again close and touch central features in both (see also Brown 1969: 24–25, 31). The emblematic deed of both is a typical trickster act and outrageous offence: they both stole from a god, Prometheus fire from Zeus, while Hermes cattle from Apollo. Furthermore, both became inventors of sacrifice, based on their theft, and also figures of knowledge, even teachers of humans. Perhaps most importantly, they are both figures of mediation and liminality, in the specific sense of mediating between the divine and human realms. However, Prometheus does not have a realm on its own, neither has epiphanies, and has nothing to do with enchantment. Also, in contrast to Prometheus, Hermes does not challenge the authority of Zeus (Rayor 2004: 8–9). Thus, Hermes can be considered as the Greek version of the kind of trickster figure that was embedded in Prometheus. It is thus quite striking that not only the Sophists but also key figures of modern Enlightenment rationalism like Diderot or

Marx took Prometheus as their idol – though perhaps not surprising, given the association of the Enlightenment with the promotion of universalistic knowledge through secret societies, analysed by Koselleck (1988).

The relationship between Hermes and Prometheus, and especially the pacifying character of Hermes is shown particularly well in Aeschylus's *Prometheus Bound*, where the cruel verdict of Zeus is transmitted by Hermes. This results in the scene, alluded to in the Preface of his dissertation by Marx and analysed in detail by Voegelin (2000), in which Prometheus reveals his hatred of the gods, while Hermes characterises it as 'no small madness' (lines 975–976). This madness is identical to the arrogance or hubris of Prometheus, the refusal to accept, thus inevitably transgress any limits, or the same as evil, given that the etymological roots of evil and hubris are shared, as seen before. Such failure to accept limits is another way of capturing evil in the trickster, while Hermes manifests the other side of the trickster, the association with boundaries – though this association can be connected to exchange being conducted on the borders between communities (Brown 1969: 40–41).

This play also contains the earliest reference to another set of crucial trickster-like figures, the Kabeiroi. Aeschylus even wrote a play entitled *The Kabeiroi*, but this got lost, and few fragments survived. We only know that this play takes place on the island of Lemnos, where the Kabeiroi not only entertained the Argonauts but got them thoroughly drunk.

The Kabeiroi as the arch-tricksters

The connection between Hermes and the Kabeiroi is also tight,[4] as in some tradition Hermes is one of them, while in others he is their father – or child. The Kabeiroi are among the most obscure deities of the Greek pantheon, not present in the classical accounts of mythology, only discussed in relatively late sources, and in a most confused way. They belonged to an archaic layer that was purposefully pushed to the background, following – according to Nietzsche – the Greek ability of overcoming tragic events by wisely ignoring them, instead of becoming entrapped in them by celebrating their memory.

Continuing our effort of bringing together the various Greek trickster figures, and in the footsteps of the recent milestone work of Sandra Blakely, we consider the Kabeiroi and the other similar obscure demon-figures of the Greek pantheon like the Telchines, the Daktyles, the Kouretes and the Korybanths as being basically the same. Kerényi (1980: 106–109) argued about the close links between Hermes and the most important *daimon* of Greek mythology, Eros, and also his father, Poros.[5] Blakely's book not only offers a comprehensive and recent overview of the surviving record, situating the Kabeiroi in the context of the other similar *daimones*, but places them in a comparative anthropological perspective by relying on African ethnographic evidence about myths and rituals related to metallurgy and smiths.

Blakely on the Kabeiroi

For Blakely the Kabeiroi are part of a group of five demons or *daimones* that share a series of features. They are all very old, tapping into a time before the Greeks, outside canonical Greek mythology, even evoking, in a vague and contradictory sort of way, memories of the Golden Age. They are certainly from the East, and from Phrygia rather than the Levant – any Phoenician connections belong to later times. They are closely associated with the quasi-mythical, pre-Greek Pelasgians. The places in Greece where they are present offer a particularly interesting list through the lens of contemporary archaeology, as it includes the islands – for the Kabeiroi, the three North-Eastern islands of Lemnos, Samothrace and Imbros, but almost for all Crete; parts of Thessaly, especially Thessaloniki, where the cult of the Kabeiroi was particularly strong, and in the Roman imperial period became the most important deities (Blakely 2006: 33–34), posing the question of which emigrants group, from the East, could have been associated with such cults; Argos, in the Doric areas, and Thebes, in Boiotia, the only place where the Kabeiroi had a temple. While the latter is a later addition,[6] the others cover, almost perfectly, the main places now associated with the spread of Neolithic in the seventh millennium BC, from Turkey (thus Phrygia) to Greece.

Being situated both in between ancient and more recent times and also between the East and the West means that they are highly liminal figures – and this is only reinforced by a third main shared feature: they are also between the human and the divine realms, recalling again Hermes but also Eros. And, indeed, they also share particularly strong ties with eroticism, or rather mere sexuality, though in a quite specific and particularly disturbing sense: the daimones are associated with some particularly revolting offence committed against the Great Goddess, something so offensive that it could not even be mentioned, thus became an *arrheton* (an unspeakable thing; or taking the form in an illicit, possibly erotic way). This already helps to explain the meagre and conflicting evidence we have about them, and also their intriguing character.[7] Their closeness to the occult again connects them to Hermes, various modalities of Hermetism, and the figure of Hermes Trismegistos. The activities of the daimones, or their followers, were always secretive, involving for example mystery rites of which the initiated was not supposed to divulge the secret.

Concerning the reason and nature of these initiation rites, another important common feature of the daimones must be mentioned: their connection to metallurgy, especially iron-making. Here we touch upon another layer of liminality, as metallurgy involves the creation of an in-between product, obtained by altering the qualities of natural objects, especially melting the stone, emblem of solidity. Thus, it also involves the problem of metamorphosis, another key feature of the *daimones*; just as another liminal moment, the period of crisis associated with the rise of metallurgy, the Bronze Age, age of warfare. This reveals a crucial difference between the East and the Greeks: while the crises brought about by metallurgy effected everyone, and the

54 *Presenting the trickster*

contrast between traditional culture and the new practice of metallurgy was also shared (Blakely 1999: 87), including the widespread tensions between the *daimones* and political authorities (Blakely 2000: 125, 2006: 227), attitudes in the two areas to metallurgy differed significantly: while in the East the new (unreal) realities were admitted into rituals and cults, producing a kind of fusion between sanctuaries and industrial sites (Blakely 1999: 87), in Greece there was no sign of transforming traditional deities into a metallurgical one, and there were no public rituals associated with metallurgy. The closest equivalent to Eastern (and also African) metallurgical cults were the daimones; they as if translated the Eastern metallurgical package into Greece (87). As a particularly important sign for this East–West contrast, attitudes to metallurgy in Athens, Ionian centre of Greek culture, and Argos, Doric centre of Eastern influences, were radically different: in Athens, iron-making was associated with magic and the charlatans (*goétes*), and considered as dirty, while in Argos it was a mark of political prestige (Blakely 2006: 213).

The secrecy associated with the Kabeiroi rhymes well with the secrecy surrounding both magicians and smiths, or metallurgical specialists. Both groups were considered as first occupations and have special initiation rites, which suggested already to Louis Gernet that the daimones are fragments of memory about the initiation rites of prehistoric metallurgists (200). In fact, the tight links between secret societies, the secret knowledge of both sacred and metallurgical transformation and metamorphosis and initiation rites must be made even stronger, as no doubt the metallurgical process itself, with the melting and re-shaping of the stone containing ore, suggested the phases to rites of passage. Not surprisingly, smiths were often the ritual specialists themselves, in the Far and Near East (Siberia, Phrygia or the Levant) as well, just as in Africa – though not in Greece.

Given that smiths just as magicians belong to a professional group as a secret society, it also meant that for any concrete community they had to be outsiders, being both itinerary and foreign. Their knowledge was not only secret but also magical. The kind of knowledge they were associated with did not simply meant skill, rather a cunning device. The term Blakely (2006: 211) mentions is *palameisin*, derived from *palamé* (originally meaning the palm of the open hand, involving both acts of violence and works of art). But *palamé* is also a term associated with Hermes (see 'To Hermes', line 110), in particular with the cunning invention of fire, an invention also assigned to the Argive culture hero (thus trickster) Palamedes, who brought to Argos achievements of civilised life as weights and measures (or limits), and also warfare (Blakely 2006: 211). The term is also used by Theognis of Megara (lines 623–624), an early lyric poet, who stated that in man there are all kinds of badness, but also virtues, and finally cunning tricks (*palamai*) that are necessary for making a living. Even more importantly, Palamedes is present in Plato's *Phaedrus* (261d), who evokes there a 'Eleatic Palamedes', characterised as a trickster, a figure widely, though not without perplexity, identified with the founder of Stoicism, Zeno.

These terms bring in a series of further associations. Palamedes almost sounds as Old Medean, or member of the Magi, who were an ancient Median tribe (Herodotus 1.101). The significance of this fact is that it identified an entire population as priests, thus capturing a priestly tribe, comparable to the Levites. The etymology of Median is middle, alluding to their liminal character, and the Medians were in fact in the middle of many things, East and West, South and North, and especially the ancient Silk Road.

Here a short linguistic excursion must be made around the term *magi* or *magus*.

The magi

The term *magi* originally denotes the priestly caste of the Persians, playing a major role in the *Histories* of Herodotus, who was surprised by their special religious importance. This immediately reveals the heart of Asia: while Asia was always more technologically advanced than Europe (Goody 2012), at least until the fall of the Byzantine Empire, the guidance of social life there become monopolised by a priestly caste, with exclusive power to perform rituals. This priestly power is not limited to the Persians, but can be found almost everywhere in Asia, including Vedic India, Tibetan Buddhism, or Levitic Palestine (a version of the various Phoenician Baal, Marduk, and other cults, and very different from prophetic teaching, whose central issue, as among others Weber and Girard realised, was that God requires mercy and justice, and not the mechanical administration of sacrifices). Such obsession with priestly power and bloody sacrifices was alien from the Greeks or the Romans, in spite of their evident and long-standing piety.

Persian *magi* represents in at once the most concrete and symbolical manner Asia in confrontation with Europe; yet, there is still more. The word *magh/i* in Old Median, describes not only the priestly caste, but an entire population. There was a Magi people. In our terminology, this is a trickster people: an entire population composed of magi, or of people who adhere to the impious trickster vision of the world – comparable to the world vision of the Sophists or the Gnostics.

Even further, in two key articles Victor H. Mair (1990, 2012), a main authority on Chinese linguistic came to argue that *magi* was the first Chinese written character, also connected with two symbols widely identified with the magi: the cross potent sign, and the so-called open female image. The cross potent sign, similar to the Maltese cross, used among others by the Templar crusaders, can be traced back to Pech-Merle cave, around 20,000 BC, a cave that is just a few miles from Pergouset cave, with its Room of Monsters (Horvath and Szakolczai 2018a: 144–146); while the open female image is again widely present, central among others to Ireland and India, associated with the goddess Lajja Gauri (Dexter and Mair 2010), but also present, unknown to Mair, in Tassili. This image, often considered as a fertility symbol, or even a kind of tribute to femininity, is rather explicitly deprecatory of women.

Professional metallurgical magic

Such *magi* connections are all the more plausible as relevant professional groups, beyond the association of smiths and Persian *magi* (Blakely 2006: 16, 125), include the *goés*. The term, originally meaning ritual specialist, with a special link to the dead (209), rooted in the word *goos* 'ritual lament for the dead' (24), became increasingly connected to magic (153),[8] gaining the meaning of charlatan, while Plato used it to denote the Sophists.[9] The special task of *goétes* was a combination of loosening and binding (210), pointing towards alchemy, with its double aim of dissolving in order to build up anew: analysis and synthesis, deconstruction and reconstruction. Daimones, metallurgy and destruction were interlinked (26), and this might be a reason for the association between daimones and physical deformity (10).

Such Greek problematisation of metallurgy contrasts with the oriental and African emphasis on the act of smelting and the evocation of parturition. This latter accentuates the confrontation between metallurgy and women. Women were not only excluded from any association with metallurgy, but the activity of smiths was closely modelled on sexuality and parturition. Here African ethnography adds a valuable help. The furnace, in Africa, was not only conceived of as a womb, a kind of matrix in which material is transformed and a new entity is born, but was explicitly built on the model of a woman, with her knees opened wide, recalling the 'open female' images mentioned above.[10] Thus, the entry to the furnace had the character of a vulva (Blakely 2006: 100–102). Such allusion was underlined by often depicting breasts on the furnace, activities being accompanied with excessively obscene songs. Smelting was sometimes accompanied with child sacrifice – new furnaces in particular were consecrated by such sacrifices.

A further common feature of the daimones is their association with dancing and music. In most cultures, singing and dancing is more connected to women than man, but the daimones are almost exclusively male. Such dancing is partly associated with consorting the Great Goddess; however, the dances of the daimones – also associated with insulting the Great Goddess – were rather warrior dances, involving frenzy, close to shamanistic possession. Plato's idea concerning divine madness was quite different, not associated with the ritualistic activities of a professional group, rather divine inspiration, thus initiative.

The Kabeiroi, in particular

While being part of the daimones, the Kabeiroi have special distinguishing features of their own. This includes small stature: they are often called or represented as dwarves, bringing in association with similar dwarfish demon-figures like the Egyptian Bes or the Pygmies.[11] Particularly important representations are the twelve dwarf 'gods', marching in a line, in the open-air sanctuary at Yazılıkaya, near Bogazkoy, about 150 miles north from Kaymakli, dated to the Hittite Empire. They are also associated with physical deformities, here recalling the lame smith-god Hephaestus, also part of widespread Indo-European myths about the lame dwarf smith, particularly important in Germanic and Nordic mythology.[12] Just as important is the testimony according to which they were troglodytes (see Herodotus 4.183), even subhuman (Blakely 2006: 52–53), a point particularly revealing if we connect their Phrygian origins with the enormous and enigmatic underground structures of Turkey. The association of Kabeiroi with darkness (Blakely 2006: 48) is perhaps another sign of their troglodyte origins.

Still further, the Kabeiroi have connections with the origins of Greeks theatre. This is partly through the Doric farce (associated in particular with Megara), a major source of comedy, in Greece just as in southern Italy – a kind of comedy that was always particularly violent, rude, vulgar, and obscene; and partly through the Satyrs (Blakely 2006: 45–47). The association between satyr plays and the origins of comedy are well known, but Satyrs are also linked with metallurgy. As craftsmen, they were working in the smithery of Hephaestus among others helping him to create Pandora – subject matter of a lost play by Sophocles (49–50). The Kabeiroi also have close connections with Prometheus and the Titans – in Lemnos and Imbros, the Kabeiroi are outright identified with the Titans (49–51).

The Kabeiroi on coins

Further information on the Kabeiroi is contained in Greek metals coins. These used as images the representative mythological character of the city minting them. As such coins were relatively late, they were bound to ignore older layers of mythology. Yet, a number of coins contain relevant images, all from islands. While the central Lemnos figure in coins is Hephaestus the Olympian deity associated with metalwork, an Imbros coin depicts Pelasgian Hermes with a Phrygian cap (Head 1964, III: 211), or Hermes as one of the Kabeiroi. Kabeiroi also appear in coins in Syros (IX: 124), Melos (IX, No.4547, an island famous for its obsidian deposits), and Thasos (III: 225, the only Greek Aegean island colony founded by Phoenicians, close to Thrace). The most striking such coin is from the Balearic islands (IX, No.16), where a dwarf Kabeiroi is shown standing and holding in one hand a stick,[13] in the other a snake.

The content of Kabeiroi arrheton knowledge

As an unspeakable knowledge is not to be conveyed, it is difficult if not impossible for us to discover this content, all the more so as initiates in classical Antiquity were quite strict in maintaining their vow of secrecy. Even Pausanias, the Hellenistic traveller and geographer, only conveys us that he participated in these rituals, but is not allowed to relay any details. Kerényi (1980: 143–182) in his classic article collects three main known features about the *arrheton* acts of the Kabeiroi: that this was connected to *hieros gamos*, or a kind of secret wedding ceremony involving the Great Goddess; in it the

58 *Presenting the trickster*

Great Goddess appears in a way that is considered as highly improper; and the Kabeiroi committed particularly atrocious, unspeakable acts. However, in light of the analysis that we would present in Chapter Four we tend to use a more extended perspective on the *arrheton* moving beyond evident violence.

A crucial piece of information in this regard is transmitted by Blakely (2012: 60–62): a recently found magnetic ring in Samothrace strongly indicates that this object played a central role in the ceremonies. Apart from the mythological significance of rings, their magnetic features are also important. Rings are associated with binding, up till the present day, but also with invisibility – one of the central features of the Kabeiroi, and of tricksters in general.[14] They are also supposed to bring wealth: the magic ring acquired by the Lydian king Gyges, which granted him the power to become invisible and procured him wealth, though only temporarily, is one of the best known stories in Herodotus's *Histories* (1.8–12), also elaborated by Plato (*Republic* 359A–360D), and a prelude to the exploits of the Phrygian kings Midas and Croesus, who both became proverbial terms for wealth. Finally, magnetic rings also play a crucial role in Plato's *Ion* (533D–E). Apart from rings, the token of invisibility was the Phrygian cap, associated with dwarves.

Such initiation rituals certainly had a sexual character, were even a kind of sacred marriage, involving acts that were for some reason unspeakable. At the corresponding level of thought, they involved reflection on flux, flow, or stream; perhaps a paradoxical reflection on the absence of reflexivity combined with sexual acts that rather liberate the unconscious, perhaps by performing acts that are otherwise impossible to do, thus unspeakable. Concerning the possible nature of such acts there is a unique text that, indirectly, offers us precious insights, 'Interpretation of Dreams' (*Oneirocritica*) by Artemidorus (Bowersock 2004).

Artemidorus's book was the best-known discussion of dreams in classical Antiquity. Foucault devoted to this the first chapter of his *Care of the Self*, in implicit contrast to Freud: according to Artemidorus the first step in understanding dreams is to recognise whether they come from the outside or are produced by the mind. However, Artemidorus also deserves special attention 'as a witness of his age' (Bowersock 2004: 54). During the Second Sophistic he was practically the only contemporary who stood by classical Greek culture, explicitly repudiating the Sophists, seeing them as not different from adulterers and forgers 'whose art is deception', and whose acts are 'fundamentally destructive of Greek identity' (58–59).

Artemidorus's terminology offers precious revelations concerning what was considered as *arrheton* in Greek culture, especially given his knowledge concerning Asia Minor (53), the area closely associated with the Kabeiroi. While, as discussing dreams, the sexual vocabulary of Artemidorus is particularly rich, even reporting acts of 'sometimes grotesque irregularity' (62), he purposefully avoided the name *eunuchos*, using instead various substitutes, and also avoiding the verbs *lesbiadzein* and *phoinikidzein*, denoting female and male homosexual acts. Even further, 'for sodomy, cunnilingus and fellatio he uses, for some reason, the same word, *arrhetopoiein*, although the context never leaves the reader any doubt as to what is going on' (62). The verb *arrhetopoiein* 'formulate something that is not sayable' is used with considerable frequency by Artemidorus in his description of sexual dreams, while it is not known outside his book.

The inference this suggests is that unspeakable rituals involve sexual acts not done in the proper manner. This poses the question why such acts are then performed in purportedly sacred rituals. The probable answer is to gain power, over those who are submitted in sexual acts.

Hieros gamos

The discussion of *hieros gamos* by Calasso, offered in one of the most important chapters of his 1988 book, which also discusses the various daimones, places the emphasis on the presumed sacrificial aspects of the rite. According to him, the unspeakable refers to the presumed original identity of sacrifice and *hieros gamos*: 'the primordial god killed itself and copulated at the same time' (Calasso 1988: 127).[15] Over time, this identity became problematic, leading to the separation of the two ceremonies.[16] In a commentary on a story by Pausanias, where a sacrilege committed by two young people (they made love in a Temple of Artemis) is avenged by the Goddess requiring the yearly sacrificial offering of two young people, Calasso restates that the significance of mysteries was an 'occult tension' between *hieros gamos* and sacrifice (323–324). This amounts to a mutual implication and secret pact: 'if Hierogamy is the secret of sacrifice, sacrifice would serve to hide it' (325). Hierogamy and sacrifice are thus two forces that at the same time suppose and oppose each other: 'Hierogamy moves towards the annulling of the law, while sacrifice provides the bloody foundation of the law'.[17] Apart from being paradoxically connected to the law, Hierogamy was also the first mode of communicating between gods and men, only ending due to the sin of Prometheus, which led to a specific, separate mode of sacrifice, leaving only the 'smoke' to the gods, while condemning men at the same time to kill and eat meat (325–326). As we have seen, Prometheus would be followed by Hermes, both as messenger of gods and wily inventor of sacrifice. Such separation and the subsequent oblivion of Hierogamy is a problem according to Calasso, as Hierogamy was the primary act, performed on the basis of divine initiative, and the act of sacrifice was only a human effort to respond. Crucially, Hierogamy lacked the destructive element that is central to sacrifice (326). It originally meant an act by which a god took possession of a goddess, penetrating its body (329, 331); and thus the act of penetration supposedly performed in an actual *hieros gamos* was the imitation of such divine acts.

However, this does not make full sense, as the intercourse between gods does not involve a body; the central feature of the divine is the invisible, as Calasso reckons (327); a divine possession of a human body is different from a *hieros gamos*, and can be represented either through the rapes of Zeus, or the possession of a mystic, among others. The rites of the Kabeiroi are therefore highly suspect, just as any act of sacrifice is, as not just occult but sinister speculation that is not based on true understanding but a mixing of the divine and the human, with the possibly quite sinister aim of inciting emotions. As if perceiving such problems, Calasso offers the last word by referring to Plutarch, a follower of Plato and also a priest of the Eleusian mysteries. From this perspective, 'Hierogamy and sacrifice are the extreme points of breathing: the air inspired is joined to the blood, feeding it, thus making it unrecognisable in the mixing (Hierogamy); while the air expired is expulsed forever (sacrifice), and is mixed to the air of the world' (331). For Plutarch – and he was 'in the know' – this was 'part of the "unspoken things"' that are the basis of every myth and liturgy, and that 'always seemed "more suspicious than the things of which one talks"' (332).[18]

It seems to us that there were evident links between the initiation rites of the Kabeiroi and the Eleusian mysteries, just as between the Kabeiroi, Prometheus, and Hermes. In our view, the initiation rites of the Kabeiroi served as negative models for the Eleusian mysteries, which most probably represented the same kind of pacification of rather obscure, obscene and violent rituals, taking out the force of the poison, just as Hermes is a certain pacification of the Magi/Gnostic/trickster figure, more present in the Kabeiroi and Prometheus. Combining the open female and *hieros gamos* images with different accounts about the possible substance of the rites, it seems to us that such rites were set up by prehistoric Magi. These implied a revealing of the 'secret' of the Great Goddess, through images presenting her private parts in a wide open way, closely recalling the infamous image of Gustave Courbet, 'The Origin of the World', and the performance of particularly vulgar and shameful sexual acts on her representatives – a sordid ceremony besmirching life-generating powers and the order of reality.

The *hieros gamos* rite was widespread in the Mediterranean region, and possible elsewhere in the Ecumene, in the sense of Voegelin (1974), though of this we know even less than about the initiation rites of the Greek mystery cults. The similarity between the Kabeiroi and male ritual dances allude to connections among the Bronze Age warrior cultures all around the region. The one-sided extolling of male virtues in the direction of unlimited warfare was just the reverse side of the Magi/Trickster culture downplaying graceful beauty and the life-giving powers of women. As a result, Antiquity at its end was infested by trickster logic, unable to get out of it on its own.

With this, Antiquity was not alone. While the distant roots of Hermes, through the Titans, the Kabeiroi and the Magi are lost in the mist of ancient times, it also extends in the other direction, towards the future, reaching into our own present. Nietzsche identified Dionysus as the key Greek mythological figure reaching the heart of modernity but, perceptive such an insight was, perhaps Hermes serves even better.

Hermes in modernity

The features of Hermes indeed strikingly embody many of the most characteristic features of modernity. Hermes is the god of speed, and what is more modern than speed, whether in communication or in transport, but also – following further hints from Michel Serres – in thinking, as quick thinking is a much prized feature of mathematics, and modern science is based on mathematics. Hermes is also the god of commerce, and what is more modern than commerce, the exchange of goods and service, main substance not only of the modern economy, but of modern society, even the entire modern world, based on the – rather questionable – idea that everything can and should be not only exchanged, but made for exchange which, as we will also see – here also with Roberto Calasso and René Girard – reveals modernity as animated by a vision of substitutability, thus sacrifice. Furthermore, Hermes is also the god of speech and language, or communication, and what is more modern than communication and information, heart of both the contemporary world and technological change, leading to the current situation where communication no longer serves to share information about lives between concrete entities, but rather is the 'in-between' that stirs everything. Even further, Hermes is outright the god associated with knowledge – though this knowledge, or his craft,[19] is a dangerous kind of knowledge, leaning close to magic, the reason why Hermes would become the protector god of alchemy – as if forecasting Alfred Gell's ideas.

It is thus not surprising that the decisive significance of Hermes for our world was realised by a series of particularly perceptive thinkers, all touched by the visionary ideas of Nietzsche. We might start the line with Thomas Mann and Károly Kerényi, who first separately, and then together, explored this significance is a series of milestone works. We can continue with Lewis Hyde, who in a pair of books, *The Gift* and *The Trickster Makes This World* (whose titles say it all, capturing both the heart of the world and its sliding away), evoked Hermes for understanding modernity, among others in a most insightful chapter on Ezra Pound (Hyde 1983: 216–272). The perhaps most relevant discussion of Hermes, however, is contained in the work of Michel Serres, whose unity is woven around the figure. In between 1969 and 1979 Serres published a series of five books, entitled *Hermes I* through *Hermes V*, which pioneered the modern study of communication, in a way only comparable to that of Gregory Bateson. Among others, in two flagship chapters of the series, selected as the first two chapters to the first English publication of his writings (Serres 1982), it presented Don Juan, an 'apparition of Hermes', as the 'first hero' of modernity, and through an analysis of Aesop's fable about the wolf and the lamb demonstrated the problematic complicity between modern rationalist philosophy and science in their destructive warfare waged against nature.

The Hermes theme is resumed in his perhaps most valuable book, *The Parasite*, published just after the *Hermes* series was concluded. The parasite is

Serres's recapitulation of the trickster figure, a word absent from the book. Its 'best definition' is offered as 'a thermal exciter', as it enters the body, infests it, being able to adapt to different hosts, but not changing its nature, only irritating it (Serres 2014: 341–343). It produces both heat and fire, water, turbulence and liquidity; it is 'an inclination to trouble, to a change of the phase of a system'; its main concern is to 'transform the state of things (*l'état des choses*) itself' (353). It is also a deviation, at the start just a minimal one, which might even disappear, but which under certain conditions, which we would name 'liminal', can grow until it 'transforms a physiological order into a new order' (358). Finally, through Molière's *Tartuffe*, Serres adds that every parasite lives by provoking crises – a choice area being the family (375). The figure of the parasite not only captures the theatre-economics-exchange nexus, as both hypocrisy and using the sacrificial mechanism is central for it – René Girard was life-long friend and main source of inspiration for Serres – but reaches into the problem of evil. While not intending to write about evil, the work turned out to be 'the book of evil, the book on the problem of evil' (164, 454). The parasite, this distant relative or rather twin brother of Hermes, in the short, concluding Epilogue to the book is recognised as evil itself, as it never stops, never ceases performing its various bodily acts, and simply imposes itself on the world, without any limits, inundating everything. Such evocation of the flood is fundamental, a metaphor often used by Serres, a version of the flux, the incommensurable. It is to the unlimited, frenetic activities of the parasite that a number of things are attributed including rumour, fury and incomprehension, violence and killing, misery and hunger, illnesses and epidemics, and also 'bestial metamorphoses' (453).

Serres brings out the frightening, demonic features inside and especially behind the figure – a touch of evil, even shadow of death. Hermes is not just a communicator and mediator, but a guide of souls, even thief of souls. Building a world, our world, on Hermes is an extremely dangerous, not to say foolish undertaking, as with Hermes nobody can ever be sure. Hermes cannot be a trusted friend, so those who invite us to 'trust' him, and his main spheres of activities – which are, as we have seen, the media, communication, words, the economy, and specialised, magical-technological knowledge – are to be suspected of having a specific agenda, promoting their own interests behind the smokescreen. This is rendered visible, still at the threshold of modernity, by Goethe's *Faust* whose Hermetic aspects, beyond the efforts of Mephistopheles to 'steal' the soul of Faust, include the recognition of the alchemic character of the modern economy (Binswanger 1994). Thus, while Goethe's 60-year-long efforts to complete his unique masterpiece started with the figure of Prometheus being behind the figure of Faust, this other 'first hero of modernity', it ended up by identifying there another trickster figure, Hermes, linking together technology and the modern economy as direct heirs to alchemy and magic, through their joint, creative-destructive promotion of the void and the flux.

In Greece, Persian Magi and secret activities were always associated, also connected to the daimones, and from about 420 in Athens such activities start to gain the meaning of magic (Bremmer 1999). Plato uses the word only once (*Republic* 572E), and his usual term for the Sophists is *goés*. But he mentions a 'secret knowledge' associated with such figures in the *Theaetetus*, the dialogue that just precedes the *Sophist*, and which offers unique hints about the content of trickster knowledge.

Notes

1 Note that he is not yet called *psychopompos* (guide of souls) here.
2 Such focus on the power of oaths is connected to curse and verbal magic, in particular magical incantations, also through the affinity of Hermes with the herald (Brown 1969: 8, 22–26, 30–31). Such incantations were central for Mauss's work on prayer. They worked as masks, transforming the face of the person uttering them into an ancestral being, as they were '"acoustic words" for supernatural utterances' (as in Murphy 2003: 151–152). Note that in old Hungarian singing incantations and hiding away are the same word (*rejt*).
3 According to Calasso (1988: 124), this in itself gives the lie to any idea of progress.
4 About the Titans being the Kabeiroi, see Kerényi (1991: 60–62).
5 The connection between Hermes and erotic desire is also emphasised in Brown (1969: 9). While Brown published his important study in 1947, it was started in 1941, and given the war conditions could not take into account the work of Kerényi, originally published in 1943.
6 Alluded to by legends that connect the foundation of Thebes, not only the sanctuary, to the move of Cadmos, a Phoenician, from Samothrace to Thebes.
7 They play a major role in *Faust II*.
8 The word *goétes* first appears in a fragment of *Phoronis*, the epic poem of Argos (Blakely 2006: 192). Hermes was also widely associated with magic, which would be a major reason why later he would become identified as the patron god of alchemists.
9 See *Symposium* 203D; *Sophist* 235A, 241B; *Statesman* 291C, 303C, but even *Republic* 280D, 283A, 598D. Interestingly, the term was both infrequent in the last works, and not present in the early Socratic dialogues.
10 See in Blakely (2006: 145–146).
11 Evidently, we do not refer to the actual ethnic group, rather to their general representation in the Mediterranean world, for example as present in the famous battle between the cranes and the Pygmies (Homer, *Iliad*, 3:1–7). The point was made in connection with the Negroid features associated with the Kabeiroi, which connect them to the Pygmies (Blakely 2006: 52) – at least, in Ancient Mediterranean imagination.
12 See Clover and Lindow (2005: 77; on Loki and dwarves, 84–85).
13 The stick or rod was an important magical instrument of Hermes, a sign of his medical magic, connecting Hermes to Asclepius (Brown 1969: 17).
14 Concerning the invisibility techniques of the *Magi*, the figure of Zalmoxis is illuminating (Herodotus 4.94–96). In order to confirm his teachings about immortality to the Thracians, in secret he built an underground dwelling where he hid for three years, disappearing from view, and so when he reappeared in the fourth year, he was believed.
15 This idea, as we'll see, is rooted in Calasso's reading of Vedic Hinduism, but we consider this story as a Gnostic misinterpretation of ancient times.

64 *Presenting the trickster*

16 As sign of their original identity, both ceremonies involve taking up the crown (Calasso 1988: 128).
17 Note that we only reproduce here the argument of Calasso, and not accept it fully – or rather accept it as the genuine basis of the Magi-Gnostic vision of the world that Calasso successfully reconstructs.
18 Some images associated with Asia Minor, like the famous Inandik Vase from the Museum of Anatolian Civilizations in Ankara, offer further help, by redirecting to the *arrheton*, discussed above. See also similar representations of the battle of the cranes and Pygmies (Blakely, 2006: 42–43; Kerényi 1980: fig. 2).
19 The Greek word used for his knowledge, *dolos*, means both trick and craft (Brown 1969: 22). This has parallels in Hungarian, where the word for purposeful acting, *cselekszik*, is derived from ruse *csel*.

4 Plato's *Theaetetus*
The Sophists and secret trickster knowledge

The *Theaetetus* is, in a very specific though highly significant sense, the liminal centre of Plato's work. The claim is not exaggerated, and can be safely supported, but its meaning must be immediately qualified. By no means is the *Theaetetus* the most important dialogue of Plato; this was not asserted in any sense; what is being claimed is that it plays a role – and a central one – as a hinge or a joint (inflexion point or saddle) in the entire oeuvre.

This is best visible in the fact that it is with *Theaetetus* – though not in it – that Plato for the first time reveals a sequential ordering of the dialogues. Otherwise, one of the most striking aspects of the dialogues is that each of them is self-contained, making no cross-reference to the others, leaving open the interpretation that all the dialogues belong equally together, as well as the claim that each is a self-contained whole – just as various combinations of these extreme poles (and possibly others). Given that Plato was interested in educating the soul, it cannot possibly be suggested that the dialogues were not built upon one another; so the reason why he failed to reveal their order has to be that – for the same educational purposes for which he wrote dialogues, and not systematic treatises – he implied that we, all of us who only read the dialogues and cannot have the gift of a personal acquaintance with Plato must make this effort on our own, so that his teaching could not be codified and thus rendered a dead word. He was amazingly successful in this manner – but then we need to explain why he took exception to his own way of proceeding with the *Theaetetus*. However, as the sequence becomes evident not from the body of this dialogue, but through its follow-ups, the *Sophist* and the *Statesman*, this is not the place to pursue this argument. The question, for this chapter and book, is what was the substance of the teaching expressed here that came up in a liminal moment of Plato's intellectual path, and that certainly influenced the substance of his last works, in contrast to the conclusive dialogue of his earlier work, culminating in the *Republic*.

This is all the more important as the hinge character of the dialogue can be maintained by a series of arguments from inside the text. Two of them, which are still connected to the place of this dialogue in the general – sequential or other – ordering of the dialogues, concern the very starting and ending of the text. The first character who appears in the dialogue – to disappear almost

66 *Presenting the trickster*

immediately, though not before revealing himself, not as a participant in the dialogue, but the one who wrote it down – is Eucleides (a disciple of Socrates, present at his death, and founder of the Megarean school of Socratic philosophy), presenting himself as just 'going down [*katabainón*]' to the harbour [*limén*], where he saw Theaetetus being carried to Athens. This is evident allusion to the *Republic* (327A), which starts by Socrates 'going down [*katebén*]' to Peiraeus, or the harbour of Athens,[1] the *Republic* being one of the central (not liminal-central) dialogues of Plato, though by no means his last word, rather the key, summary dialogue of his middle period. The significance of the reference to a port or harbour is also underlined by the *Symposium*, where the telling of the story about the transmission of the dialogue takes place also at a port, this time in the old port of Athens, Phaleron.[2] At the other end, the dialogue finishes off by Socrates leaving to respond to the suit brought against him by Meletus. This evokes *Euthypro*, traditionally considered as the first dialogue of Plato, just as the dialogues around the trial of Socrates, which take up the centre stage in the early Socratic dialogues. All these clear allusions lead to the point that this dialogue was destined, by Plato, to explicitly mark the transition to a new stage of his thinking – by evoking the core centre of his thinking, so far.

This is reinforced by another central feature of the dialogue, the modality of its presentation, where the parallels are particularly strong with *Phaedrus* and the *Symposium*, or two of the other dialogues that are considered to span the transition space from the *Republic* to the six late dialogues. This concerns their distancing, at once reflexive and performative (theatrical) character. Just as in the *Symposium*, and also in *Parmenides*, Socrates and his interlocutors do not enter the scene talking, *in medias res*, rather there is an elaborate set-up by which the transmission mechanism of the dialogue is transcribed, thus making plain the radical difference between being present when the dialogue is actually taking place, and its lame, limping, written down version, a faded copy of the original – but still a necessary exercise, if taken with a proper degree of care. Furthermore, and similarly now to *Phaedrus*, the dialogue has a meta-character, there problematising the writing down of a discussion, while this one problematising knowledge itself. Still, and in a somewhat paradoxical way, such distancing is not only an exercise in reflexivity, but at the same time in theatricality, as the transmission mechanisms are explicitly performative or theatrical. Even further, in this case such theatricality is heightened, and is given a specific spin, with the starting scene taking place not in or near Athens, rather in distant Megara, a town famous for its mime plays – which has its own relevance, given Plato's alleged life-long interest in the Sophronic mimes.[3]

The hinge character of the play can be further undermined by taking a closer look on the term 'harbour [*limén*]'; a word with special importance on its own. A port, of course, is an extremely liminal place. But there is absolutely no reason for Plato to bring in the port of Megara as scene for introducing the dialogue; and, furthermore, to designate it by the generic name 'port [*limén*]'. The word must have its own importance.

The Greek word *limén* is formally identical with Latin *limen* 'beam in doorframe', etymological root of liminal; while the Greek and Latin words share some etymology. Given our argument about the liminal character of this dialogue this cannot be accidental, and requires a further investigation into these two terms; their correlated and exact etymologies.

According to Liddell and Scott (1951) *limén* not only means 'harbour', and in its metaphorically extended sense 'safe haven, retreat, refuge', but also 'gathering place, receptacle', while in Thessaly and Cyprus (thus the archaeologically most archaic parts of Greece) this is the term used for the agora. It is also applied to a very concrete receptacle, source of birth, the womb. The term is closely related to a similar word, *leimón*, whose basic meaning is meadow, but also stands for, in a vulgar sense, the female private part, and in an extended – and somewhat puzzling – metaphorical sense for any bright surface. The Greek etymological dictionary (Beekes 2010) is uncertain about the roots, arguing for moistness, evoking the Latin term *limus*, and also possible connections with two similar Greek terms, *leimax* 'slug' and *leibó* 'libation'.

Even in Latin (de Vaan 2008), we have to do with a pair of related words. The situation is even more complex, as dictionaries consider that there are two identical words spelt *limus*, one meaning 'mud, slime', being connected to *limax* 'snug, snail', a word shared with Greek (see also Italian *lumaca* or Russian *slimak*); while the other 'transverse, oblique', this being etymologically connected not to the other, but to *limen*. Given the officially recognised closeness of this group of Greek and Latin words, one might argue that if a well-argued semantic closeness can be established, then purely formalistic arguments to wedge a gap between the entire complex might become less tenable. The proper perspective, we argue, is again archaeological; we only need to move behind the buildings of classical Antiquity, to the Neolithic and its passage tombs, or even back to the Palaeolithic and its caves. Such passage tombs, and cave entries, bring together a certain gathering place at or near the entrance, scenery of rituals, and having an antechamber or port-like character; the more narrow and often muddy, moist and slimy entrance to the inner cave; and the inner chambers of the cave or the passage tomb, genuine safe haven and receptacle, recalling the uterus.[4] It can easily be understood how such a privileged liminal place, with the transformation of the Palaeolithic walking culture into the sea-faring cultures of the Mediterranean, was eventually transferred to ports, thus creating both manifold linguistic affiliations and associations, but also difficulties concerning the recognition of these links.

That such considerations, about the uterus, receptacle or matrix character of the port of Megara, central not as the place of the dialogue but for its eventual transmission, are not accidental is reinforced by a central feature of the modality of the dialogue, the manner in which Socrates conceives there his role in the acquisition of knowledge. He is not a possessor of knowledge, a wise man, rather only a midwife, helping to bring forth the knowledge that his interlocutors, in fact everyone, already have, inside, in a kind of womb or matrix (150B–E). In doing so, he plays on a set of dichotomies, focusing centrally on the male/female difference, where men with their knowledge are assigned a secondary, imitative role to women, the ones who are actually, concretely productive, fertile, capable of bringing forth real beings. The role of Socrates as a midwife, in fact, is three times imitative, or 'hysteretic', lagging behind, as he is imitating his mother, who was a genuine midwife, as even midwives can only be women; but only those women can be midwives who are no longer fertile themselves, in this being similar to men; however, and as a further distinction, and reinforcing in the third step the male/female difference, they cannot be simply barren, only past their fertile age. The procuring of knowledge is thus assigned a secondary, even clearly mimetic and epigone role by Socrates, to be pursued by those who cannot bring forth in actual reality anything, following up on the *Symposium*, a close precedent to this dialogue, where Socrates was assigned a secondary role even in matters of a particular knowledge, concerning *Eros* (love), as compared to Diotima, not a midwife but a female prophetess, and intrinsically tied to both beauty – the heart of Plato's world vision – and the generation of children. Thus, this dialogue implies the culminating insight that one should rather be weary of those men who are too much fixated with possessing or producing knowledge, and especially those who want to create some kind of ascendancy for the possessors of knowledge, given that this is only secondary to the more important matter, which is the generation of a new life. This implies a radical contrast with the Magi vision of the world, proliferated among others by the Kabeiroi, also guilty of some unspeakable offence against the Great Mother – an unspeakable (*arrheton*) offence which they evidently turned to a secret (*arrheton* or *aporrheton*) knowledge.

Thus, all this has basic relevance for the question of secret knowledge, or the efforts of Socrates to render evident the vacuity of the claims of those who create credit and power to themselves by pretending to be exclusive possessors of such hidden, secret knowledge. It takes us back to Pergouset and Tassili, the guardians of memory of Çatalhöyük or Nietzsche's ascetic priests – or image-magic, generating non-being.

The troubles with knowledge

The central theme of the dialogue, thus, is knowledge. However, we can cut the excitement short, and sparing the reader to go through in search for an answer through what is otherwise one of the longest dialogues of Plato – especially that far, preceded only by the *Republic* – by revealing that no such answer is given there. Furthermore, this is not only one of the longest dialogues, but also the last (or sort of) in which Socrates is present as the main character. As promised, he'll return next morning at the beginning of the *Sophist*, but there the leading role would be soon taken up by the enigmatic Eleatic Stranger.

In the standard Plato literature, it is considered as something like evidence that the central issue here is the transition, purely as a matter of content, between the theory of Forms, as presented in the *Republic* and also *Phaedo* (and other dialogues), to Plato's later position, the question being the extent to which the changed his mind, and whether he dismissed completely the earlier theory of Forms or not. This issue certainly has its importance, which cannot be pursued here; but it cannot be the full story. The reason for the elaborate reflexive mediation and theatrical scenery of the dialogue, and the related intermediary dialogues, must be incorporated in any serious analysis, and cannot just be considered as a trivial matter of transition, just as it is done by various transitiologists in the social and political sciences. A distinction must be made between the content and the modality of knowledge, following on the footsteps of Foucault's (1966) distinction between *savoir* and *connaissance*, the latter being the knowledge-content, while the former being concerned with the manner in which what is to be known is conceptualised. It is in this context that Foucault famously introduced the *episteme*, and epistemic changes, capturing the shifts in the very idea of how knowledge was conceived in Europe between the 16th and 19th centuries.

Taking inspiration from the spirit, though not necessary from the words of Foucault, let me now attempt to reconstruct the way the *Theaetetus* grapples with issues related to this shift in Plato's own thinking.

Starting with basic terminology, the word used by Plato for knowledge is *episteme*, and not *gnosis*; the latter term only appears four times, and does not carry any special weight, while this is the dialogue which uses the word *episteme* by far the most time in Plato's entire oeuvre. The etymological root is in the word 'stand', but arguably much more important for Plato – especially through the concluding part of the dialogue – is the related word *epistasis* 'stopping, stoppage', implying a quite vehement stopping of motion, in order to examine and attentively observe a thing. Apart from its evident connection with knowledge as inquiry, this has crucial significance for the dialogue due to two different reasons. First, it implies a general contrast with motion, or flux, the central content of the secret knowledge; and second, such a stopping of a flux or flow will be central for Plato's introduction of the syllable as a central issue in the meaning and use of language.

Turning to matters of content, the *Theaetetus* is about knowledge; and the best way to start the discussion is by recognising the point, significant not only due to matters of content, but also form: this dialogue is not only the farewell to Socrates as our guide into the thinking of Plato, but also represents a return to a major formal characteristics of the earlier dialogues, their inconclusive character. However, this is with a major difference: while the early dialogues were about genuinely substantive issues, like courage, virtue (*areté*), or temperance (*sophrosyné*), where the main point was – made particularly clear in the middle dialogues concerned with love – that such matters can never be definitely put into words, now the topic was knowledge itself, something that is almost exclusively a concern of words, especially if we add other signs and images. Knowledge does not exist without human instruments, and central among such instruments are words; so it is twice paradoxical, highly puzzling and troublesome, that words cannot even fully understand themselves –

especially if we consider that one of the dialogues immediately preceding the *Theaetetus* was *Cratylus*, or a dialogue explicitly about words. Thus, put simply, we cannot know knowledge.

The dialogue, however, and at the very start of its substantial part, not only defines knowledge as its target, but comes to present, and as central to its argument, a kind of secret knowledge.

Secret knowledge in the *Theaetetus*

At an early stage in the dialogue, Plato/Socrates makes a stunning claim about Protagoras[5] that created quite a headache to interpreters since: he claimed that Protagoras possessed a 'secret doctrine [*mystéria legein*]' (156a3–4) that was not revealed publicly, where Protagoras mostly worked, only transmitted 'in secret [*aporrhéto*] to his pupils' (152c10). The common view about this claim is that it is a fiction (Sedley 2004: 39); consulting the two main commentaries singled out for attention by Sedley, one argues that '[t]he suggestion that Protagoras secretly taught the doctrine which follows [concerning the flux] is almost certainly not meant to be taken seriously' (McDowell 1973: 121), while the other (Burnyeat 1990) simply ignores this passage.

However, there are a number of good reasons why the idea should be taken seriously. To begin with, the idea of an originary flux was taken up by Newton, at the heart of his world vision, and it has indeed become the backbone of the empirical philosophy of Locke, arguing that any knowledge humans gain is based on sense perception, so it is the ideas Plato attributes to Protagoras that seems to be close to the modern scientific vision of the world, and not those of Plato. It is thus not so surprising that it is increasingly argued that Plato was wrong in his confrontation with Protagoras, and we moderns should rather be – or even in fact are – following the Sophists, and not Plato. This view is only reinforced by the argument made in the *Laws*, where Plato argues, in contrast to the claim of Protagoras that man is the measure of all things, that rather the divine is the measure. Surely, we moderns agree with Protagoras, and nowhere more than here.

Second, and as an indirect but crucial corroboration of the secret transmission, there is something strange with the disciples of Heraclitus. While Heraclitus indeed said that 'everything moves [*panta rhei*]', he also said many other things, and this was by no means the heart of his doctrine, which rather focused on the measure of a divine cosmic order. His supposed disciples thus got his ideas seriously wrong already at the time of Socrates and Plato, and indeed it would be this vision of Heraclitus that would be transmitted in the standard history of philosophy, up to Hegel. How this could have happened, and how the false teaching attributed to Heraclitus actually came to be identical to the secret doctrine attributed by Plato to Protagoras can be explained – and such an eventuality *should* be taken seriously – by assuming that the Sophists, and in particular their founding leader, Protagoras, were indeed operating by initiating their students into a secret or mystery doctrine. Finally, from studies in anthropology just as from the history of religions we know that this was indeed the case how priests and sorcerers, possessors of ritualistic knowledge operated. Here we only need to add that tricksters and sorcerers are one and the same thing, as Plato already realised, rendered evident by his use of the term *goés*, maybe alongside the same bipolar continuum already discussed.

Thus, we need to take seriously Plato's claims about secret knowledge; and must start to do so by considering his exact terminology, or the words used – all the more so as words were the theme of one the most direct predecessors of this dialogue, the *Cratylus*, which again must be taken more literally seriously, as it has been again recently argued by David Sedley (2003).

Plato actually used two different words for this secret doctrine: for the mode of activity of Protagoras, telling the real truth to his pupils in secret, he uses the term *aporrhétos* (152c10); while for the content of these teachings, he uses the term 'secret doctrines [*mustéria*]'. Both terms, and especially their use by Plato, merit closer scrutiny.

Mustéria stands for not just anything mysterious or secret, but for the secret performance of religious rituals, closely connected to initiation ceremonies. The most famous such rituals were the Eleusian mysteries, but the first references to the term are actually from Heraclitus, fragment 14 ('The mysteries practiced among men are unholy mysteries'), and from Herodotus (II.51), referring specifically to the Kabeiroi. It just captures the heart of the non-philosophical or pre-philosophical, non-rational knowledge in contrast to which philosophy emerged as a form of discourse – already before Plato; and representing a much stronger contrast to philosophy than myths are. Plato used myths in his dialogues, but never compared his teaching to mysteries to which one had to become initiated. In fact, the term is only used once in his other dialogues, in *Meno*, and in a non-emphatic context. Thus, his claim about a secret mystery doctrine in the arch-Sophist Protagoras is highly charged. It is quite problematic to consider it as simply a way to make the idea of Protagoras look stronger (Lee 2005: 77). If anything, the charge attributes them sinister qualities, and arguably quite intentional harm. There is a double issue here: on the one hand, the task of philosophy is clearly different from hidden religious ceremonies, whatever purpose and value could be behind them; but second, and even further, such traditions are one thing, but the efforts of foreigners – and we should never forget that the Sophists were not natives – to a secret mystery cult cannot but be sinister in intention and effect.

These points are reinforced by the use of the other term, the adjective *aporrhétos*.[6] The word first appears in the *Phaedo* (62B), and in a most significant context, as the secret doctrine evoked here is nothing else than the idea of the body being a prison (of the soul); a Gnostic and alchemic idea frequently, and mistakenly, attributed to Plato himself, about how to catch and refashion a corrupted body by implanting a new soul in it. However, here, both in the concrete context and the broader context of the other uses of the word it is revealed as the teaching to which Plato is opposed. In the

72 *Presenting the trickster*

Republic the term is used twice. One is irrelevant for our purposes, but the other (378A) is an important advice about certain things not to be spoken – not because their content is secret, but because the audience could be unprepared or immature – like persons who are thoughtless, for example due to being too young.

The occurrence in *Cratylus* (413A) is close in meaning to that in the *Theaetetus* but does not add anything new. The three first uses in the *Laws* are quite technical. The fourth and last occurrence, however, towards the very end of the dialogue (968e4–5), thus at the end of Plato's last work (the *Laws* ends at 969D), is again highly significant. It is a partial correction of the passage in the *Republic* analysed above; not a change of content, only a precision concerning modality. In the *Republic* Plato used the word *aporrhétos* in a somewhat imprecise sense, conflating the secret with what temporarily, or due to certain conditions, cannot be uttered, for which he generally uses the word *arrhéton*. Now he separates the two meanings, by introducing a new word, *aprorrhétos*, an *hapax* in classical Antiquity (nobody else ever used this word), making a distinction between indescribable and imprescribable. This latter term does not have the connotation of secrecy, is rather coined by Plato to denote ideas that cannot be communicated prematurely, or 'ought not to be divulged beforehand' (Cooper 1997: 1616).[7]

Trickster knowledge

Still, what is the main characteristic of the trickster as a knowledgeable figure? Such a question/approach immediately hits a paradox, as the trickster figure over the enormous space and time where it makes its appearance – basically: everywhere in the planet and in its entire history that can be traced, back to 33,000 years – reveals two fundamentally opposite basic features. On the one hand, Trickster is endowed with shrewd and cunning intelligence, so it is unusually smart; on the other, it is a hopeless dupe, an idiot incapable for proper emotions, having no taste and no mindfulness. No matter how hard one can try, these two features cannot be either explained away or reconciled; in fact, they are already there, hinted at through the double meaning of a trick, which implies both rationality and imitation. The trickster is therefore fundamentally bipolar.

This also means that its opposite features do not so much represent irreconcilable opposites, rather two poles of behaviour in between it continuously swings. The same trickster might appear in one situation a complete dupe and idiot, incapable of understanding anything, or performing the most basic actions, just that it would switch, in a nick of time, to the radically opposite behaviour, suddenly inventing a seemingly rational and congenial solution, and mobilising people for reaching that aim. But this bipolarity, and such swings between the extremes, are already hinted at in the two basic meanings of doing a trick, a cunning plot and a mere joke, as one of the most frequent and evident modes of conduct of tricksters is that a proposition they make can be immediately, in case they encounter significant resistance and hostility, turned into a mere joke, claiming that 'I did not mean it seriously', thus transforming its opponent from a person of integrity with a courage to stand up into an idiot who simply failed to understand a joke.

Another crucial feature of trickster knowledge is a duality and oscillation between open, public and hidden, secret. Trickster, on the one hand, evidently performs all its activities in public, lives in and for publicity, cannot have any influence if not through such public performances. Yet, on the other hand, the public face of the trickster is just another ruse, as the most important activities of trickster are conducted behind the scenes, in the darkness, especially as concerns the business they deal among themselves; or their plotting. Trickster knowledge is always fundamentally secret, because it has to hide away its destructive nature.

Here we approach the heart of the *Theaetetus*, while we also return, from a new angle, to the strange plot at the start of the dialogue. As, returning again to features of the trickster as a being, in contrast to the nature of the knowledge it possesses, the trickster is never direct or straight, rather always acts obliquely. Such obliqueness, in fact, returns to the very etymological root of 'limen', as the term does not simply mean a lintel, but some kind of oblique action. The paradoxical connection between the threshold and obliqueness can be understood through the trickster figure.

Knowledge and its secrets

The dialogue, as it is well known, is about knowledge, which further underlines its importance – philosophy, to be sure, is much about knowledge and truth. It is also a particularly inconclusive dialogue, the last of the inconclusive Socratic dialogues, in a way the last of the Socratic dialogues *tout court* – as the next two dialogues will be held not by Socrates, but the Eleatic Stranger – the founder of the Eleatic school being Parmenides, Plato's other teacher and discussed together with Heraclitus in this dialogue; while Parmenides also appears, together with his main student Zeno, in the dialogue *Parmenides*. Yet, while not offering a definition of knowledge – but for Plato, as it was already pointed out through the early dialogues, nothing could be defined – the dialogue offers a number of crucial ideas concerning the gaining of knowledge, in between the *Republic, Phaedrus* and the *Symposium*, on the one hand, the *Sophist*, the *Statesman*, and *Philebus*, on the other; in particular, a crucial discussion of the nature of a secret knowledge, and its holders.

The holders of this secret knowledge, so radically different from the knowledge promoted by Socrates/Plato both in form – as it was not secret; and in content – as we'll see are the Sophists. Given that the Sophists operated mostly in the agora, or in the open public sphere, one might be surprised to learn that they also held a secret knowledge. However, then as well as now, or just as in the period of the Enlightenment, the two were going well together, as the *pretence* that everything should be displayed and discussed in the

74 *Presenting the trickster*

open, in front of everybody else, was just a smokescreen for the real initiated to cajole everybody *else* to reveal their thoughts openly, so that this could be appropriated and also they could be judged on the basis of their genuine ideas, while the promoters of open discussion could safely plot in the background. The position of Plato was radically different, as while he was not afraid of a public discussion, he frankly admitted that there were things that could not be divulged in this way, as could only lead to misunderstandings.

The content of this secret knowledge is also surprising, as this concerns the flux, or the idea that everything always being in motion is the great hidden secret of the universe: so nothing is stable. This position is attributed to Heraclitus, through his student Cratylus, who then evidently transmitted this to Protagoras. This descent has its own importance, as Heraclitus was not a Sophist, and this particular saying was by no means central for him. In fact, the central terms of his philosophy are about measure and order, *metros* and *logos*, and are quite close to the philosophy of Plato, who evidently was his student. It also should be noted that Hegel, and the entire German idealist tradition, would also identify Heraclitus with the saying of *panta rhei* (everything moves), providing a further indication that this tradition is a continuation of Sophistic, in contrast to the hermeneutical tradition, to be traced to Schleiermacher. The point of Plato rather is that the Sophists, par excellence mimes, quickly came to imitate the philosophy of Heraclitus as well, picking up some elements of it, spinning these out of context, and integrating it with their own Sophistry.

The most direct and specific discussion of the secret knowledge occurs at the start of the dialogue, just after the first efforts of the young Theaetetus to respond to the question 'what knowledge is'. While this first response, not surprisingly,[8] is offered in terms of geometry, Socrates notes that the question concerns not this or that knowledge content, but the nature of what knowledge as such is.[9] It is after the first serious response of Theaetetus, that knowledge is identical to perception, that Socrates brings in the secret knowledge of the Sophists, arguing that the idea that all knowledge is mere sense perception is the same as the secret knowledge of the Sophists, that all is motion, nothing is stable; at its bottom or limit the universe is a flux (152A–160E).[10] This, however, is simply absurd, as there must be a real essence of our thoughts, in harmony (*symphonei*) with each other (154E), just as the real thing must be equal to itself (155A), as otherwise simply no knowledge would be possible. At this stage the head of young Theaetetus starts to spin, but Socrates orders him to get his act together, pointing out that he should not talk like the uninitiated who only think that nothing exist except what they can touch by their hands;[11] contrasting this with the other – schismogenic – extreme by the holders of the secret knowledge, who argue that beyond the apparent reality there is only eternal motion. It is in contrast to both these positions that Socrates/Plato tries to unravel what it really means to know.

It first leads him to dismiss the position that knowledge is equal to sense perception, or something that can be obtained merely from the outside, as this cannot solve the problem of dreams, or illusions. Beyond mere perception, there emerges the reality of the memory (163D–E; 166B); and beyond mere words, the issue of respecting the homology or correspondences between real things (164C–5A).

When Socrates returns to the question of flux and motion (179D–E), it is Theodorus who mentions that it is difficult to assess what the Sophists say about motion, as they indeed are always in motion, difficult to pin down (179E). In pursuing the investigation, Socrates first sets up a distinction between the ancients, who concealed the meaning of the flux from the multitude in poetry, and the moderns,[12] who are – ironically – deemed wiser, and of whom two schools are presented: that of Parmenides, for whom all is one, denying any motion; and that of Heraclitus, for whom all is flux, thus denying stability. Plato then moves beyond his own teachers – or, rather, to be precise, he is moving beyond their exaggerated, misrepresented and sophistically disfigured ideas. Here, and beyond the secret knowledge of the flux, Plato formulates a few crucial points about knowledge. To start with, he renders evident the stable unity that exists behind our perceptions, thus securing the inner power we all have inside ourselves, and names it as the soul – making it evident that the word used does not matter (184D–E). Second, he argues that the soul directly grasps the essential character of things, which cannot be reduced to sense perception (186A). Third, he connects the knowledge gained by this way not to sensations, but 'the process of reasoning (*sullogismos*) about them' (186D); truth therefore lies not in perception or in sensations, but in reasoning. Finally, he offers a crucial insight into the nature of thinking (*dianoeisthai*), defined as 'the talk which the soul has with itself' (189E), or a kind of dialogue with oneself, which culminates in 'arriv[ing] at a decision (*orisasa*)', ending the stage of doubt and reaching silence with oneself. This is not equivalent to a judgment, meaning a summary evaluation, whether of others or even of oneself, but of returning to the kind of natural peace that is the basis of a full and healthy human personality.

This, however, is not the end of the dialogue, and for a number of reasons. To start with, there is the question concerning the possibility of a false opinion. This, on the one hand, implies Cartesian doubt – an issue which is not possible to solve, but which is simply wrongly posed; on the other, it concerns the reasons for the emergence of such false opinions. It is here that, apart from evident errors that are inevitable but indeed would be sorted out by time we can return to the interference from the trickster. This includes misleading in concrete instances, but much more serious are the various tricks used to undermine the ability of making decision – one of the worst of which is generalised Cartesian doubt. We can now return to the point concerning why the entire undertaking of Cartesian doubt is wrongly posed. This is because our need to make decisions, to solve the issues of our life, cannot be justified by and reduced to general, decontextualised matters, as it involves first of all care for our concerns. About this, no ultimate knowledge can be gained – perhaps, apart from the fact of our mortality; but if we

76 *Presenting the trickster*

never end questioning, turning it into an endless postponement of decisions, we certainly lose. Thus, we must doubt when the conditions of our life give us a good reason; and similarly, we must stop doubting when the continuation of the investigation would threaten our virtue. That is what matters – and this is not a question of universal, context-free knowledge.

Returning to Plato, it is thus not surprising that the dialogue is inconclusive, as there is no possibility of a knowledge beyond doubt – except that we are doubting, which is the tautology by which Descartes solved his – indeed his – problem, by mistakenly identifying thinking with doubting, an error of which we all suffer the consequences in our everyday life when – for example – managerialism and economic theory cancel trust out of existence. Part of the problem is that thinking is necessarily done through words, but words can never do full justice to reality. Thus, though Socrates/Plato already refuted the idea that knowledge is identical to words or naming, here at the end, once he gave the best answer he could do – and that probably could possibly be done – to the question, he ends the dialogue with a specific and quite momentous linguistic discussion – carrying just as important hints as the starting geometrical references were.

The start is offered by another, and last, return to the original question concerning what knowledge is.[13] At stake is the nature of the primary elements of which things are composed, and the argument is that such primary elements can't be explained – any knowledge can only concern their composition. We can notice here that Plato returns to the problem of the incommensurable as the real irrational, *alogos* or *arrheton*: decomposing elements until they return to the flux is the wrong strategy, as in this way all proper measure, and commensurability, is lost. Decomposition or division is thus equal to destruction. Knowledge, and reasoning, can only be connected to the harmonious combination of elements, or entities, that already exist as such. It cannot start by their supposed, thorough, universalising decomposition.

It is in this way that Plato now returns to words, to language, and its basic components: the elements as letters (*stoikheion*), and their combinations as syllables (*syllabé*) (202E).[14] At the start, and by referring to his own name, Socrates first brings the young Theaetetus to admit that a letter is unknowable, a mere sound, but a syllable is knowable (being a combination of two letters). This leads them to discuss the question of the part and whole (204E), and of divisibility (205D), leading to the paradox that the syllable is both elementary and composite.

The meaning of this digression appears increasingly unclear, as Socrates uses the term element all but indiscriminately for real world objects, for numbers, and for language, seemingly ending in the paradox that language is the key to knowledge and understanding – without language, there can be no talk about knowledge; yet, language itself, or at least its key elements, the letter and the syllable, seem to lie beyond understanding, 'equally irrational [*alogon*] and unknowable [*agnoston*]' (205e3–4), as the syllable, like the letter, is also one and indivisible (*ameristos*; 205c2).

The paradox is resolved in two crucial summary arguments, which then make the usual indeterminate ending seem even necessary. The first is based on a crucial distinction between (cognitive) knowledge and recognition:[15] while it indeed does not make sense of talking about knowing the letter 'a', when we learn writing we all make much efforts, in our childhood, to learn the alphabet in order to recognise (*diagignoskein*; 206a6) what a letter is. The elusive quest for absolute knowledge cannot reach an end, but it is quite easy to explain what we mean by recognition (206B).[16] The second argument offers a truly striking corollary of the section, and in a way of the entire dialogue. It offers a metaphor for clear thinking by characterising talking as a 'stream (*rhoé*) that flows through the lips' (206D). This renders evident the significance of a syllable, this linguistic invention of Plato, as it is the combination of a vowel – which simply flows, emitted by the mouth as an air wave frequency; and a consonant – which in some way stops the stream of the vowel, thus ends the meaningless, unending flow, procuring a meaning to the combination of the vowel and the consonant(s), the flux and the obstacle, the unlimited and the limit. Thus, it not only summarises the discussion about the knowledge of language, but also returns to the central issue of secret knowledge, the eternal motion or flux.

It indeed helps to conclude this chapter as well, by bringing together the two central ideas of the dialogue, the soul as the central seat of knowing, and the syllable as the true basis of language, both combining the flux (or the unlimited) and the limit, in a very specific way, thus being indestructible.

Conclusion: revisiting the indestructible

The two crucial terms offered by Plato in the dialogue about knowledge are the soul and the syllable. The properly thinking soul is the centre of understanding, thus of knowledge; while the syllable, with its combination of vowels and consonants, is the basis of language that renders understanding possible. It is their combination that produces something that, in many ways, resists the flux. The Sophist challenge concerning their secret knowledge is thus met: the real, genuine knowledge is not that everything is a flux; this is only a state of the world that does not take into account the mind, the control of the soul; or, the soul exists and is real in so far as it is controlled, like the divine – and language. In fact, the secret knowledge is nonsensical: to say all is flux is to produce a linguistic statement, which ignores its own nature, but pretends to undermine our certainty in the existence of our mindful soul, and whatever can be apprehended through such understanding, by a trick.

The careful soul and the syllable are also connected by being both stops in the flux, thus offering measure, and so the basis of our reality. They were also brought together in Vedic Hinduism, both considered as indestructible (*aksara*, or able to resist the flow, *ksara*). Given that the indestructibility (or immortality) of the soul was one of Plato's main ideas, this establishes a quite striking parallel between Plato and the Vedas. Nevertheless, the Vedic idea was part of a worldview radically opposed to Plato's vision of harmonious beauty, as expressed in the *Timaeus*, or mindfulness (*phronesis*), as expressed in the *Republic*, rather party of a Gnostic-like position, questioning the very value of life and the world. Thus, in our search for the from-inside perspective about the trickster, we need to extend the investigation to Vedic Hinduism.

Notes

1 See the importance of going under (*Untergang*) for Nietzsche, both in *Zarathustra* and *Gay Science*, significant also for liminality, as 'transition' in German is *Übergang*.
2 About this, see Szakolczai (2013b).
3 We should also note the connection between Megara, the Doric farce, and the Kabeiroi.
4 The cave also had its evident significance for the *Republic*. There, however, the converting force of *eros* (love), was not yet present, just as the crucial reference connecting love with beauty and the generation of children.
5 Protagoras the Sophist is the antique flux theorist who claimed that there are two opposing argument on every subject (see Seneca's Letter 88). Protagoras probably continues the Ionian doctrine that things are mixtures of opposites, thus things can be blended in various proportions.
6 This adjective in general is more or less synonymous to *arrheton* (see Burkert 1987: 9, 137), except that Plato uses the latter word in the trivial sense of not saying something, while the formal in reference to some knowledge that is considered as hidden or secret.
7 Such a distinction is central for the Tübingen school of Plato hermeneutics; e.g. see Szlezák (1999: 62–63, 111–112). Thus, in so far as Tübingen school view of Plato's secret doctrine concerns a certain specific content that Plato reserved only for the initiates, this is clearly wrong, as would identify Plato with the Sophists. However, and most evidently, Plato did hold the view that a presumed free and open discussion of properly philosophical themes was sheer demagogy.
8 This is because Theaetetus, like Theodore, was a specialist in geometry. Theaetetus – presented at the start of the dialogue as dying, specifically as being carried [*pheromenó*] (a term that was gain its significance in the dialogue, as one of the main modes of motion, the other being 'alteration [*alloiósis*]', see 181D), mortally wounded, to Athens – is reputed, according to Book X of Euclid, as founder of the theory of irrational numbers. The first person who discovered the problem of irrationality was Hippasus of Metapontum, a Pythagorean who because of this was expelled from the school, and soon died. For a discussion of these facts, containing – as usual – a particularly incisive commentary, see Serres (1982: 129–133).
9 This is the difference between *connaissance* and *savoir* in Foucault's (1966) terminology.
10 See in particular the excellent discussion entitled 'The "Cold Wind" Argument; and the Theory of Flux: 152a–160e' by Sophie Grace Chappell (2013).
11 Socrates, like Plato, was indeed an initiate into the mysteries.
12 The term used for moderns is *hysteron*, equivalent to latecomers or epigones.
13 The recurrent question 'What is knowledge?' is a constant device in the dialogue.
14 These words indeed became the standard terms in Greek for letter and syllable, terms that did not exist before this dialogue. The first term also meant 'in a form of sun-dial, the shadow of the gnomon, the length of which in feet indicated the time of day', thus playing a central role in geography. As *sullabé* also means 'grip, hold in wrestling', perhaps this was another fortunate borrowing from the terminology of Plato's favourite sport. At any rate, the term is hardly used by Plato outside this dialogue and its pair *Cratylus*.
15 About recognition, see Pizzorno (2000, 2007, 2008).
16 Note that the standard Loeb Classical Library translates *stoikheión* as 'elements' not 'letters' here.

5 Vedic tricksterology

Introduction

The Kabeiroi are a small group of quasi-divinities, belonging to a remote though not the oldest but quite unclear layer of Greek mythology. Their influence, except in so far as preserved and transmitted through Hermes, was thus mostly marginal (though occasionally also liminal) and overall fading. The magi of Iran, however, not only gained influence in Greece and – as the three biblical Magi – even in Christianity, in manners that are still to be explored, but – as we saw – quite widely over Asia. Even further, among the Medians, a close kin of the Persians and in empire-building antecedents of the Persian Empire, it was even the designation not just of a priestly caste, but of an entire social group (Herodotus 1.101). The magi also played a central role in the Persian Empire, though there their influence became shadowed by the Zoroastrian religion. However, arguably, the most important religion where the world vision of Kabeiroi-like magi gained overwhelming influence is Vedic India – a religion who roots are lost in obscurity, but which was much connected to the magi.[1]

The study of the Vedas, of course, is an enormous field, and a labyrinth that one enters at one's peril. It can be particularly controversial, to say the least, to discuss Hinduism not as one of the main world religions, in the footsteps of Max Weber, but by pursuing traces of the anthropologically based idea of the trickster, following the Kabeiroi and the magi. We'll venture to do so by taking as our guide the work of Calasso (2010) on the earliest Vedic text, the *Satapatha Brahmana*.

The rise of Vedic Hinduism is one of the many extraordinary events that happened to this planet. We have lost sense of this extraordinariness as India simply exists, it is now the most populous country in the world, also one of the oldest civilisations, having a kind of unique religion which it is still debated whether it is a world religion as – though having an enormous amount of followers – has no missionary zeal, in contrast to Christianity, Islam or Buddhism, and its adherents – apart from fringe minorities – are almost exclusively limited to the Indian peninsula. It has become plain evidence – thus its striking character escapes us.

80 *Presenting the trickster*

A central aspect of this exceptionality concerns the extremely old, archaic character of Hinduism. It is evidently a survival from an incredibly distant time, hardly changing anything over long millennia. What gave it its incredible resilience?

The rise of the civilisation can be traced to the second millennium BC, but it is very difficult to gain a precise understanding, as material remains are extremely scarce – in contrast to other large and lasting civilisations Vedic Hinduism had no interest in building temples – and there were no historical tracks kept. Furthermore, its emergence was not autochthonous, but due to the arrival of a strange and distant people, the Aryans, who gained ascendance over the inhabitants not by force, through conquest, but evidently solely through the power of their knowledge. To increase perplexity, their language, evidently unchanging again since millennia, is Indo-European, thus situated thousands of miles away from all other Indo-Europeans – except for the Iranians, with their magi.

Our guiding hypothesis targets this similar singularity. We argue that the world vision embodied in Vedic Hinduism is even much older that it is usually assumed, and can be traced back to the Room of Monsters in Pergouset cave (dated around 31,000 years BC) and the Shaft Scene (dated around 16,000 years BC). Thus, Hinduism is an entire civilisation generated by the ascetic artists and ritualistic priests.

The core of Vedic Hinduism is an extraordinary, and extraordinarily negative, gloomy vision of the world. According to this world vision life not only has certain inescapable negative sides, involving pain, suffering, injury, even – ultimately, inevitably – death, but life itself is nothing but a life of death – a permanent, lasting, living death. Living a truthful life from this perspective has no sense, as everyday life itself is nothing but the realm of untruth, illusion, *máyá*, life being itself a wound, and so one can only escape death by escaping life (see Calasso 2010: 113, 224, 287, 317–318). Given all this, it is more than puzzling how this terrible and terrifying vision of the world could not only have become accepted by an entire people – and of an enormous area, a sub-continent in itself, which then became the most populous region of the entire planet – but also those propagating such a vision could become legitimately accepted, and without any recourse to violence, as undisputed rulers of this area.

The reason, as always in the case of vicious circles, can be approached from two sides – as the closing of a trap always implies that short-circuiting can only proceed by the joining of two elements, implying a willing consent of the victim to its own destruction. On the one hand, the proponents of this world view – in the Vedic case, the Brahmans, but in this book we'll call them, in the sense of a Weberian 'ideal type', simply as *Magi* – not only offer their gloomy vision, but also suggest a way out and remedy which focuses on the scrupulous performance of meticulously detailed rituals of sacrifice, to be performed strictly under their guidance (Calasso 2010: 287ff.). On the other, the success of getting the – absurd – Vedic world vision accepted required more than a general susceptibility on the part of those who personally experienced some suffering, thus magnify their own experiences into a timeless universal. A civilisation cannot be built just on such an error.

This reason can be perceived through apprehending Vedic reasoning. The main reason while life itself is to be considered as untruth is not due to the inevitability of accidental pains, but is rooted in the most basic fact of life itself, eating, which in many cases requires killing. But in itself even this argument could not be sufficient, as humans were arguably killing and eating animals for many hundreds of thousands of years. So how could a logic of culpabilisation, resulting in a debt culture, substituting a gift culture, take root in a culture, at its very heart, which with a single masterstroke deprecates the entire world, life, nature and everything, while at the same time blaming every single human being, considering them as accountable culprits – guilty simply because of having bodies?!

Before going into further details, let us consider three historical instances relevant for putting this question in a proper perspective, including at once the heart of the present, some of the most relevant broader contemporaries of Vedic Hinduism, and its most distant origins.

Concerning the present, the most important, indeed inevitable, reference point is Nietzsche's work, and its very centre, the *Genealogy of Morals*, with its focus on guilt, debt, and bad consciousness, leading to the diagnosis of modern European decadence and nihilism, culmination of his last thoughts. Nietzsche's intuition that the revaluation of values, at the heart of our contemporary condition, can be rooted in some ascetic priestly machinations is extremely well taken; just as the hint that the distant sources of this can be found in Hindu culture. Even the perception that from there, its has been transmitted to modernity, is well taken, though the identification of Christianity as the culprit is certainly inacceptable – though aspects of historical Christianity are by no means blameless. Indeed, Christianity plays a central role in the second level, concerning the broad contemporaries of Hinduism – contemporaries with respect to the axial age, understanding this in the broadest sense. Here we refer to the joint conviction, shared by Judaism and Christianity, but also Hinduism and Greek mythology, that in the distant past there was something like a Golden Age; but that this was lost due to some kind of foundational error or original sin. Our claim is that the existence of this very broad and extremely old theme, and which cannot be taken lightly, creates an eternal possibility that certain groups and movements can take the argument up, intensify the related feelings, and can either turn it against certain individuals and groups – those identified as guilty for the loss of the Golden Age; or – and here we reach into the more sophisticated, but at the same time arguably the more dangerous case – that such guilt is turned inwards, identifying the guilty not as them, but us: each and every one of us. It is this argument that was taken to its extreme by Hinduism: we are guilty simply because and in so far as we live – or as we eat.

82 *Presenting the trickster*

However, as we suggested, there is a third level; and this is the level that for us is the most important, an inevitable and unsurpassable starting point for every serious analysis: this is the perspective of the late Palaeolithic, as evidenced by cave art. For the purposes of this book, the central concerns can be resumed in the following manner. To start with, beyond artistic beauty and technical virtuosity, though by no means downplaying these concerns, these images demonstrate a world vision that can be rightly considered as the vision of a Golden Age, by people who either still lived there, or who had evidence of it in living memory. But the fact that it was depicted, and that is was aiming literally eternity, also signals that this world, and world vision, came under threat. We argue that this threat was connected to a then recent technical – not yet technological – innovation, the discovery of the spearthrower, and the unfair advantage this gave humans over their prey. The knowledge gained of making and using a spear was recognised as an irreversible development; it was not possible to unmake it; and yet, some people then living evidently realised that this was a huge threat to their world, and their mode of living. Cave art was not a discovery of *Homo sapiens*, rather immortalised the vision of the world before the discovery of efficient weapons.

The problem of meat-eating and what is behind it

Vedic metaphysics was built on the problematisation of eating animal flesh (Calasso 2010: 83). Around this, an entire culture of debt and guilt was developed, the tightly woven and evidently inescapable circle of Vedic thinking. The entry point is a trivial justification of meat eating: we eat meat, and cannot help not eating meat, because it offers pleasure. We should notice that, evident as this seems, this is already not quite right, implying an artificial separation of means and ends, typical of world-hostile Gnostic thinking, as we eat meat simply because this is part of our nature – just as we are sexually active not only because it gives us pleasure, but because this is part of our nature, a way to have children and families. Our nature, our being, is a complex and in some ways evidently mysterious interweaving of nature and culture, necessity and pleasure: a tightly woven web into which all of us our born, since time immemorial, thus which we need to take as given, thus a gift, even though – beyond our parents and grandparents – we cannot identify who gave us this gift, and so any human culture associates this with the divine, the gods, or God. This is while all human cultures, originally and fundamentally, were gift cultures. But here we try to unravel the emergence of a debt culture – even, we claim, the emergence of guilt culture, to be traced through Vedic Hinduism – and behind this, as we'll see, to the Palaeolithic trickster-magi. What is specific to such debt culture is that this mysterious, at once natural and cultural web is taken apart, with the ostentatious purpose of explaining it, in order to orient our conduct better, consciously and rationally according to such findings; but which, instead, only results in a thorough entrapment in a guilt and debt culture. This is – and here we need to pay very close attention – a direct consequence of the purported effort to explain, rationally, as part of a doctrine and knowledge, something that simply cannot be explained, and which always remains a mystery: why are we what we are? Why do we have a language and a culture? Why do we need to eat, drink, and love? Even worse, such metaphysical system of entrapment (which is by no means equal to awareness about the divine, or something similar) only works if it starts by an artificial focus on one element in one part of the entire nature–culture–human–divine interface. In the case of Vedic Hinduism, this is meat-eating.

The justification of the obsession goes in two directions: one is connected to pleasure, presumed consequence and mental purpose of eating meat, while the other with the preceding act of killing – in order to eat animal flesh, we need to kill other bodies. The next step, in the first part of the circle, is to problematise pleasure, any pleasure, leading to the ideal of a life lived without any pleasures, leading to the renouncer saint as main figure of the sacred. At the same time, the other part of the circle joins into a problematisation of killing (Calasso 2010: 359–366). Here, as we already indicated, we touch upon a very old, and justified concern, and also one that can be observed in most of the various traditions, to be taken back safely to prehistory. It is visible in ethnographically collected stories about killing the bear. Central to such stories is the use of euphemisms about killing;[2] the pretence that the animal was not killed, but killed itself, by some act of stupidity – everyone knows that this is false, yet it is not simply a trick, or a lie, but a way to maintain one's face, and one's belief in the goodness of life in this world, by trying to minimise the scope of evidently necessary violence; or the even more exaggerated pretence that the animal consented to its death – an idea also present in sacrificial practices, here clearly imitating hunting practices, where it was considered that an animal could only be sacrificed if it clearly manifested its consent to the act.

The two half-circles, as if in a symbolon, are joined by both being inevitable facts of life – part of us having bodies. We feel pleasure by eating or erotic acts, as it is good, and it is good that we feel pleasure, as without eating or sexual activity we – whether as a concrete being, or as a community – would cease to live. Similarly, as we are not scavengers, we must kill some animals, even though this is not a nice thing to do, and we should therefore proceed which as much care with such killing, and the minimal manner, as possible. Caring for pleasures and pains, rights and duties requires measures and attention to limits. But this is definitely not the direction taken by Vedic Hinduism, which rather arrived at, by fitting together the two halves, the exact opposite position: if this is life, then life is bad, the world is bad, it is a mistake that we exist, that this world exists, and thus our real duty is to escape this world, our own world, as quickly and fully as it is possible. This is what Nietzsche identified as nihilism, Max Weber as the religious rejection of the world, and Eric Voegelin as Gnosticism; and this is a consequence of starting not with the Maussian idea about life as presence of gift-relations, rather the kind of guilt and debt culture again identified by Nietzsche, in his *Genealogy of Morals*. We would add that this also amounts to a hostility

84 *Presenting the trickster*

against forms, and the body. So there is indeed a paradox there, at once a desire for and hostility toward the body, as it is also expressed in the famous poem of Catullus, 'Odi et amo' ('I Love and I Hate').

The danger of reconstructing any system of belief is becoming entrapped by it, enchanted by its own legitimation. The Vedic effort to problematise meat-eating ostensibly serves the purposes of defending life. Yet, its ultimate outcome is the most world-rejecting form of religiosity, an explicit suggestion to escape the world by throwing away life by attacking the body – so something evidently is wrong with these pure defenders of life. Through the figure of the trickster-magi as a figure touched by the kiss of death, even a living dead, we can understand that the purported defence of life is motivated by an unparalleled hostility to life, a ferocious will to destroy the body, bearer of form, thus securing a return to the nothingness of the flux. The trickster-magi are united with the flux, hybrid, chimera-people, the 'many-headed beast', like 'the Chimaera or Scylla or Cerberus' (*Republic* 588D) and divinisers, who lost their own will and determination, and thus are set to impose their own deprived condition on the entire world.

It is in this undertaking that we can locate the origins of sacrifice, and also self-consciousness.

The rise of self-consciousness

Just as Nietzsche considered this nihilistic debt culture central for the rise of self-consciousness, Calasso also reconstructs this Vedic debt culture as generative of a kind of consciousness (Calasso 2010: 399ff) – and with striking results, from the proper perspective of Palaeolithic archaeology. Here in Calasso's account a central role is played by rituals of sacrifice. Thus, we need to enter the heart of this Vedic ritual, through Calasso's 2010 book *Ardour*. However, strikingly, the arguably most important idea of Calasso in this regard, a stunning intuition, is already contained in the first, 1983 volume of his series, and thus it could be considered as an implicit guiding idea of the whole. Here, in his first attempt to get at the bottom of the act of sacrifice, much relying on the ideas of Girard and Mauss, but not bound by them, he starts from two crucial recognitions. The first is that the performance of a ritual act of sacrifice is a par excellence self-conscious act, possibly the very origin of self-consciousness, and the reason why self-consciousness is inevitably a bad consciousness, as 'whoever acts in this way contemplates oneself as acting' (Calasso 1983: 180). Second, sacrifice is not the origin of exchange, rather – quite the contrary – it is a certain kind of exchange, or substitution, that rendered sacrifice possible. This substitution is a purely mental act, and originally implied not the giving of names, rather is based on the 'forming mental images' (185). Thus, sacrifice can be defined as an act by which giving and taking enters the process of consciousness (185).

We argue that the full significance of this insight can be understood through the monster images of Pergouset cave; a point all the more important as, in our view, the entire world view and metaphysics of Vedic Buddhism can be taken back, in quite minute details, to the Shaft Scene of Lascaux and the Room of Monsters in Pergouset cave – distant sources of the nihilistic, Gnostic, body-rejecting *magi* vision of the world. The novelty of these two epochal depictions, together with a series of other images from prehistory, is that – using the technique of representation first developed in Chauvet, and continued in countless other caves, but betraying its spirit – these depicted images not in order to capture, represent and transmit a vision of the world focusing on the given character of our lives amidst all those graceful beauties of nature granted us and the invisible powers behind, rather on the one hand to shock and entrap viewers in composite, unrealistic images, while on the other hand offer elements of a secret doctrine that, in radical contrast to the ruling Palaeolithic vision of the world, evidently presented life, and the world, from it reversed side, as full of terrible, painful, frightening events and realities. Sacrifice was only rendered possible by such false and fake exchanges, the idea that the powers of our mind can be used to establish substitutions between different parts of our reality – operations that are simply absurd, as every single thing in our reality has its irreplaceable and unrepeatable concreteness – as any animal, any plant, even any rock, is part of a lineage that comes before it and which will be continued by those that come, much as a consequence of its own acts and responsibilities, after it.

Vedic mentality

The underlying mentality of Vedic Hinduism can be traced back to prehistory, while also shows striking affinities with modern Western rationalism. It forms a tight circle, shown among others by correspondence being one of its central concepts, shared with alchemy and its destructive zeal against the body. It also has a singular, privileged point of entry, from where this circle can be reconstructed, and also its deeply problematic aspects rendered evident, the singular privilege accorded to the intellect.

Modern psychology, in the footsteps of Dilthey's philosophy, makes a distinction between the cognitive, emotive and conative aspects of the mind. Concrete human experience assumes their balanced unity. In the case of Vedic mentality, the balance is strongly skewed towards the cognitive. Emotions are viewed with little sympathy, considered as childish or female, not to be relied upon by adult males when guiding their actions.[3] But, similarly, will or decision-making power is also downgraded, emphasis being singularly placed on the work of the intellect. Everything must be thought out in advance, pre-set procedures must be scrupulously followed, nothing should be left to emotions, impulses, the presumed whimsies of the moment. The underlying attitude is a thorough mistrust of oneself, in one's own emotions and the ability to make the right decisions.

Such excessive emphasis on cognitive factors results in a hypertrophy of consciousness.[4] It constitutes a circular system, and it is accidental in what order we explore its interconnected aspects and symptom. One is a general loss of confidence in oneself, leading to widespread uncertainty, a failure to have the otherwise almost natural ability to do the right thing at the right moment on the basis of one's own powers. The related matter, as if corresponding to a Hegelian master-serf dialectic, which Serres considered circular, is the ascent to power of those with special powers of the intellect. The most important consequence, however, closely corresponding to undermining the self-confidence of each and every normal human being, is the rising importance of substitutability.

Substitutability and concreteness are two radically opposed modes of living. The second, in every sense of the word, is the natural condition. This means that naturally, in nature, everything is concrete, given and not substitutable. It exists at a particular time and place, and fills its mission and destiny in so far as it is there, whether as a non-living object, a plant or an animal, or a human being. There are no two things that are completely identical in the world, not even two tree leaves or two snowflakes. Any substitution assumes an intellectual operation, a kind of abstraction from one or other aspects of two objects, so that they could be made comparable, and thus substitutable.

Substitution, as a principle, is therefore a further ruse of those who are in the know; who have the mental powers of rendering, first in thinking, and then in actual reality, through various techniques, of which agriculture and then metallurgy are the basic models, various objects all but identical, thus interchangeable. Such interchangeability is helped by the characteristics of words and images, as the same word or image can certainly stand for, or represent, different concrete bodies. Substitutability is thus the precondition of exchange, but it can also lead to the construction of new bodies by the combination of various words and images. Such combinations further undermine the sense of reality, rendering people living in their concrete situations confused and powerless, and assign further power to those capable for such technical manipulations. It is the tricky unreality of substitution that is captured in money: in the fortunate, twice Goethean expression of Jean-Christophe Agnew (1986: 71–72), money is a 'sorcerer's apprentice'; it is 'alchemy and roguery conflated and abstracted'.

The ultimate consequences of the rising force of substitutability concern matters of life and death. Life, most evidently, is not the result of a mental operation, cannot come into being through a substitution, but requires very concrete and generous acts. Similarly, anything concrete that dies is irreplaceable in its concreteness – even if death happens, being part of nature. The question concerns the way the new logic of substitutability would eventually interfere with such basic natural processes. It is here that we return to the debt–guilt culture to which the body is an obstacle to be destroyed, and rituals of sacrifice.

Life is the continuity of giving of gifts, and the natural proliferation of such lives, based on a fundamental unity of experience: we follow our principled heart and our mindful feelings, which naturally guides us to the right decisions, as they mature in the right moment, and in case can be corrected or modified by our reasoning power, based not simply on one's own wisdom gained from previous experiences, but inherited from virtuous characters. However, the Vedic prioritisation of consciousness renders one uncertain; life is no longer centred on gifts but is dominated by all kind of anxieties about performing the right acts in the right way. Fundamental for this new, unreal mode of living is the induced feeling – induced by conscious knowledge – that this life we live is not a gift, rather a burden; and furthermore, that our continuous existence is an accumulation of debts. We are born, thus we are indebted to our parents, but even more to the gods; and in order to continue living, we keep accumulating debts. And here the circle of mere consciousness, the obligation of not just acting but act purposefully and consciously, become joined to the obligation of self-consciousness, or the creation of a special, moralising quasi-entity behind the human being, which furthermore is not simply based on awareness, or some kind of conscience, but on the consciousness of being in debt, thus guilty. Thus, the presumed identity between consciousness and conscience, fatefully present in some European languages,[5] is based on this circular Vedic mentality of connecting (conscious) existence to (moral) guilt, started with the excessive weight attributed to the intellect, as otherwise mindful human existence would not become problematised.

However, in order to close the circle and render the system fully working an element is still missing, and this is sacrifice. The connection between substitutability, exchange and sacrifice is central not only for Vedic Hinduism, but also infiltrated into the modern world. How this happened is still a mystery, so we need to investigate Vedic sacrifice further.

Vedic sacrifice

Hinduism already for Mauss offered a prime model for understanding sacrifice, bringing out its nature with particular clarity. The first and central feature of any ritual of sacrifice is destruction (Calasso 2010: 244). This is perhaps the single most important difference between gift-giving and sacrifice, even though both contain an offering, even captured in the German word used for sacrifice, *Opferung*. A gift given and accepted must be preserved; the destruction of a gift is the greatest offence. A sacrifice, however, only becomes a sacrifice if the object offered is destroyed. Second, a sacrifice is primarily a gesture (243). The destruction involved with a sacrificial act cannot be done in any way one pleases, but must involve a well-defined and specific gesture by which the act of destruction is completed – the libation is poured out, or the victim is killed. This gesture, especially if it involves blood, or killing, must be performed in an open public space, in front of others who can observe and control that the right procedure is followed. Thus, while a religious act, sacrifice is closely connected to theatrical performance, or theatricality. This is a very special and also singularly unique connection, as no other act of killing, just as no other religious act is supposed to be theatrical; quite on the contrary. Yet, while a sacrifice is theatrical, it is also real: the victim is actually killed. Such similarity between the priest and the actor again already was noted by Nietzsche.

88 *Presenting the trickster*

Furthermore, a sacrifice also must follow rigorous procedures. Every single momentum is a ritual of sacrifice is strictly regulated – this is why a sacrifice can be defined not only as an act of theatrical performance, but also as a process or a procedure (Calasso 2010: 383). Rituals, in the sense of Victor Turner, involve participation. But the efficiency of a sacrificial ritual depends not on gaining the full participation of those present – apart from the victim and the officiating priest, everybody is happy to only watch; but on strict adherence to procedurality. It is only in this way that an act of killing, or destruction, works as a sacrificial act – and, in fact, a sacrifice always works: it is a fully efficient ritual.

However, we have to stop here and ask what this efficiency means; and how much it actually is a consequence of such ritual exactness. It is the vectorial outcome of three factors: first, the shock produced by the fact that blood is spilled, so a life is taken away; second, the fact that this was anticipated, not a surprise, a foregone conclusion – an anticipation that only accentuates the shock effect, far from attenuating it, and still working on the psyche; and finally, more at the level of consciousness, the elaborate procedure to the followed that both makes the outcome fixed and justifies the procedure at the level of the consciousness. A sacrifice is only a sacrifice if consciousness is a constituent part of the act, and if everybody involved and present knows that it is a sacrifice – strangely enough, involving the victim itself, who is supposed to consent to such an act.[6] Thus, a sacrifice is a 'controlled catastrophe' (Calasso 2010: 298). Finally, and most importantly, an act of sacrifice implies contemplating oneself: 'a sacrificial act is any act in which one who acts contemplates oneself while acting' (Calasso 1983: 180).

Sacrificial mentality

Calasso considers Vedic Hinduism as prime example for sacrificial mentality. However, as his prime source is Mauss, whose work on sacrifice was basically a comparison of Vedic and Levitic rituals, and just as he relies also on Mauss's own prime source, Sylvain Lévi, who was a main experts on such rituals, and especially the *Satapatha Brahmana*, main theme of *Ardor*, Levitic sacrificial rituals – much discussed, from a comparative anthropological perspective, among others, by Girard and Mary Douglas – are also of prime importance. Though Calasso says very little about this, the links between the Brahmanist and Abrahamist sacrificial mentality will be of prime importance for this book.[7]

However, Calasso repeatedly states that sacrifice was considered to secure any undertaking (Calasso 2010: 433; Calasso 2016: 96), and traces this rite much further back in history, to the Palaeolithic, indeed – just as Girard – to the very origins of humanity. His work contains four basic points. To begin with, and to some extent following some suggestions from Meuli, Calasso gives credit to the idea that hunting is somehow the background to sacrifice (Calasso 2010: 378). This is based on similar stories in Vedic Hinduism and

Greek mythology, involving major deities, hunting, and the antelope. We can also add that the most important sacrifice in Vedic religion is the horse sacrifice (18), and the horse is the central figure of Palaeolithic paintings. Second, the underlying reason is the connection between guilt over killing and pleasure derived from eating meat. This is one of the central and also, according to us, most problematic ideas of Calasso, as here he simply accepts the Vedic vision of the world, supposedly confirmed by recent archaeological evidence about the conversion of humans, in the remote past, first from a vegetarian to a scavenger meat-eating, and then to a predatory diet. However, evidence for such a conversion is rather controversial, and it seems quite probable that humans, or humanoids, were meat-eaters, and even predators, going back to millions of years. In our reading, the idea of an original guilt concerning such remote processes is far-fetched, and risks of taking the Vedic justification at face value. Instead of starting from Hinduism, or any other of the more recent traditions as primary, we rather take the world vision as captured in cave paintings as primary – a vision compatible with the logic of giving, and not of sacrificial rites. The guilt on which Brahmans and other priestly religions played was not due to human meat-eating, or even hunting, rather the technological development associated with the spear thrower, or unjust long-distance killing.

The third main point is quite close to Girard's ideas, and concerns the connection between sacrificial rites and desire, especially its rootedness in mimetic rivalries (Calasso 2010: 301–302). The final point concerns the connection between sacrifice and metallurgy, not elaborated in detail, but alluded to (Calasso 1983: 155, 171), and which gains its significance by the connection between metallurgy and alchemy, but also metamorphosis – two points much discussed by Calasso, though the connections with metallurgy are overlooked.

The most important ideas of Calasso on sacrifice concern a triangle between the Vedic mentality justifying sacrificial rites; its contrast with the mentality on hunting and sacrifice that transpires from Greek thinking, especially mythology; and the extent to which the modern world, especially in so far as based on rationalist thought exhibits a sacrificial mentality that, strikingly, is quite close to Vedic Hinduism.

Concerning Vedic Hinduism, sacrifice is the core of the Vedic world vision, and the Hindu way of living. Indeed, it provides the link between the two, through a circular justification. Given that for about three millennia this animates the life of one of the biggest countries and oldest civilisations of the world, it is evident that we need to tread with much care, recalling again Bateson, now about the treading of angels, and with respect for such an achievement. And yet, given the perceived importance of this way of living and thinking for the present, even for the destiny of our world, we need to think. Thus, in the following, we will attempt reconstruct, still following Calasso, the underlying logic of this 'sacrificial vision' (Calasso 2010: ch. 16).

The sacrificial vision

We characterised, following Calasso, the Vedic vision of the world as sacrificial. This means that according to this vision the very creation of the world was due to sacrifice, was an act of sacrifice; that the performance of rituals of sacrifice is therefore necessary for the continuous survival of the world; and that such a myth of origin both justify the way the world is, and the particular – Hindu – way of life that is in line with such vision of the world. The relevance of all this is not just through the apparent contrast with our present – which is evident; but also to the striking parallels with our 'rational' ways, which is much less so.

In the figure of Prajapati Vedic Hinduism has a most peculiar creator god, radically different not only from that of the monotheistic traditions, but also of the similar figures of most other cultural traditions. Creation here is a lonely act of utter pain. Both terms are extremely important as. While every creative act often involves painful work, the memory of any significant and meaningful bringing into the world is never dominated, in healthy occasions, by such utter recollections of pain. It is also particularly strange concerning an original deity. But the second, reinforcing aspect is even stranger, the sense of utter loneliness, and even the repeated experience of being rejected – as Prajapati is not only alone when creating, but is even rejected and immediately attacked, after, and in fact would end its life – an absurdity for most other traditions – again rejected and alone, unacknowledged and unrecognised. Just as strange are some of the acts associated with the first moments of creation. These involve an attack on his life by his first son *Agni* (fire), just as his attempted rape of his first real daughter, thus offering a striking Freudian scenario of parricide and incest at the origins of the world. Sacrifice is indeed the first word of the world, whispered to Prajapati by his first, spiritual daughter as a way of escape. But, though Prajapati escapes now, he won't escape eventually, and the real act of creation would materialise out of his decomposing body. Thus, not surprisingly, for Vedic Hinduism a world created out of pain and death *is* nothing else but a world of suffering and death, with the only possibility of liberation being escaping – as the world anyway is nothing else but untruth and illusion itself.

What sense can we make out of this story? What could be its experiential basis? Of course, with the means of mere science, nothing can be said about this, as we do not have a record about such experiences. However, such a strange and unique vision must have been rooted in some experiences; and, indeed, the background evoked is quite suggestive. Furthermore, and following the hints from Calasso, such experiences must be taken back to the Palaeolithic; and still following hints by Calasso, and the spirit of Plato, such originary scenes represent mental images. Thus, even if we do not have written accounts about such experiences, perhaps it is possible to find images that can be connected to them. After all, the origins of Vedic mentality, given their eventual impact, must have had their own significance. So we need to look for such traces, in prehistory, among the many such images that have been discovered since the end of the 19th century; and among the most important and striking of such images.

Concerning the possible experiential basis, the idea of being alone, rejected and unrecognised by all, is common experience of errants, especially those with a strong mind or imagination. The two are indeed connected, as being personally or socially marginalised, through some or other bodily or character deficiencies, is often combined with particularly intense mental activities. The reconstruction of such a figure is central for Nietzsche's *Genealogy of Morals*, just as for the anthropological figure of the trickster – another errant outcast, furthermore often considered as the second founder of the world, but one who has particularly strong powers of imagination. Thus, the experiences behind Prajapati's creation of the world can be the experiences of an outcast who resented his exclusion and responded to this by a mental act of creation – musing about the possible origin of the world, possibly accompanied by various visions, among others vision of parricide and incest, which – and here Freud can be taken on his words – often accompany dreams of wish-fulfilment; dreams that visit particularly those who are, or feel themselves, excluded.

Thus, in our reading the Vedic world-creation myth is actually a purely mental operation – but how could this have been effective in any way? Only if somehow this experience found a particularly powerful way in which it could have been transmitted, against the other storyline, held and kept by those from whom Prajapati felt excluded, or prehistoric reality. In our reading – and while we have no proof, we consider it as the right and duty of academics to formulate ideas, even if they cannot be tested as hypotheses; perhaps, even more then – this can be captured in two crucial secondary founding instances of Palaeolithic cave art, the Room of Monsters in Pergouset cave and the Shaft Scene of Lascaux; and in the manifold trickster figures that can be shown in a few other restricted, alternative caves.[8]

But what is the main content of this alternative, Gnostic vision of the world that became the dominant vision in Vedic Hinduism? It is nothing else but a vision based on sin, guilt, debt and death, or what Nietzsche so perceptibly identified as the revaluation of values: the condemnation of the world, our beautiful world as it is, as an illusion and error, and the conjuring up of a second reality as the real one. Let's now review the central aspects of this revaluation of values, as it transpires through Calasso's Nietzsche-inspired work.

In order to guess the first step we only have to put ourselves in the place of a trickster. The trickster by definition is an outsider and outcast, and if we start with the perspective of a well-functioning community – and we should have this as our starting point, instead of an absurd, Hobbesian, war of all against all; or an even more absurd Girardian starting point of a *collapse* of order, as in order to collapse, a proper order must first of all exist,[9] then the trickster is a genuine enemy of the people, and is bound to be considered as the first person to be considered as the culprit if something is going wrong, being guilty by character (hubris). Left on its own, the trickster might lick his wounds because of it – as indeed nobody is responsible for one's character – but can't do much about it, and does not stand a real chance to reverse this evaluation. For this, a genuine revaluation of values has to be produced, and accepted; and this can only start by reversing the very self-evident situation of guilt, arguing that, quite on the contrary, it is not he, the trickster, who is bound to be guilty, but everybody, and almost by the nature of things, is guilty, even of an original sin. But how is this so? And how could everybody accept this?

Guilt and the related idea of debt are omnipresent in Vedic thinking; sacrificial thinking is organised around it. Guilt is not due to a concrete act committed or an event happening in some remote but concrete historical time; everybody is guilty, and forever, men and gods equally; guilt is part of the nature of things, is the nature of things, the character of the created world, that was due to pain, and only produces pain and suffering. The created world is not good, but bad, the guilt for it is to be expiated by sacrifice, and since nature has no inherent values, it is quite justified to consider nature itself as a sacrificial victim.

Such sinfulness, or guilt, can be perceived at the very heart of human nature: humans need to eat, and eating meat gives particular pleasure, but eating meat assumes the prior killing of the animal, and killing is violent, thus bad, so our nature, human nature, is bad itself, even twice: because eating meat presupposes killing, and because we not only need meat, but feel pleasure for it. Such problematisation of meat-eating – at the heart of Vedic thinking – is joined to a problematisation of sexuality, closely connected to hunting: the pleasure derived from killing and eating the prey and from consuming a sexual act are thought to be similar, just as consuming meat and consuming sex are present even in the term flesh, and consumption, just as killing, are about destruction. We need to hunt, conquer, subjugate, kill, consume, destroy, in order to live and to perpetuate ourselves. Thus, by simply living, due to our nature, we are sinful, lustful, continuously producing guilt, for which we continuously need to perform expiatory sacrifices.

However, here we bump into another most tricky issue. Our guilt is due to killing, or destruction; but an act of sacrifice is also destruction, often even a killing, so only perpetuates destructivity. Thus, sacrifice, seen from this light, is not so much the expiation of guilt, rather itself makes us guilty. Here we enter the vicious circle that Calasso identifies as being at the very bottom of Vedic thinking; but it also recalls that sacrifice is nothing but a ruse or trick (Calasso 1983: 181; Calasso 2010; 2016: 38–39). Here Calasso is in evident difficulty, as the idea that sacrifice is a mere scam is standard Enlightenment accusation, while Calasso is at pains to emphasise the seriousness of sacrifice as a practice, yet the very reconstructing of the Vedic logic leads to the same inference – a problem quite similar to Girard's (sacrifice is violent, but it at least controls violence; so the disappearance of sacrificial rites only escalates violence). The way out, in a sense, is that in Vedic thinking the belief in the existence of powers external to humans is still maintained, so there is genuine religiosity and at crucial points this mitigates the otherwise radically Gnostic or world-rejecting vision of Hinduism. For Calasso, this is best visible with the story about the mustard seed at the bottom of the heart, with its evident Gospel equivalences.

The emergence of rituals of sacrifice, we argued, was not the origin of culture, rather expression of the resentful vision of world characteristic of tricksters, and also a ruse to deviate attention from their possible acts and thus guilt. The full-scale revaluation of values is that everyone else is guilty, all men and gods; the real world and the divine is full of evil and guilt, except for the tricksters. The corollary is the apotheosis of the tricksters as the pure ones.[10] He is the one who is correct, while all others are corrupt. Their task is to correct creation, in particular the bodies created, for their further perfection.

Still, how can this be accepted? This can partly be due to guilt about technologically efficient long-distance killing. But there is also another issue, related to knowledge and self-consciousness. The trickster is the eternal outcast and outsider, who does not participate, but looks at everything that goes on around it, in nature and in social life, from the outside, so that occasionally it could intrude, in the best possible manner for itself. The sacrificial act offers the possibility of raising such external, conscious awareness to another level by making it imperative that the sacrificer contemplate himself, in the very moment of acting, reinforcing a split consciousness, and thus giving rise to the emergence of self-consciousness (Calasso 2010: 105). Such a focus on consciousness complements the external, negative vision of the world, and together constitutes the heart of the Gnostic mentality, consisting of a split self – split both from the external world and internally; a hostile, resentful vision of this not external (by nature) but externalised world; and finally the rise of consciousness as the self-consciousness of this split self. It is this vision of the world, and of the human being, that would become the core of modernity, whether in rationalism, founded by Descartes's highly theatrical contemplation of his own mind in the act of thinking, replacing thinking itself by the split dualism implied in doubting; or in romanticism, inaugurated by the similar split thinking of Jean Paul (Johann Paul Friedrich Richter).[11]

From split self-consciousness to Gnostic world-rejection

Sacrifice contributes to the consolidation and strengthening of trickster self-consciousness by reinforcing a schism and duplication in the actor, comparable to Foucault's ideas about duplicated representation. A sacrifice is an act, but an act in which the actor is not just performing an act of destruction, but does it consciously, contemplating the act, at the same time of committing it, thus also contemplates itself in performing the act. Sacrifice is thus profoundly intertwined with knowledge, and of a very particular type – helping to identify what is trickster knowledge, a central concern for tricksterology.

In trying to capture the nature of this knowledge and showing its close connections with Gnosticism, we start from a distinction between knowledge and belief. Knowledge is fundamentally tied to visible and objective aspects of the world, while belief starts from the recognition of forces that exist outside us, but are invisible.

We can consider as pure knowledge – technically, trickster knowledge, or the kind of knowledge considered as Gnosticism – the sum of those views concerning the world, or nature, that can be gained from the position of the isolated and world-hostile individual who gains strength through the self-consciousness obtained and fortified through acts of sacrifice – a re-externalisation of forced, as externally constrained, self-sacrifice. The central issue concerns the starting point, or the presuppositions, for gaining such knowledge. In synchronicity with the basic stance of the isolated and deprived individual, the basis of such knowledge involves neither concrete, actual experiences undergone in real life in the real world – as we have seen, the position of the knower assumes that such real experiences cannot be relied upon; and nor does it assume a direct communication from the divine, as the fully isolated individual does not trust the divine any more than fellow humans or the world. Instead, and merely generalising its own experience, it is assumed that genuine knowledge can only be gained by first undergoing pain – instead of following the self-evident pleasures of the world; and then, by performing operations by and through the mind alone.

As always, we should not forget basics; and the first and foremost of such basics is that the trickster is always only considered as a second founder of the world. In Vedic thought, which is by no means the oldest human tradition, only – perhaps – the oldest that has come to be written down in its entirety, and from the trickster perspective, it is this position that is transposed into foundational and original, but this should by no means be accepted as originary. It can be extremely old – in fact, we believe that this can be traced to Pergouset cave, thus over 30,000 years ago; but the world-view of Chauvet cave is much older, extending way back to Neanderthal times. Thus, the central tools of such mental operations, words and images, including their central confluence, were not discovered by the Vedic sages; what they did was to assign new values to these tools of the mind and the operations that can be performed with them. Words emerged as expressions of experiences and tools of mutual understanding; however, and in line with their general vision of the world, in Vedic thinking words came to be considered as acts of violence done to the world – also much in line with the idea that the first word of Vac, helping Prajapati, her father, was sacrifice. Similarly, images were made back at the time of Chauvet cave, at least, and the aim of such images was to evoke the beauty of the world. In Vedic thinking, however, emphasis was placed on the mental character of the images and, just as in the case of words, emphasis was placed on the way such images not simply represent but substitute real objects, thus doing violence to them.

The question of substitution is absolutely central for Calasso's work and his understanding of the modern world, thus his related arguments must be carefully reconstructed and scrutinised.

Substitution

For Calasso, substitution, which is 'the most powerful act of the mind' (Calasso 2016: 130), involves two types of operation which (and this is a crucial implication, involving a kind of substitution on the square) can themselves be 'substituted with each other' (Calasso 1983: 273). In one case, '*a* standing for *b*' implies that *a* literally 'annihilates *b*, kills it, sometimes to discover its functioning', while in the other case it means that *a* symbolically stands for, or represents *b* (273; see also 181), from which it is, or has become, distant. He traces the origins of such substitution not to the act of naming, but – before this, and constitutive of naming – to the formation of mental images, which can again, in both senses, 'stand for' the entities they capture in images (185).[12] In contrast to Plato, Calasso does not connect such images to the memory, but in both cases adds a crucial comment about bifurcation – the same term that, we have seen, was already central for Serres. The formation of mental images helps the originary bifurcation of the psyche, meaning the separation between an act and its contemplation, central to sacrifice – but where again the interpretation of Calasso veers too far from Plato and too close to the Vedic ritualists.[13]

The main rival of substitution, its enemy brother – as there aren't many modes of thinking – is connection (Calasso 2010: 422). This latter, operating on the basic principle of analogy, always precedes substitution, while substitution has affinities with the digital, and its basic means is codification. They also correspond to two basic elements of both nature and the mind: the continuous and the discrete (509).

In spite of their radical difference, being opposite poles, substitution and connection are also present together, stir each other up, with and through imitation and metamorphosis (Calasso 2016: 126). Thus, before moving further, we need to resume Calasso's ideas about these two central terms.

Imitation and metamorphosis

Concerning imitation, Calasso much relies on Girard, focusing on the conflict, rivalry and violence inherent in the act of imitation, mimesis, or emulation. Metamorphosis, or transformation, however, as used by Calasso, is a much more complex and problematic idea. It can be understood through imitation, to which it is tightly connected. If imitation means to copy or follow somebody, or the way of the actor, metamorphosis means to outright transform into someone or something else (see the Greek mythological figure Proteus, illustrating metamorphosis, so central for early modern actors; Agnew 1986). In one of the best of his many *bon mots*, Calasso claims that if the man of imitation, or the comedian, is the main enemy of Nietzsche, then the man of metamorphosis, associated with the *goés* (magus, trickster, a word also used for the Sophists) is the main enemy of Plato (Calasso 2016: 128). Metamorphosis is thus the extreme version of imitation (122): or, 'When pushed to the extreme, imitation is metamorphic' (125). The result is invasion, a key feature of mutual parasitic and trickster interference and intrusion: 'In metamorphosis the imitator invades an entity from which it lets itself become invaded' (125). This can lead to a desperate situation from which there is no way back, thus when a metamorphosis, instead of liberating and expanding someone, rather imprisons it (125–126).

The tight links, yet differences between imitation and metamorphosis also can be shown through their relation to learning: in so far as learning relies on imitation, man is and stays a slow learner, but his powers of learning can be extended through metamorphosis, or imagining himself in the place of others (Calasso 2016: 124; see also 127–128).[14] This is because man learns not only by imitation, but also by possession (a central theme of Calasso), and possession is the basis of metamorphosis (124).

The central issue is whether we consider such metamorphosis as real or as merely a product of the mind. Calasso, taking perhaps too literally the claim of Pausanias about a past ('golden') age of metamorphosis (Calasso 2016: 225), argues for the real existence of such an age – the idea that the late Palaeolithic, in fact, *was* such an age (15), confirmed by his reading of cave art, which was not an act of magic, rather of metamorphosis (27). However, following Plato, we consider metamorphosis as itself nothing else than a form of magic, and make a basic distinction between the main body of cave paintings, which in our reading were expressions of a quite Platonic vision of the world, based on the *thaumazein* 'wonder' experience, that was not an act of magic, or (self-)transformation, but a wonder at the beauty of the world; and the rather very few composite images, including the ones Calasso characterises as the master of animals images, which were rather the makings of the Palaeolithic trickster. Playful imitation of animal gestures and voices, even the pretence of being a bear, a fox, or any other animal, is of course fine. But Palaeolithic man, in his great wisdom, we presume, knew it well that representing such a figure in an image can be problematic, as it can inspire a fixation into such a position, along the lines of the trickster fixer, and it is better to be avoided. It was not avoided by those who indeed jumped into another shape, and thus transmogrified themselves into a trickster. They were few and far between for long; however, eventually their power came. Thus, in our view, the late Palaeolithic was not the age of metamorphosis, rather the – indeed lost – Golden Age; the real age of the trickster only came with the Bronze and especially the Iron Ages – including, in the footsteps of Max Weber's diagnosis at the end of his *Economic History* lectures, the age of modernity.

We can now revisit the links between connection and substitution, and imitation and metamorphosis, in some of the most important pages that Calasso ever wrote (Calasso 2016: 126–135). The violence implied by imitation, as discussed by Girard, focuses on the conflict emerging between different subjects that come to desire, through imitation, the same objects, or objectified beings. However, in a different manner, imitation, by searching for the perfect copy, can lead to the eventual substitution of the real by a copy, which is violence on its own, making evident 'the latent violence of every imitation' (126–127). This is particularly problematic for the union of modern science and technology, which aims at producing the perfect copy, not realising that, if successful, that would imply the radical annihilation of the original – even the very possibility of originality, thus authenticity. Thus, radical correspondence and substitution (through imitation) by the perfect copy implies the similarly radical and irreversible detachment of the original from itself, as a kind of split. This leads to a not just irreversible but limitless process, as 'imitation does not pose limits to itself' (129); the exact meaning of the mathematical sense of the point of singularity, which Calasso evoked elsewhere, and which also incorporates, though from a distance and not asserting it, the concept of singularity as exposed by Ray Kurzweil (see Calasso 2017: 78–79). Such infinite process of imitation and substitution, which seems to be our destiny, given the path taken by Western rational thought, lead to two results, equally absurd and desperate: on the one hand, the self-divinisation, or *theosis*, of the man of knowledge (Calasso 2016: 128–129); on the other, the destruction of the concrete, which from the perspective of the expanding logic of substitutability becomes the 'negligible' (*trascurabile*), or whatever from the perspective of the universal and general is considered as being of minuscule value.

Both these concepts need to be presented in some detail, taking into account the other places in Calasso's books where they are discussed.

The negligible

The question of the negligible (*trascurabile*) is discussed in two different books, published 33 years apart. The themes, seemingly, are radically different: in one, it is about the designation of the sacrificial victim (Calasso 1983: 191–193), while in the other about dealing with the problem what and how is to be excluded even by a perfect machine when it offers a close reproduction of reality (Calasso 2016: 128–134). However, as Calasso shows, all but identifying sacrifice and substitution, the two problems are revealed as the same. Indeed, the main reference points evoked just before in both cases are also identical and quite portentous: they are Nietzsche and Christ (being among the few occasions when Calasso evokes Christ), but also foundational figures of philosophy, Descartes and Plato.

Starting with the first, the problem is the designation of the sacrificial victim, a central issue for Girard as well, but where we need to add, and centrally, the figure of the trickster, as in our interpretation tricksters are choice subjects to be identified, and not without a reason, as being guilty of messing things up, thus their trick to invent a mode of designating somebody else as victim. Such affinity between designation and trickster even comes out of Calasso's analyses, as in both cases the discussion ends with the problem of deceit (*inganno*) necessarily involved in such designation. Calasso argues that the problem is not limited to sacrificial thought, but also centrally involves modern philosophy, where the problem of sacrifice is explicitly central, including Hegel, Schopenhauer, Kierkegaard and Nietzsche (Calasso 1983: 191). While it is not discussed explicitly in the strand of epistemological rationalism, it is centrally present even there, though in an altered form. When Descartes talks about the negligible – thus, what can be safely left out when thinking about order – is nothing else but the victim. Citing Simone Weil, Calasso argues that this marks the passage from the finite to the infinite.

Calasso then applies the term to the Vedic thinking of correspondences and the infinite arguments about substitution and sacrifice, pointing it out that all this talk does not alter the irreversible fact that whoever was a designated victim became killed, so is little more than a pious lie. The section ends with a phrase bringing together sacrifice and the negligible: 'the world without gods again reveals itself as a world of compulsory esoterism [*esoterismo coatto*]' (Calasso 1983: 193).

The second section helps to render all this clearer. Its discussion of Turing and the negligible starts by a simple question: how is the negligible born? The answer involves the passage from analogical to digital, leading Calasso to a number of inferences, as – given that the analogical is continuous, while the digital is discrete – this passage is a modality of the passage from finite to infinite. Thus, a simple technical-technological issue directly takes us into the heart of the sacrifice/substitution nexus: the passage operates through substitution, which is essential for the working of any machinery. A machine imitates the mind, which can only work if it ignores something. Thus, '[t]he *negligible* is the key to every efficiency' (Calasso 2016: 132). It is also identical with the residue of Vedic thinking, just as it is the basis of science. We thus live in '*the realm of substitution*' (133; emphasis original), the real question being whether we are aware of what we ignore in this manner. Turing was well aware that the mind was not a machine consisting of discreet states, like his universal machine of 1935, so a machine can only simulate the mind, and simulation, in one of its meanings, is identical to faking, deceiving, or falsity. Yet, the spirit, so to speak, was liberated from the bottle. The potential consequences were drawn by Simone Weil is some comments departing from Bourbaki: experimental science escapes the problem posed by two experiments never producing identical results through the idea of the negligible, '[b]ut the negligible is the world' (Calasso 2016: 134). Calasso adds that this idea is identical to the Vedic vision concerning the residue being the world; and the ensuing commentary starts with the problem of deceiving. But, before doing so, he also evokes another comment by Weil, and from the same page, where Weil recalls that the idea of analogy was central for the Greeks, as this – or rationality in the sense of ratio, or just proportionality – served as a bridge between finite and infinite. It also leads to the problem of deification, of divinisation, another major problem for the Greeks, while asserted by Hermeticism and alchemy, and implicitly by modern technology.

Self-divinisation (*theosis*)

Self-divinisation is a central idea for Hindu, and in general oriental, spirituality. It means the way by which the illuminated ones can leave this world of suffering and death (Calasso 2010: 287–288). It is also discussed in the same pages as the negligible (Calasso 2016: 128–129).

But how are the negligible and self-divinisation connected? They are indeed the logical, opposite but tightly connected outcomes of the substitution/connection/imitation/metamorphosis nexus, as explored by Calasso. This nexus, once set in motion, and passing beyond a certain limit, produces an irreversible process which, on the one hand, regards everything concretely existing as a nuisance in the path of the march of the whole, and on the other justifies the undertaking by the deification of the select few who become the victors of the process. Both deification and the neglect of the concrete individual were anathemas for the Greeks, who on the one hand abhorred the idea that humans can imitate the deities, and on the other respected the full freedom of every concrete individual member and family of the community. They are also evidently in line with oriental thought, where the concrete was overlooked in the name of the whole, while divinisation pursued by the select few was the explicit aim of spirituality.

The question concerns the place of the modern West in this map. Strikingly, as Calasso's ideas render it evident, without naming it, modernity increasingly follows the oriental model. This is best seen through the alchemic technology/fairground economy/democratic public sphere nexus, where the concrete human beings, in their local world, are ignored and overrun by general considerations of the public, whether measured by voting or purchasing power, while the ideas of transhumanism and artificial intelligence increasingly propose a certain divinisation of man (Calasso 2017: 75–87; Horvath et al. 2019).

The building up of this nexus is particularly visible in the metaphors of weaving and the spider, central for the trickster tales discussed before, and also present, prominently, in Calasso's work, through terms like *tessitura* (weaving, texture), *legame* and *vincolo* (bond, tie), and *ricucire la trama* (stitch the weft) (Calasso 1983: 181; Calasso 2010: 420).

Conclusion

The contrast between belief and knowledge, or prophets and priests, reaches its culmination in the atmosphere of the world-view emanating out of Vedic Hinduism. In introducing the contrast between the rudimentary character of Vedic material civilisation and the enormous complexity of the mental universe built around it, Calasso (2010: 25) states that even such a cautious and terse scholar as Louis Renou was constrained to characterise it by the phrase 'the Vedas move in panicky terror'. It is the same terror that animates Gnostic systems of belief, which are so far from the Greek vision of intermingling between gods and their world. Calasso argues that the Vedic vision of the

100 *Presenting the trickster*

world closely recalls Gnosis, except that, while in the West this remained – at least until modernity, we would add – a heretic, minority undercurrent, in Vedic Hinduism it became the official dogma. The origins of Gnosis are tentatively associated with the Iranian plateau (Calasso 2016: 291), implying a connection with the *magi*. The following, incisive characterisation of Gnostics argues that between them there is always an air of familiarity, even when they are adversaries. They only show emotions as a mask, but do not feel them, preserving an 'invincible remoteness (*disaderenza*)' to their surroundings, which is difficult to perceive, and only another initiate can notice it;[15] they are 'self-sufficient, stranger to the world, indifferent to merits and virtues, tending to being amoral, cosmopolite' (291). Gnosticism brings in the problem of evil, even placing evil inside the soul (294). It systematically ignores beauty and virtue (296–297), placing emphasis on salvation through knowledge and underplaying the importance of belief that has affinities with perceiving the graceful beauty and harmony in the world and the pursuit of a life of virtue as the key to happiness. The central chapter of this book, about men of knowledge and predators (115–181), is much devoted to the detailed exploration of this alternative affinity, in the footsteps of Plato's association of the Sophists with hunting, as an activity of catching victims.

We can now return, at the end of this chapter, and of Part I, to the striking similarity between the philosophies, and worldviews, of Plato and the Vedas. How is it possible that the indestructibility of the soul, and of the syllable, led Plato to his beatific vision of the world in the *Timaeus* and the *Symposium*, while in the Vedas such indestructibility was compatible with a gloomy, sacrificial vision of the world as a place of endless suffering?

The answer lies in a proper reckoning with the meaning of our limits. Our two central, indestructible features are that we have a soul, an essence setting limits to the infinite flow out there in the world, as presumable material of divine essence; and that we have language, a way of producing sound-waves in a measured, limited manner, rendering understanding possible. We know that we exist, and that therefore there is existence, there are things and not just nothing – the central question, the real mystery for Leibniz and thinkers influenced by him, like Voegelin and Serres, and not by Cartesian doubt; but we cannot fully venture into this mystery, as that lies beyond our limited being. All our understanding is based on language, thus we cannot overpass the limits of language – we cannot even know the origins of language, as we cannot talk about language without using language. A reduction of communication to mathematics, outside language, poses the problem that mathematics is itself a language, but most importantly that anything produced by artificial intelligence would miss the other crucial aspect of understanding, the proper soul. Proponents of artificial intelligence argue that by the language of pure science and pure mathematics they can produce (i.e. imitate) human intelligence; not that they are capable of generating a concrete soul. So they pretend that the soul does not exist, only impulses. However, if we start from the position that the soul exists, which is the basic stance of nature, a view of which Plato only gave the clearest account, but which is shared across the globe, then the minuscule limit of modern technology, its ignoring the virtuous soul, becomes a colossal error. The pretence of human limitlessness, and the gaining of absolute, unlimited knowledge, is thus a ridiculous though highly dangerous as potentially destructive idea – a return to the kind of flux in which nothing can be said to exist. Modern science at its ultimate limits and with its utmost efforts does not reach out to hold the key for everything, rather to nothing or nothingness, chaos itself, a situation to which it threatens to return our world – a mortal threat which Aby Warburg perfectly perceived, about a century ago, in his 'Ritual of the Serpent'. This is because any knowledge that reaches outside our limits and measures is by definition incommensurable, unspeakable or irrational. Thus, from the Greek perspective, the reckless fiddling with the zero, the diagonal of the square, and even the square root of minus one, or modern technologised science, with it anger to transform everything solid, is not rational, rather the height of irrationality (*asymmetros, alogos*). Thus, in the spirit of Max Weber's inquiry, the problem of irrational rationality must be extended from capitalism to modern science.

Thus, we now turn to Part II, which will pursue the traces of the trickster, this figure of utter limitlessness in history, until we arrive at the full-scale reassertion of such demonic limitlessness in modernity, the theme of the concluding part of this book.

Notes

1 Apart from general linguistic concerns about Indo-Iranian or Indo-Aryan language, crucial common elements touching upon the earliest central features of Hinduism include horse sacrifice (for horse sacrifice by Magi, see Herodotus 7.113) and the word *soma* (intoxicating drink, central for Hindu rituals).
2 This is also present in Vedic Hinduism, indicating that this tradition seamlessly fits into immemorial practices.
3 The extreme male bias of Hinduism is shown by the fact that while life expectancy, for natural reasons, is higher for females than males in all areas of the world, for long India and Pakistan were the only two countries where this was reversed.
4 See again Nietzsche's *Genealogy of Morals*.
5 The worst case is French *conscience*, which also implies consciousness as – arguably due to Cartesian rationalism – the new, rationalistic term 'consciousness' did not become separate from 'conscience'. In Hungarian, *tudat* consciousness and *lelkiismeret* conscience (literally, acquaintance with one's soul) hardly have a common letter.
6 Thus, Stalinist forged trials requiring the admission of guilt by the victims, broadcast all around the countries were technically following sacrificial procedures.
7 On difference between priestly and prophetic, see Max Weber.
8 This will be further discussed in the first chapter of the second part, based on a series of prior publications (Horvath 2013; Horvath and Szakolczai 2018a; Szakolczai 2017).
9 Just as the origin of language, the origin of order is lost in the mist of history, but just as language has come into being, and is simply marvellous, showing no

102 *Presenting the trickster*

   evident sign of development, rather in many cases showing definite signs of decay, the same must be assumed of order.
10 For European equivalents, see the medieval Cathars and Bogumils, the Puritans, and the Communists.
11 For details, see Szakolczai (2009, 2016).
12 About such centrality of images, see also Calasso (2010: 202–204).
13 In the other case the meaning remains enigmatic, but is similarly connected to the split of the mind with an act of self-consciousness.
14 Note that this implies to transform the other person into a mere place-holder, thus by definition a nullity.
15 Calasso's Tiepolo book contains many evident analogies.

Part II
Tracking trickster traces: evil machinations

6 Prehistoric trickster
Archaic outlines of evil

It is one of the commonplaces of the literature on the trickster that the figure is extremely old, probably a survival of prehistoric times. This is based on what most trickster tales tell. However, anthropologists then return to the stories as told now by people, as this is their professional duty (while mythologists study the stories told by people a long time ago). But what was actually the prehistoric trickster? How did it look like? While such questions seem impossible to answer, we argue in this book that there are some surviving testimonies that help to start answering. They are some images that survived in caves, among many other Palaeolithic images. Thus, in this second part, we will attempt an archaeology of trickster knowledge – this time not only in the sense of Foucault, but also in the standard, disciplinary sense of archaeology. However, at first, we need to specify the manner in which we'll be doing so.

The trickster as a figure of in-betweenness, and thus in this sense of non-reality, was central in situating the figure in contrast to reality. Another key feature, close to this first, captures again, in a certain way, the heart of the human and the divine, as it is indeed language, and knowledge. Plants live, animals move and feel, but they do not really speak, and are incapable for knowledge, in the sense as we understand this word – while god, or the gods, possess full, almost infinite knowledge, and the distinguishing feature of humans as humans is again knowledge as speech. What, then, is specific about the knowledge and language held and used by the trickster?

The answer follows from the previous point, of in-between-ness – in fact, this term, which is all but equivalent for liminality, is in our view perhaps the key word of the modern world, and the title of the series in which this book is published. The trickster is in between in knowledge, as always, even in between the human and the divine, the kind of in-between-ness that defines the unreality of the trickster. The knowledge and the language skills of the trickster are again in between human and divine knowledge: in every possible senses of the term. The trickster does not have full divine knowledge, but has ample knowledge about death, destruction and regeneration; about Eros and Tartarus. The Homeric hymn 'To Hermes' is particularly instructive: the first thing Hermes asks for Apollo is the knowledge of the future, of prophecy or divination (a word that says it all); but Apollo does not give it to him. The trickster knows some things that the gods know, and which surpasses ordinary human knowledge; but not everything. On the other hand, the trickster has no full human knowledge as such, as the trickster cannot know what only humans can acquire, through their experiences, in the full meaning of the word: mindfulness (*phronesis*).

The in-between is thus just a word, capturing and describing in words not something that exists, but the non-reality that is there between and after concrete beings; then it can be intuited that this in-between exists; that we do have interests; and that such interests not simply exist, but are central for existence, in particular central for our existence: Eros, the moving force of the world. So what is the nature of this 'in-between' trickster knowledge that does not transmit full, intact divine knowledge to the humans, only the part of it, if not a perverted version Eros?[1]

The trickster and Eros

The relationship between trickery and Eros is one of the most longstanding controversies in human thought, the question of oppressive Eros being originally Plato's dilemma, concerning the dynamism that mediates between people and the objects of their desire. The *Symposium* leaned towards the primacy of elevated love, a wondering on the beauty of love, friendship and intimacy, but the sexual snare, the dumb monotonous incubus of Eros in its robbing bestiality in pursuit of possessive unification is also present in his works. Eros could be vulgar evil, if it is not handled with noble care, in view to virtue and improvement. Only in a harmonious agreement on goodness can Eros flourish, but mutuality in equal disgrace or deception only brings errors. These defects offer only a semblance, an imitation of the authentic, as telling things without reality ruins thinking. There is also a clear parallelism concerning the relationship between ritual and Eros on the one hand, and ritual and divinisation on the other, as the bringing of the divine flux into the body happens through Hierogamy (see p. 59 above). Still, a communication can only happen between equal partners, so the question is whether such connection was first established artificially in a ritual, or happened in a natural way through liminal crises. Furthermore, while the ritual indeed is derived from liminality, Eros is not a direct descendent of liminality and clearly predates everything existing. Eros is part of the flux, and man also has to enter the liminal flux in order to get in touch with Eros. It is thus necessary to review more closely the connections between Eros, ritual, and the trickster, especially the sacrificing trickster, a central concern for us. It is here that the strange crossing-over between prehistoric ritual and Eros, stumbled upon by the trickster, can be clarified.

The central question concerns the kind of ritual sacrifice Eros represents. Eros is like a breath of wind or some echo rebounding from smooth, hard surfaces, which returns to the source from which it issued, to the soul, bringing a stream of sensuals. It passes back into its possessors through their eyes, which is its natural route to the soul, as Plato explained it in *Phaedrus*, and also in *Alcibiades*. Eros arrives, generating excitement in its possessors. It waters the passages of effluences and causes desires to grow, filling the soul of their possessors with love. This is the desire that is imitated by rituals, a kind of sensual flow that is terrible, wild, and lawless by its own. So rituals are most potent instruments for invoking Eros with their copulating, fractioning rhythm and sounds, but paradoxically even by their mechanical procedurality, all of which find their way into the inner recesses of the soul. Rituals are the simplest and most effective methods of turning Eros around, if they are able to implant sensuals in the participants. Indeed they are based on the understanding that humans already have capacities for such sensuals, but these are improperly aligned, so the ritual is needed to turn them to the right way. In fact, rituals are an effective technique, but as always, efficiency is a double-edged sword, and rituals can train people for the right as well as the wrong behaviour – leaving aside the problematic character of any such implanting. So many rituals are made to implant into people's minds a kind of understanding that for most part is the very opposite of those which they had before the rituals, which the ritualists wish them to have. These should be indelibly and unalterably imprinted on the minds, giving a strong enough impulse so that they would lead their lives afterwards accordingly. Preference is for the strongest possible sensuals in order to evoke the presence of Eros. As a result, rituals often involve bloody sacrifice, castration, or other mutilation as well, a kind of destructive liberation.

The procedure of castration is simple: an operator seized the genitalia parts to be removed with one hand and struck them off with another, in order to attract Eros. It is based on a cunning knowledge of Eros and its desires: how can Eros be approached and handled, the circumstances and the conditions under which Eros becomes particularly fierce or calm, what provokes satisfaction in Eros, and what procedures makes it tame or wild, vulgar. Operators in charge of such rituals handle Eros as if endowed with the power of manipulation and the gift of swift execution. Rituals bend themselves into a constant, mechanical link with their targets, producing the same effects all the time, with a well-fed Eros destined for evil constrains, the exact destiny to be decided by the operators.

Prehistoric trickster images

Eros as a trickster appeared in Palaeolithic images already with its complete attributes, and it never really progressed or changed up to the present day.[2] Hunchback, phallic, big pointed nose, rounded eyes, protuberances, pointed head are as many mime attributes – no modification in the pattern, or at any rate any of these faded away during tens of thousands of years, still visible in the Megaran Mime, the Phlyakes actor, or Pulcinella of Commedia dell'Arte. It was a uterus being – far removed from the world of reality, with its forms and borders; something in-between being and non-being: misshaped, unformed, miscarried. It also often acted in a mute way, a main feature of pantomime until

108 *Tracking trickster traces*

our days. Nevertheless, it became the forerunner of acquisition, driven by an untameable urge to possess others' properties, a kind of lawless one, outcast and outsider, ever on the margin, as shown on Figure 6.1: the transparent, colourless, but ever present evil. Note that what we see in this and the following figures are the trickster's image as evoked by the erotic rituals.

The trickster reduces all its arguments to labelling its position in-between territories. It shows revulsion and resentment at the sight of new arrivals. It is present in Palaeolithic, Mesolithic and Neolithic images alike. Sometimes

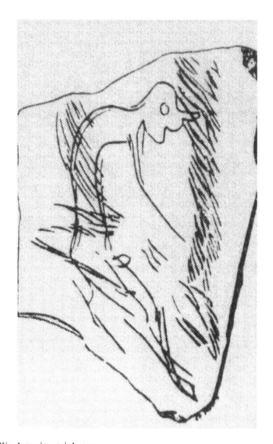

Figure 6.1 Phallic Isturitz trickster.
Phallic Trickster from Isturitz cave, Spain; Magdalenian stone incision. These submissive yet aggressive, compassionate and tyrannical characters are best described as trickster figures, whose phallic, alert, oversexualised attentiveness has been depicted in engravings already in Magdalenian caves, around 12,000 BC. It is alert for every mimesis, intersection, symbiosis, metamorphosis or union with people, ideas, events or opportunities. Its desire for union and expansion is infinite. Its beady eyes, pointed nose, protruding mouth, receding chins and pointed bald head are bridging about 14,000 years, offering a view of the world as a field of pitiless invasions and terrifying obsessions.
Source: Saint-Périer (1935)

it wears skinny outfits, often consisting of stripes, in order to show its hybrid, animal–human type. It may have an animal profile, with a doggish muse or a bird's beak, a skinny scalp or a fuzzy hair, accordingly to how it desires to show its intact closeness to the bestial world. Whether it is standing up, with an erect phallus, or is running with the phallus hanging on its side, there is always eagerness in his hungry, swift figure, or in his swollen tummy – mirrored in its hunchback – for demanding more, due to its acquisitive appetite. Its insignificance needs be filled with things so that he could seem to become existent.

This next trickster (Figure 6.2), depicted many thousands of years later, has a big belly, a long, sensual nose, a doggish muse and standing, doggish ears – to feel and hear in the widest possible way (note that the god of death is a dog for the Egyptians, just as the guardian of the gates of Hades is for the Greeks, given that they are unclean, gobbling up any dead organism) – and piercing eyes: a rogue, a rascal, a disgrace; impostor, ragamuffin, the wretched one, following Radin's description of the Trickster; but also highly sensitive, responsive, and expansive in its soft, swift appearance. It has an over presence, but is strangely colourless, recalling Détienne and Vernant's (1978) octopus for its readiness to catch the victim from its hide to feed itself. The big belly is not there by accident; digestion indicates absorption, annihilation – not a complete one, rather a transformative one. The threshold does not indicate the elimination of one's state; rather it indicates the condition of our passing from one world to another (about the transformative aspects of the Tassili murals, see Horvath, 2015b). The trickster's belly and phallus is a kind of bridge; it transforms one into another existence. We can recall here the example of the eunuch: as Aristotle (*Generation of Animals*, 5.7)

Figure 6.2 Big-bellied trickster at Tassili, with tail and hanging phallus; Neolithic mural painting.
Source: Lhote (1959, fig. 45)

explained, castration is a transformation that changes the form and character of animals, as well as humans. The multiplicity of transformations is stretching from the different states of realities into their partial or total mixture onto an artefact, a process called technology, or better to say, a fabrication of resemblances. The trickster holds a Y-shaped bone, the sign of *steresis* (discussed in Horvath 2019c), meaning the perverted matrix, the ever-circling one, not linear generation. It is striped, another sign of hybridity. The trickster has a phallic penchant, a tantrum-like qualm for possessing and consuming everything, as if to compensate for its sterile insignificance by unlimited inclination. Amorous inclinations fill always the trickster's thought; it is full of desire for other kind of corporality, including food and drink as well, swelled up by desire and the will to generate.

We have repeatedly referred to the trickster as a mime. This connection needs to be explored in some detail.

The trickster and the mime

Let's start with the most classic work. At the start of his *Poetics* Aristotle defined as the central concern of all forms of art as a kind of *imitation*. While much of modern art can be characterised by a desperate effort to escape such imitation, and while modern philosophy similarly ignores imitation, recognising the centrality of imitation is also a central part of the contemporary intellectual landscape, among others due to the work of Girard. Without entering a full discussion on the nature of imitation, what Aristotle says and implies, in the footsteps of Plato's *Ion* and *Republic*, is that whoever is engaged in producing and experiencing works of art, and especially the one who is performing them, or is engaged in a kind of miming, takes a step removed from mindful activities. At the basic level for Aristotle 'imitation' means to follow a form that one is lacking.

But Aristotle should be complemented here, using contemporary knowledge in sociology and anthropology, following especially the lead of the Cambridge ritualists, thus returning to the question of rituals. Art imitates real life in an organised and formalised way; and a crucial practice that enacts and thus alters reality through miming activities are the rituals. Various forms of art evidently grew out of rituals, of which theatre is one of the most interesting and best-studied example, already offering important hints concerning the possible real-life effects of artistic performances. Rituals are set up in order to assist the main crises or other moments of transition in social and human life. They negotiate between different realms of reality and states of being, and proceed mostly through formalised acts in which individuals go through the motions that was led before them by the example of a practically infinite series of generations; thus, it should not be surprising if ritualistic imitations themselves alter reality. Such a bringing in of rituals immediately leads to two questions. The first concerns the links between ritualised Eros and the trickster; while the second the relationship between Eros, mime, sacrifice, and the Palaeolithic trickster images.

Prehistoric trickster 111

To the trickster making and mimicry are the same. It mimes the forms, using various signs – it is always expert in art, or artificial creation, a mechaniota –, stuffing itself with the cosmological order of harmony, saturating geometrical designs, flooding the matrix, packing reality until transforming it, eventually leading to the technological world of today. As a result of its ceaseless mimetic activities technology became an end in itself, within which the world of forms lost its benign meaning, its kindly disposition, its graciosity. And to all those who were inside this favourable and propitious nature existence was lost, and there was no return; the little figure of the Isturitz engraving itself demonstrates the awakening of Eros and the cancelling of a possible continuity, until somebody starts a reverse move of care and mindfulness. There can be no return by itself once the mechanism has started, reaching to the core of geometry. Here we are, in between elements of rituals, or rather to say Satyr plays, in the terminology of Classical Greece, which for so long were performed outside sacred theatre, as were not considered part of the festivities and not subjected to general judgement. Satyr plays are based on mere relations, on the various detrimental effects of the satyrs, and on the mockery of the established order, involving nakedness, animal skin, mask and bristling hair. Changing position by fantastic skipping and jumping were the accustomed rule.

In Palaeolithic times hundreds of kilometres of cave insides became places of a dizzying drama. They became sites of exuberant, ostentatious displays with richly decorated, resplendent hair-dress, elaborate caps and florid forms, strikingly bold pictures, brilliant engravings. In Figure 6.3 the trickster is taking the face of dog, bird, or lion, on a human neck and erect pose, thus becoming a hybrid. Such hybridity can be seen particularly well in the flamboyant phallic figure of the last image, with beak-like nose and pointed cap, in excited gestures. Its short-sleeved dress has nothing to do with our clogged, animal-skinned stereotype of Palaeolithic man: he is dashingly theatrical, even showy, just like the left corner image, with extravagant strips of shawl. Be careful, this show has the same purpose as every theatre: it is a transformative play, as the second image shows: the human profile inside the animal face is marked by an outward, extravagant display of the mime.[3]

Theatricalised ritual originally was identical to sacrifice, whether in Hinduism, the Mediterranean, or in pre-Columbian America. And just as theatre implies substitution, between the actor and the role it plays, a kind of transformation or metamorphosis, the same kind of transformation is alluded at in these images. Metamorphosis and theatre are almost the same things; the Greek mythological figure of metamorphosis, Proteus, was a figure central for actors, even in early-modern England (Agnew 1986: 9, 14). The images shown in Figure 6.4, through their similarly hybrid character, belong to the same complex, even if no trace of bloody sacrifice was yet found in the Palaeolithic; signs of a trickster mentality of substitutability eating into the body of the real.

Turning to Figure 6.4, it shows the trickster absorbed into the head of a dog. The dog-man lower part, with its thighs and arms, retains human features, but the head, with its articulated muzzle and forms of eyes is a dog's

112 *Tracking trickster traces*

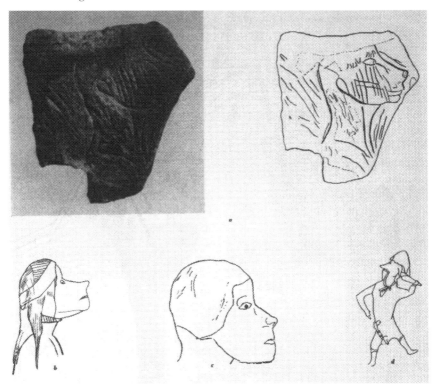

Figure 6.3 Mime trickster in the La Marche cave: the animal profile.
Source: Péricard and Lwoff (1940: 116–167); Lwoff (1941: 150, 153, 1943: 168)

one. Inside the dog's head, however, the head of a trickster is drawn, with beady eyes and a big, sensitive nose. This is not a mask, but the reproduction of absorption. There is no division line on the body that could indicate that the trickster is wearing a mask;[4] the body is complete, a dog with a human body. It represents a complete and definite acquisition, where the long-nosed, beady-eyed, large-eared man is transformed into a dog: snuffling, tasting and hearing the world with the eyes, ears, mouth and tongue of a dog, thus becoming a hybrid. Man and dog became one body: the man absorbed the dog, the dog absorbed the man; a new power was born, which is separate from reality where both man and dog have a definite space and time, an assigned life and an area where they are same with themselves. Here, all their co-ordination, localisation, function, confirmation and foundation have gone, and it has been transformed into a trickster, into a transcendental man-dog mixture; pushed out of reality, its own, given, inner relatedness. They became servants of another will, separate from their own inner composition, having lost the full capacity of sensory apparatus – only the voracious appetite remained the same. Here ritual as sorcery is at work, which alone could bring

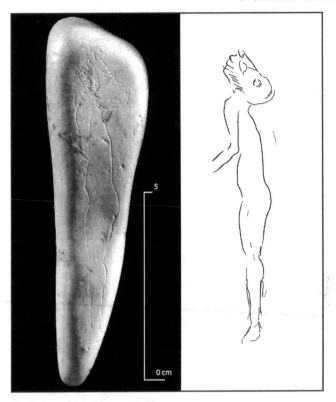

Figure 6.4 The Dog–Man hybrid trickster, Gourdan cave, Dordogne, bone incision.
Source: 'Les abris sculptés de la Préhistoire', www.culture.fr

forth this metamorphic becoming. Only a transformative show, the magical modality of trickster activity is able to activate this kind of immaterial process of merging together separate natural entities, to combine the hunter's skill of the dog with the skill of the man as a clever modifier. Eros as transformer was not only Plato's concern. Ovid's *Metamorphoses* is based on this as well, the transformation of the naked and violated into somebody or something else than before by the force of Eros, which is manifesting many kinds of efforts that inside the context of reality would be strictly prohibited, or plainly impossible. However, through the trick of transformation, such activities could be carried on, ecstatically, by intoxication, beyond any reasonable limit.

The next image analysed, a lumpy figurine from the Neolithic Grimes Graves flint mine in Norfolk, England (now in the British Museum), explores the same issue of erotic transformation. While the authenticity of the image is debated, the figure is timeless in its type. The image of the neck-less figurine has a crudely executed head with rounded, animal eyes, nose and mouth, lumpish breasts, uneven nipples and a protuberant belly. It is a hunchback, with its crude arms oriented towards its intimate part, leaving no doubt what is the focus of its

114 *Tracking trickster traces*

inclination. Its trickster message is about the insignificance of generation, as everything can be endlessly reproduced, emphasised both by the hollow void carved into the bottom of the figurine and its huge hunchback, which repeats the uterus form. It is echoed by a cruel, sarcastic smile, dismissing the vanity of everything, as nothing is real, just a repetition. Many of its attributes are coming back later with the Pulcinella figures, like the hunchback, pointed head or cap, huge belly, sexual hybridity.

The trickster wishes to eat, drink and bedding, searching for any experience that brings pleasure and enjoyment, though this is always combined with a misgiving or an anxiety that all might not be well, and certainly will not end well. Trickster is in uncertainty about the world, does not really know it, does not really understand it, its knowledge is remorsefully restricted to its desires, as seen in the belly sculptures at the site of Lepinski Vir (Figure 6.5).

Figure 6.5 Phallic Mesolithic figurine, Lepinski Vir, Serbia, *c*.6000 BC.
Source: Wikimedia Commons, https://creativecommons.org/licenses/by-sa/3.0/deed.en

The figure is profoundly phallic, even its open mouth expresses laxity, a desire to be penetrated. Its open, rounded, animal eyes are blank and paralysed by impulses. It is bald and neck-less, holding his erect phallus with both hands. The whole rounded figure recalls the uterus form.

Every aspect of this Mesolithic site repeats geometrical patters, including the circle, trapezoid, and triangle. Most importantly, the shape and orientation of the entrances are Y-like hook forms, indicating intersection or bifurcation. The angle or bifurcation could be in the middle, or in the upper or lower left, indicating the matrix where the entering characters are meeting with the departing characters before their transformation. This angle is the sign of constant of production, of the dynamical equation that accounts for the acceleration of growth, which is the special occupation of the trickster who invaded this central place of the matrix. Most likely it did so by seducing others, or inflicting damages on them in this or in other ways, as it completely lacks in attributes or forces that make life ongoing and especially easy-going, as we said it before.

All in all, these images of the evil about the relativity of forms attempt to take up any guise by which victims can be easily captured. The weird gloom of the images renders any benign connotation impossible, but they do not demonstrate the opposite either, rather something mixed. They are not explicitly malignant, though have a somewhat detrimental effect, sometimes directly harmful, and never really harmless: there is always a definite danger that they will be infective, tending to exert an imitative influence that facilitates looseness, the giving up of measures and boundaries. They are not gentle or kind, but still try to sing to the soul with a certain mildness, or with a relaxed menace, intimating with a wink or a nod that there is nothing to do, this is what we are, trying to provoke a favourable sentiment, with the desire of opening up and embracing everything, without constraints. This sentiment could only come about when the reality of the artist became altered, resumed under another existence and especially a new, different idea, the needs of acquisitiveness. The point is that this sentiment could be threatening to the kindly disposition to reality, to its favourable borders and forms that give proportion and harmony to it, exactly by its universalism. As it drew its life from tension, from confusing the clement and the benign, it can now turn this into a recurrent and evolutionary growth, into a new layer of unified development. Now, under its new guise, it is the trickster again that promotes peace and masters kindness, set to create a world without conflicts by resolving it into global muteness.

Eros and sacrifice

In order to pursue Eros's path further, let's try to see what kind of actions have the joint character of provoking erotic sensuals and destruction of the bodies at the same time. And here, it is easy to ascertain, sacrificial offerings can play a central role. Aristotle's ideas concerning the link between pity, the desire to help and wanting to embrace, and fear in producing the tragic effect, and even the mutual reference of the two emotions to each other are, at one level, eminently plausible. And yet, the tightness of such a connection is problematic, even beyond – though not independently of – the rather bleak view of a consuming nature implied by it, and poses the question of the exact conditions under which such a connection could be established. Why would somebody feeling pity, sympathy and compassion, would need to relate such a feeling to oneself? This is not due to sincere compassion for the life or fate of somebody else; rather, it is part of a love that is artificially incited, urging for union in a way of self-denial. Is sacrifice thus closer to Eros than to terror? Can they even be the same? Under what conditions may such emotional cross-references make sense?

Perhaps the answer is that the desire to help also has an erotic character. It is here that, quite strikingly, rituals of sacrifice come into view, and in an almost exclusive manner. Such a ritual not only meets perfectly the bill, but it is also difficult to think about other situations where a similarly tight link could be established between the evocation of passive feelings of terror and active, erotic desire for union with a giving, help-offering sensual. This assumes the position of a mere spectator of such rituals, not the position of the victim, but only such positions are effective, as the position of the victim disappears with the completion of the sacrificial act. And such a perspective has particular significance, as this is the perspective of not only of the spectator, but also of Eros, or the flux as sensual. They both feel, so the sensuals establish a communality between them.

Here the careless, thoughtless, ecstatic Eros feelings, which indeed recall a time of the jesters and fools, rogues and clowns, with their mocking and cruelty, become dominant. Mocking aims to hurt; mocking humiliates; mocking is violent, and is anyhow without solution. Mocking is therefore frighteningly close to the sacrificial ritual, it is terroristic, reflects and perpetuates a sense of helplessness. Ultimately, as Nietzsche was so well aware of it, laughing is a way of 'killing'; or, according to Baudelaire, laughter is outright satanic. Carnival mocking manages to get around this problem by being strictly mutual – whoever is mocking somebody else can immediately mocked by others; yet, in any such practice, mocking is the expression of helplessness and uselessness. The second problem, cruelty, is strictly connected to it, and indeed violence can be considered as a modality that can accompany almost any kind of carnivalesque behaviour: whatever begins as a good clean fun can spill out of its boundaries – especially because a central aspect of the carnival is to overthrow and question such boundaries, any boundaries – but then, it is evident that some boundaries must be maintained; presumably those borderlines, boundaries and prohibitions that were observed.

And here we reach the heart of the problem, that cannot be theoretically solved, and at the same time cannot be assumed away: that Eros by itself has nothing to do with beings – they are for each other – it is just a sensual assistance for filiation, but has no independent role. In one sense, this concerns assumptions or preconceptions of conditioning, which was Plato's education for good. In a more sensitive manner, this concerns the exact combination of the survival of genuine forms of sensuals (as Pascal expressed it by the 'reasons of the heart') and more corroded, corrupted and depraved forms of desires and inclinations, which are produced by machinations. However, the question also touches upon the irruption of Eros into the sterile and useless practices and modes of existence evoked and disseminated by the operators. The question now concerns who these operators are.

These operators were not simply outside the ordinary framework of social life, but – in the logic of the Platonic chain of being – are at a third remove from it. At first remove are out of ordinary events, whether natural disasters, social and political crises, or moments of transition in human and natural life, where within a short period the entire framework of life is temporarily altered; and at second remove are those rituals that try to assist humans in responding to such challenges, or easing the strains of transitions. The radically difference is that in their operation their action was reduced to evoking Eros. We know that a theatre is something like a mimetic sacrifice – which becomes most visible through the central role played by the tragic, fateful death of the hero, and often actual rituals of sacrifice, in classical Greek tragedy. But a theatrical presentation ended, and did not shed blood. This is a relatively simple point, but the reverse possibility carries an implication which is both very significant for this book and highly troubling: if a theatre is a fake sacrifice, then the operators, or whose entire life is devoted to sacrificial rituals, must live for their whole life in an unreal, artificial manners. As it will be discussed in detail in the next chapter, we consider that these operators became operators through their living under ground, as troglodytes. While, contrary to a long-held view, man did not live in caves in Palaeolithic times, with the rise of the Neolithic an enormous mental shift took place towards self-denial, and some people in fact decided to dwell deep inside underground structures that they themselves excavated.

Far from losing participation, the troglodyte mind implies an excess of it; and it is this excess that makes it, beyond rituals, a constant presence in everyday life. Thus, it can appear real, even excessively real, even though its existence is radically outside of the logic of normal everyday life, as it is more dead than living.

And it is here that the troglodyte is caught in-between two opposite excesses, as an outgrowth of rituals: it wants to embrace death while also making contact and become connected by Eros, the two as if marking the opposite ends of a Y. This implies that, on the one hand the troglodyte ends up by becoming the living dead of pure sensuality, while on the other it leads to a growing terror provoked a desperation that it is unable to resolve, can only transform it, by a strange and genuinely perverted transmogrification into the escalation of soul snatching.

Notes

1 These sections much rely on Horvath (2013) and Szakolczai (2013).
2 The discussion in this section relies on Horvath (2019a) and Horvath and Szakolczai (2018a).
3 A striking repetition of these pointed nose images can be seen in Tassili (see Horvath and Szakolczai 2018a: 140–142).
4 On the mask, with a particular focus on it generating possession, see Pizzorno (2010).

7 The troglodytes
Evil proto-scientific methods for transformation

> But in Europe each of us senses that Greece cannot be confused with Sumer and its tablets.
>
> Marcel Détienne, *The Greeks and Us* (Détienne 2007: 126)

Trickster is just a word, and no single word can do justice to such an extremely complex character as the trickster figure of comparative anthropology, mythology and folktales. Its range extends from simple storytellers and circus clowns through all kinds of folktale characters and classical heroes (or rather anti-heroes), prominently including Homer, Shakespeare, Goethe and Dickens, to demonic figures of absolute evil. The name thus cannot possibly do justice to the full character. Yet, it is significant, especially in capturing the kind of knowledge that is characteristic of the trickster, thus we have to start with it. Yet, the word, with its focus on the act of tricking, has its own significance when the figure is applied to the modern world, especially concerning the manifold historical sources of modernity, in particular the difference of the Greeks, already much discussed in this book.

A trick, in its current meaning, is a quite ambivalent noun, as it combines two senses. One is 'a cunning act or scheme intended to deceive or outwit someone', a stratagem, ploy, ruse, scheme, device, manoeuvre, machination, and – not necessarily, but quite centrally – implies quite nasty and malevolent deceit, treachery, or cheating. At the same time, it has a similar but less serious meaning as 'a skilful act performed for entertainment or amusement', thus a trick performed for pure and explicit entertainment; something that is not done in real life, only in its imitation. Given such ambivalence and complexity, it is not surprising that the etymology of the word is quite uncertain: into English, it came from French; but the source of the old French word is uncertain; perhaps it is from Latin, but the roots of the supposed Latin source term *tricæ* 'trifles, nonsense, a tangle of difficulties' is similarly uncertain. At any rate, there are no real Latin or Greek predecessors for the term, and in French, just as in Italian, the term has a rather more limited and specific meaning than in modern English. Significantly, the expression 'to do the trick' in the sense of 'accomplishing one's purpose' is modern – from 1812; and originates in the US.

The two senses are brought together by the fact that both meanings imply a certain kind of knowledge. One might say that anything one does implies knowledge, in some way; but the knowledge assumed by a trick has a number of very particular features. To start with, the kind of knowledge assumed to successfully perform a trick is extremely close to what we have come to called as rational, but not mindful or careful. This implies, first of all, the possession of a very special kind of knowledge that is not available to everyone; which must be acquired, by some special means – whether by long training, by a special kind of introduction or initiation, or simply by accidentally gaining some relevant piece of information. Second, it implies a rank division between those who possess this knowledge and those who do not; a kind of binary social stratification that cuts across any other social separating lines. Third, a connected to both previous, yet adding a further and crucial angle, it implies non-participation, or a position of exteriority. Whoever does a trick on somebody else does not belong to the reality of those on whom or to whom the trick for performed; they for him become mere objects of the tricks, whether only a spectators, or as actual victims. We are not really supposed to do a trick to any of the persons we love, or only like or respect; this can only be justified if the trick was only done not seriously, as a joke – and even joking with somebody, even in the most casual and innocent case, has something improper about it.

A trick, therefore, is an act performed by certain people possessing a special skill in front of, or even on others who lack those skills, and are therefore either simply spectators of the act, or even its suffering objects. Its application therefore is similar to rationality – a trick could be defined as a special modality of applied rational thought. This is perhaps very close to the sense in which magic, art and technology are connected, in their similar bringing about of enchantment, according to the ideas of Alfred Gell. However, a trick is not identical to rationality, not to mention reason, as it has a second, just as crucial but opposite feature: a trick is always imitative. Anybody doing a trick has something not fully real about it; it might apply a certain knowledge, but the kind of knowledge that is a trick always lacks something, thus it is unreal, as lacking kind sympathy.

The point is crucial, and perhaps can be illuminated through another example, again focusing on the strongest of sympathy and compassion, on Eros. Plato's Eros belongs to the Forms or Ideas: 'he who loves the beautiful is called a lover because he partakes of it' (*Phaedrus* 249E, trans. Jowett). In Plato's understanding, Eros is held to be a participation, a serious aspiration for possessing the good, even without reciprocity, without acquisition or appetite. Hence, it does not belong to a lower order of reaction and stimulus sensuals, but to mindfulness.

This Eros is excluded in the case of a seduction, where the seducer is interested only in a concrete end; while the case of mutual seduction, when both sides from the start are just interested in a limited and non-existential relationship, might be a perfect illustration of corruption as a condition of corruptness, in the etymological sense of a 'joint break' – and even this, of course, might go astray. The central issue is that tricking is not simply imitative, but – just in the case of rationality – it implies a very special kind of imitation; an imitation that is not done in fully good faith, respectfully. And here we can turn to the third main feature of the trick, apart from its paradoxical joint involving of rationality and imitation. This is that tricking also involves leading in some way – which is again highly paradoxical, as imitating implies to follow and not to lead. And yet, the term 'lead' was already deployed before, and even its character was specified, such as in the word 'seduce', which etymologically means nothing else than lead apart, or mislead.

The paradox can be explained by the same set-up that was already implied in the performance exactly in the double sense of this word of a trick. Whoever does, or performs, a trick, stands apart from those for whom, or on whom, the trick is performed; so there is a complete end-means separation, just as in rational thinking; and so the one who does the deed leads the others. This of course is highly paradoxical, as somebody doing a trick set himself outside the existential link with the others; thus, is the person least capable of leading them. Yet, by placing oneself outside, he also gained something; a kind of knowledge not available to those who stay inside; and the striking capability to gain leadership is a consequence of the possession of this knowledge. Thus, the rational, imitative, and leading aspects of tricking compose a full circle.

Still, a crucial element is missing, which is exactly the other component of knowledge: the question of recognition, or re-cognition, beyond mere cognition. The performance of tricks implies knowledge; still, under normal conditions, people would realise the trick as being just a trick. This is evident in the case of a special, ritual or theatrical performance, or a mere story; but even if somebody pulls a trick in real life, the not genuine, or fake character of the behaviours can be spotted, under normal conditions. Confusing the genuine and the fake is a mistake, and right in the etymological sense of a mis-take, or misunderstanding, misinterpreting, taking somebody in error – committing an error. A trick can thus only work, only be effective, under particular conditions.

In order to understand such conditions, and the use to be made of them, we need to shift our attention from the trick as an act to the figure of the trickster. To start with, trickster knowledge, while does not simply reflect the being of the trickster, certainly is not separate from it, thus in a way reproduces the ambivalences of the trickster, first of all in the sense that it is not possible to assign it a single, specific characterisation. Still, in spite of the manifoldness of trickster figures across a variety of times and places, impossible to resume in a single profile, all tricksters share a basic, though fully negative feature: tricksters do not belong anywhere, do not participate in any community, do not share anything, especially respectful feelings, also because they do not really have these feelings – though they might fake them, just as they fake, copy, imitate or mimic everything, this being one of their central tricks. This sheer negativity, as the absolute origin of tricksterness, however, immediately produces a radical dualism, between them, those who belong somewhere, anybody, and the trickster, as all tricksters are fundamentally singular, even idiosyncratic, and profoundly lonely. This existential dualism of course animates the bipolarity of the trickster's unnatural nature.

This close identification of the trickster with the outsider existence of the trickster, its radical dualism and bipolarity also implies that it has no substance, no integrity, no unity, is rather broken, a fractured, fragmented, ruptured being, split in half, this being captured in fundamental terms applicable to the trickster like ambivalence or doubt. Such a broken existence also gives another meaning to the trickster being outside everything, at least everything that belongs to normal life, and can be resumed by another constitutive dualism of the trickster, the contrast between being and non-being, existence and non-existence, which means that its bipolarity can be captured not simply by the numbers, but zero – the non-number of non-being. Finally, through the zero, or the nil, we can assign another, ultimate non-number to the trickster, which is infinity, and which can be best approached as the number of trickster growth, or the modality of the escalation of trickster knowledge, as any number divided by zero yields infinity, capturing the fact that the trickster produces – and can only produce – growth through the trick of division, or the destruction of mindfulness, while in reality division is always an operation of diminishing.

Trickster knowledge thus is always dualistic, which also implies that thinkers, or forms of spirituality, which specifically focus on dualisms and dichotomies are by definition modalities of trickster thought – except if they are explicitly aware that in real life such dichotomies and dualistic choices are characteristic of specific liminal moments. Characteristically, they maintain another dualism and this the contrast between the open and the secret part of their knowledge, often vocally support the complete openness and freedom of any knowledge and information, promoting without any reserve a free and open public sphere, ignoring or denying the ambivalence of communication, captured for example in the figure of Hermes, central for Greek mythology. However, on the other, among themselves, they always transmit their real tricks secretly, as part of a plotting. This was first identified by Plato, through the destructive element of the Sophist blackmail of total openness in the public sphere of contemporary Athens, and the extreme difficulty involved in identifying and resisting Sophists is one of his most important and persistent, though still little understood concerns.

The third main feature of trickster knowledge, after its pervasive dualism and the bipolarity between openness and secrecy, is its similarly unreserved universalism. Universal knowledge is another typical trickster trap – a verbal magic impossible to oppose, and yet which, when proposed and followed, starts a series of irreversible and deeply upsetting processes. Here anything universal is caught in a game of oscillation between infinity and the zero. The problem, therefore, is not whether such a knowledge is true or not, but that our lives are not universal, but real.

Fourth, trickster knowledge is also fundamentally transformative. This includes the trickster's ability to transform itself – where transformations into animal shape, and gender change of Dionysus, are among the most widely recognised features of the trickster; but also to inaugurate genuine transformations in the world as such – one of the reasons why the trickster is widely called a second founder of the world, see Lewis Hyde's book. The key idea is to create by destruction – an idea central to modern technology and capitalism, as captured in the term 'creative destruction', coined by Schumpeter as an explicit apology of capitalism; but can be traced back to alchemy, and hermetic knowledge in general (Yates 1964, 1975a, 1975b, 1992), and to the source of alchemy, metallurgy – visible in the religious and ritual role of blacksmith figures all around the world, and their evident 'trickster' character (Blakely 2006; Horvath 2013, 2015). It is the idea, and actual reality, of creative destruction that sets off a perverted linear transformation process, transforming linearity into circularity (Horvath 2019a), putting into motion the kind of irresistible transformation that is captured in the term integral reality by Baudrillard (2013; see Germain 2019), also conceptualised by Heidegger (2017: 3, 35–37, 191, 206–207, 210) through the distinction between destruction and devastation, and their links through machination. The outcome is unreality (Szakolczai 2016, 2017).

The last aspect of trickster knowledge, closing the circles in a seemingly unassailable and irresistible manner, is the attempted destruction of the soul through the manipulation of consent. Trickster logic differs from mere oppression, repression, exploitation and suppression by gaining the willing contribution of those affected and afflicted in orchestrating their own downfall. The destruction of the soul is a central issue of prehistoric troglodyte settlements.

Introducing the troglodytes

Troglodyte is a Greek word for underground people who live in caves or holes. The term depicts people who not just enter but even dwell in caves or similar places where others hardly go, as they are dark, humid and exclude the sun.[1] Such figures, could be dwarf-like and associated with magic, are present in many traditions all around the planet. Australia is a particularly interesting case, where it is connected to dream-time. Marcel Mauss discussed this in his unfinished doctoral dissertation on prayer, but this had a strange fate, as the version published by him in a few private copies ended around this point abruptly, while its eventual publication in his collected works ended even more abruptly, literally mid-sentence, '*ou comme on les appelle dans ...*' ('as they are called in ...'; see Mauss 1968: 477), after revealing that they lived in great caves, in the depths of the earth. The last half-page published by Mauss is available in the recent English translation, rendering first public the 'hidden' text, identifying these people as the 'invisible ones', painted all over with red. They are the 'men of the earth', an expression closely recalling Plato's 'earth-born race' (*gegenes; Statesman* 271A), who are

124 *Tracking trickster traces*

> the permanent souls of the totemic species, the principle of all fruitfulness. They come out from their underground lairs by night, to reach the surface ... where they once lived. With their magic weapons they hunt game on the surface of the earth and take it back underground where they eat it raw ... The formula is part of a process of magic. It is magic itself. It unites the bodies and spirits of the divine species and prompts these animated bodies, these ancestors resurrected in all their fabulous strength, to participate in the actions performed in their presence and to propagate the animal species as they have previously done in mythical times.
>
> (Mauss 2003: 96)

Greeks had a special dislike of the underground. In the Homeric hymn 'To Hermes' the underground is described as punishment in the following way by Apollo, after was deceived by Hermes: 'For I will take and cast you into dusky Tartarus and awful hopeless darkness, and neither your mother nor your father shall free you or bring you up again to the light, but you will wander under the earth and be the leader amongst little folk' (lines 256–259). As a footnote explains, those underground 'retain the state of growth – whether childhood or manhood – in which they are at the moment of leaving the upper world' (as in Hesiod 1977: 383). Those who dwell there live beneath the airy-light earth, in the dark dampness, in cruel bonds of grief and anguish, 'away from all the gods' (Hesiod, *Theogony*, 813).

Kaymakli is one of Cappadocia's many troglodyte systems. Its paths lead through several chambers down, to about 80m below, until reaching water level. It contains several shafts that traverse vertically all floor (see www.goreme.com/kaymakli-underground-city.php for an underground plan of the Kaymakli structure).

Kaymakli's underground structure belongs to no known culture or civilisation. It is empty of meaning and significances. No pictures or portable objects were found there. The name of its dwellers, troglodyte, is itself a name of surprise, given to those who suddenly enter to and appear from somewhere, and are 'not like us'. Troglodytes differ from city dwellers or hut builders, walkers or the settled: the troglodyte is a third kind of category, the secluded outsider. This expression provides a link between their physical appearances, their activities and their reputations. Troglodytes can be found all over the earth, from Egypt and East of the Red Sea,[2] from the Balkans through Italy to Northern Spain. However, the trickster troglodyte is a constant mental type. The troglodyte is an imposing and sombre villain, who deceive their mother's hopes, like Hephaestus.[3] Tricksters are not simply born, they are rather transformed, multiplying in pernicious and infamous ways, bringing forth new interests through poisonous connections, building networks of debauchery. They are those who ventured into the bowels of hell, occupying underground caves, groping amid shadows performing shameful magic, stealing the sensuals[4] of the souls as a way of payment to their demons – at least, this was the opinion about them.

These forces of the underground appeared as irresistible and infinite, never dying and never growing old, rather fiercely productive and manifesting themselves in various appearances that made them even more relentless, fearful and strong. When Hesiod described Tartarus (*Theogony*, lines 712–818), it seemed to be rather the geometric form of a Y, keeping these forces inside itself, than a natural phenomenon, recalling the way a funnel gradually lets a liquid through its opening to a jar: '[r]ound it runs a fence of bronze, and night spreads in triple line all about it like a neck-circlet, while above grow the roots of the earth and unfruitful sea ... And they may not go out; for Poseidon fixed gates of bronze upon it, and a wall runs all round it on every side' (726–733). This underground is fenced and feared, it has a content with dangerous, destructive potentials, which is at the same time – or perhaps due to the same reason – a generative substance, following the logic of creative destruction; even the origins and destiny, 'the sources and ends', of everything on earth and even in the sky: 'And there, all in their order, are the sources and ends of gloomy earth and misty Tartarus and the unfruitful sea and starry heaven' (736–738).

This generative source is a great abyss underneath, regulated by gates in the unreachable depth of the earth, where human artefacts mean nothing at all. Whosoever is carried there lies breathless, voiceless and soulless in a mute fluxing, overshadowed by the heavy trance of transformation. From there, there is no escape; once one is seized, it is held fast, with an iron will, and a pitiless want devours anybody trying to go out of the gates. In transformation, when characters are in the process of becoming something else than they are, reality is ruled out, as a new version is continually shaped in the process, ad infinitum, in a place where 'the awful snake guards the apples all of gold in the secret places of the dark earth at its great bounds' (334–335), and transforms, matrixes death into life.

Troglodytes can be thought of as acting out the Tartarus. In the soft tuff limestone often several levels of circulating paths were carved, as if snaking around the grim and hideous. Their system is similar to the diffusive Tartarus motive (as seen in Hesiod's description above), though even more tortuous, changing direction several times, but its shape is similarly Y like. As the cross map shows, using the case of Kaymakli in Cappadocia, Central Anatolia, now Turkey, one of the 36 troglodyte systems of the region, it was easier to get inside them than to leave them. The path leads downward, through several chambers, and then descends to the first level below. Kaymakli has countless low, narrow and sloping passages, distributed on several floors below the ground level, where the hollow receptacles are organised around shafts.[5] They reach about 80 metres below ground level, passing through all floors, thus their shape recalls that of the square root.[6] Kaymakli should be conceived of as modelled after Tartarus, though in much smaller scale. The depth of 80 metres is just over the water level of the disappeared Neo-Tethys ocean, with the large stratovolcanoes of Erciyes Dagi and Hasan Dagi, sites of important obsidian deposits being nearby.[7]

126 *Tracking trickster traces*

The volcanoes in the background give a reminiscence to Typhoeus (Hesiod, *Theogony*, 820–868), the dark, flickering-tongued snake-headed giant, with hundred kinds of voices shouting from its several heads, who came to reign over men until Zeus defeated him and buried him under a volcano.[8] Imitating Tartarus as a model may sound surprising, but the cautions operation required for working in isolation, slowly opening up the earth from level to level until the water level is reached in the depth of 80m-s, while attentively dissecting the structure with canals and vertical shafts is worth to notice, and certainly requires some explanation – but originally also a model.[9] Furthermore, the original operators certainly searched for something, which was emitting signs, having a breath and vitality. They wanted to reach and touch it, feeling its vibration in their web that grew thicker with every year of digging down the earth through ever smaller observing and controlling zones until they reached the water level. When they reached it, the sky and the water was again connected, and anything that was once buried under the 80 m high solid layer disappeared through their vertical shaft that brought down the air and the sky to the fluid water level, to their meeting point, in order to meet with Echidna, the human headed snake monster of mythology, or the dragon in alchemy: that 'shine with points of light' (204).

This has an interesting reminiscence in alchemical thinking, as the poems of the Byzantine alchemist Theophrastos, from the 7th century AD, show:

> A dragon springs therefrom which, when exposed
> In horse's excrement for twenty days,
> Devours his tail till naught thereof remains.
> This dragon, whom they Ouroboros call,
> Is white in looks and spotted in his skin,
> And has a form and shape most strange to see.
> When he was born he sprang from out the warm
> And humid substance of united things.
> The close embrace of male and female kind,
> – A union which occurred within the sea –
> Brought forth this dragon, as already said;
> A monster scorching all the earth with fire,
> With all his might and panoply displayed,
> He swims and comes unto a place within
> The currents of the Nile; his gleaming skin
> And all the bands which girdle him around
> Are bright as gold and shine with points of light,
> This dragon seize and slay with skilful art
> Within the sea, and wield with speed thy knife
> With double edges hot and moist, and then,
> His carcass having cleft in twain, lift out
> The gall and bear away its blackened form,
> All heavy with the weight of earthy bile;

> Great clouds of steaming mist ascend therefrom
> And these become on rising dense enough
> To bear away the dragon from the sea
> And lift him upward to a station warm,
> The moisture of the air his lightened shape
> And form sustaining; be most careful then
> All burning of his substance to avoid
> And change its nature to a stream divine
> (as in Browne 1920: 204)

Evidently this dragon was slain, its black and heavy, acid soul was separated and poured into separate hollows of 'gaping urn' (205), and when its stream stops to flow, then it clean is from any impurity. The process of purification results in the bright, unspeakable marvel of all its wealth:

> With quenching draughts;
> then pour the mercury
> Into a gaping urn and when its stream
> Of sacred fluid stops to flow, then wash
> Away with care the blackened dross of earth.
> Thus having brightened what the darkness hid
> Within the dragon's entrails thou wilt bring
> A mystery unspeakable to light;
> For it will shine exceeding bright and clear,
> And, being tinged a perfect white throughout,
> Will be revealed with wondrous brilliancy,
> Its blackness having all been changed to white;
> For when the cloud-sent water flows thereon
> It cleanses every dark and earthy stain.
> Thus he doth easily release himself
> By drinking nectar, though completely dead;
> He poureth out to mortals all his wealth
> And by his help the Earth-born are sustained
> Abundantly in life, when they have found
> The wondrous mystery, which, being fixed
> Will turn to silver, dazzling bright in kind,
> A metal having naught of earthy taint,
> So brilliant, clear and wonderfully white.
> (as in Browne 1920: 205)

The importance of such operations for transformation is further confirmed by the Palaeolithic Shaft scene (see Horvath 2013). The aim is to rotate rapidly the victim, accelerating the spinning process,[10] 'with all the bands which girdle him around' (as in Browne 1920: 204). This Y, 'with double edges hot and moist' encircling the creature until him 'having cleft in twain' (204), released his soul. Here in Kaymakli the structure corresponded with this aim. The first floor was the oldest, having a particular gate, that could be closed by a 'millstone',[11] or a round-form stone, on one side of the closure, which led to the 'operational theatre', a chapel-like hollow with a nave and apses. These chamber structures are repeated on the other floors, until at a certain level a huge andesite 'altar' was created. Due to its height, it was impossible to bring it from the outside. Its 57 hollows, each with a diameter of about 10 centimetres, had a particular operational meaning, either for keeping the 'sacred fluid' of the soul, or for any other kind of transformational purpose connected with it: that 'poureth out to mortals all his wealth' (205).

The troglodyte underneath architectural system is never flat, horizontal, but a well-like, vertical space of the Y, with interlinking and crossing eclipses of dig-outs, constituting regular cycling webs around the shafts. These shafts are the central tubes, and together with the receptacle hollows with which they are surrounded, they show a functional rationale. The dig-out passages, with

Figure 7.1 Cross view of several floors together and the millstone gate in the right middle. Kaymakli, Cappadocia.
Note the several peepholes for strict, continuous observance, one of the most characteristic features of this troglodyte system. It also closely recalls the underground structure of Hal Saflieni, in Malta.
Source: © Nevit Dilmen, Wikimedia Commons, https://creativecommons.org/licenses/by-sa/3.0/deed.en.

their architectural circling around a central space and the theatre-like appearance of the 'operational theatre' on the second floor, surrounded by seating platforms in a U shape, indicate the spectacle-like character of the activities performed down there, even if this only meant a continuous tracking of the sneaking paths of the dig outs – we do not know. But they have judged the process in one way or another, working in alienation, inside the dark labyrinth, in the non-society of the underground, aiming to manufacture something, as part of a fearful and risky enterprise. Indeed, the activities literally undertaken there,[12] were beyond human capacities. They were assisted by the powers of Tartarus, or better say, by the interplay of two similar wills that filled the gaps inside the process, two aspects of the same attributes to amend wretchedness. Both the punished Titans and the troglodytes shared the hunger for acquiring the other, the Titans needing the forms of beings, while the operators wanted fluxes from them. The Titans were locked there by Zeus, while troglodytes, like an army of blind and ferocious termites in repressed, intractable human form attacked the earth with mile-long dig-outs to catch something in the damp darkness, unable to escape anymore from the bellies of the earth, earning nothing but losing the meaning of their life there, only spreading merciless violence and imposing terror on beings. From the very beginning their acquisitive position determined their end.

But what was the model that was followed here? Is it possible that the void can stimulate action or contact, and what is more, eager to do that, without having bodies or even a surface, or is it possible that one can escape from one's body? Magic says, yes; but if so, in what ways, and with what consequences one can escape from the body, or enact his own body for another soul to live in it, or sending his own soul to occupy a different body? Birth and death are two possible answers for this question. The first means the entering of the soul into the body, due to the capability of the soul to take all kind of possible forms, while the second its escaping, but with a distinctive difference between the limit and the unlimited, or what is dying and what is immortal. So, and still, how to infuse a soul, whether dead or living, into a body? And how to do the opposite, to fly the soul out of it? Is the possible to answer the sensual, shared vibration of the fluxes, whether it is called soul, air, wind or sounds, even blood, as the Greeks believed? The soul becomes infused into its own body, and its move is caused by the dense effluences of the air.[13] The body functions as distillatory of the flux's original density. So it might have been the infusion of a soul flux into the body that was occurring there, as this is contained in an enigmatic line of Empedocles (fragm. 111): 'Thou shalt bring back from Hades the life of a dead man'. As heat is derived from the sun, movement is derived from bodies, and both are affected by sensuals. However, by itself the soul is not capable to move, while the body itself is not capable for having senses. It is dead when the soul departed from it. Only if they are in sufficient closeness, when they get in contact with each other, is motion able to dissolve and inflame the air. The closeness of the effluences of solid bodies in rapid motion is able to heat up the air around of them, this is why dances and other rhythmic movements are so essential in evoking the flux of spirits in rituals. In this way bodies are able to change flux density. Even the fluxes of the air might be dissolved by the action of bodies nearby.

With the help of sympathising effluences that now serve for the sake of the living dead, as in distillation (liquefying and then evaporating), the soul of the bodies[14] can be driven from its solid form, making it to die first and then as a second step reanimated into a new being and existence. This is the way bodies (including human bodies) can become the thing distilling or the thing distilled. Humans themselves can become the vessels undergoing distillation and so transformation, and then the exaltation that dwells within the transformed one, the one whose soul became condensed into a new body. This has become nothing else but a living dead, the possessed one, the ghostly image of the living one, evidently losing the sensuals of sympathy and friendship towards life in this distorted, reduced existence.

But at least we can understand the underground structure as an organ of transformation, as the movement inside the structure is the transportation of the effluences from one body to another. Such transportation is the actual meaning of energy. Thus, we argue that in this way we can explain how the enactment of this energy influences the whole process first from the bodies to the perceptor (Tartarus), and the ultimately to the agents (troglodytes), from life to death and vice versa. On the one hand, these were the effluences emanating from Troglodyte bodies going down into the Tartarus and giving rise to fluxes that played an important role in setting up a correspondence of sensuals between them; on the other, these correspondences between sympathising fluxes also developed into energies for articulating a flow of the supply of sensuals for transformation. This was a phantom movement, not real but still existing, having its own power to destroy or revitalise. Furthermore, this movement had a circular nature, requiring always new and new souls to be involved and digested. The troglodytes seem to be fully aware of the nature of this move – why would there be gates everywhere otherwise? They serve to stop or block the energy flow and urge the accumulation of fluxes. In any case, it is precisely the gates and the shafts in the underground system that serve to control the effluences, 'to change its nature' (Browne 1920: 204). Through movements we can witness how effluences flow to life, how they in turn transport other effluences into transformation, and how ultimately they come to generate new existences: the living dead, as we claim.

The living dead live in dissipation, lacking any restraint, engaged in self-indulgence, give themselves up to debauchery. Once their minds and good feelings became sickened and grown strange, they could only be soothed by the excitement of the awful and the exhilarating, as if sucking sensuals from the living. The one who alters nature, whose way of reaching knowledge is perverse, whose existence in short is an error, is the one who gains its reputation as a trickster: cunning, degraded, primitive and brutal character, whose attitude is a demanding dissatisfaction, a dull dumbness. The dwellers of these rough-hewn habitations, deprived of light and clear breath, were believed to be enslaved by demons. Thus, became an anonymous people, where nobody has a name or a self, just a rugged appearance. Yet, they were reckless magicians who transform beings and have the power to be in any guise they wish. For the Greeks, this asphyxiation of underground darkness bore hateful doom and death, bare blame; only we call it the trickster (Hesiod, *Theogony*, 213–220); painful woe, ruthless, avenging fates, dreaded anger and indignation, parts of a hateful age and a hard-hearted strife. Even in Hesiod's dry, unromantic description of the children of the doomed night we can perceive traces of the abhorrence of his people towards strangers, who did fearful deeds that bore fearful sorrows, resulting in endless fighting, lawlessness and ruin, as contained in his *Theogony*, written around 700–650 BC.

If the troglodytes were involved in specific secret activities of transformation, then some of their typical activities could be understood better, as they were the early, first producers of wine, beer, cheese, or bread, just as they were involved in metal making or dyeing – the use of dye for changing the colour of something permanently is a transformative manipulation. Of course this is not the full list, as other activities were done in secret. The simple logic behind them is always the same: how and when to cut short a particular fermentation process, or to say the progress of the body, and snatch its soul, the form of a young, virile, virtuous man, destined to live an accomplished life in full, with his own family and children, and instead to become deceived and enslaved in deprived disintegration. In general, matter is exposed to heat that makes it lose its constraints and to leave its soul. Then, as a second step, in this death-like state, when fermentation already started but not yet ended with a complete death, fermentation is artificially stopped, thus rendered permanent in one way or another. The outcome is the living dead state, archetype of the trickster. Their coarse features, unpleasant and cold appearances frightened the people around them. They looked like seductive reptiles in human form – rife with magic in their dopamine frazzled zombies appearance. They were stained and emptied, vacuous: men of many demons, operators of dark forces deviated from nature in the underground.

Here, at Kaymakli there are several layers into the bowels of the earth, gates for emphasising the closure and the secrecy of the infinite in the transformation process. Most of the passageways were linked to some strategic points in the outside world, or to secret escape routes into the surface, so the closures were not linked to the troglodytes themselves, rather to the special content they have liberated and captured, which continuously filled the hollows and cups with its dynamism. These dark burrows hosted a series of honeycomb cups: 'All heavy with the weight of earthy bile' (204), big and small, around a number of central pits, providing a place for souls during transformation. Little cubby holes housed receptacles, snug little alcoves that emerged out of the transformation process, which also enacted hundreds of another holes in the walls, repeating and imitating the bringing forth generation in nature, strengthening the effects of transformation by the intertwined sneaking passages. This was an effective logic, so well thought out that endless

Figure 7.2 Kaymakli underground passages.
The Kaymakli troglodyte system, designed for transformation, the way of lost souls in the passages. Its outlook is amazingly similar to the maze type corridors of the Rome catacombs of Domitilia, Priscilla or San Callisco.
Source: © Nevit Dilmen, Wikimedia Commons, https://creativecommons.org/licenses/by-sa/3.0/deed.en.

burying chambers repeated it, indicating the soul's survival-production, from Egypt to the Etruscans, or from pagan Rome to the Christian.

Yet, this Kaymakli troglodyte underground structure is so unspecific, its purpose is so hazy, its paths are drawn into the darkness, into the damp sightlessness, without decorations and ornamental features, with no indication of burial purposes or anything similar, that we need to conclude from the remaining facts, from the ample and empty receptacles all around the walls, ceilings and pavements, and the watched character of every movement inside its body that it was, as it seemed to be: nothing. Kaymakli is the production of nothing. A soul making factory, we should say, following Aristotle's definition of the soul, who claimed that the soul has such a small matter content that it has no real existence outside the body, it is nothing: just a light pattern of structure, the form which gives a vital cohesion to the body.

The gestation of matter is its incubating period before birth, when the body gets its soul, while it is still inside its uterus. Forms are material quintessence, but not in themselves material, only carry the image pattern from one correspondence to another during their materialisation in effluences. They search for resonance to fit the similarly shaped sensuals in others in the receptacle body. Souls have no real independent existence, rather are sensual, imaginative properties of matter; when they manifest themselves in bodies through effluences. The soul gives spiritual cohesion to the body, like the void gives volume and stability to the matrix: a kind of invisible, but sensual property. Characters are born from this unity and can bring their essence from one generation to another, there is heredity, relating patterns transmitted to the next generation. Heredity is the ability of the soul to transmit into descendants all the inheritance it gained during life. It is derived from a line of ancestors, as birth furnishes beings with their form, a firm rule without possibility of substitution. When this property of the soul is disturbed, the set of given relations that were inherited, existing through the line of sensuals are suspended. But if we look at a body as a matrix, we only see the surface of this volume, though a kind, distinct character, but neither the body nor the soul is valid without the other. They are non-functional, devoid of any organic development without the other one; body and soul must be in correspondence in nature, in hereditariness, but here in Kaymakli we see an artificial set-up: a factory of soul gestation, invoking the soul out of the body, and using as if an independent object.

Figure 7.3 Kaymakli's andesite floor stone, with the 57 soul hollows.
Source: © Nevit Dilmen, Wikimedia Commons, https://creativecommons.org/licenses/by-sa/3.0/deed.en.

In the centre of the Kaymakli system, in its main chamber, there is a massive rock with receptacles, not unlike the sarcophagus vaults in Pharaonic Egyptian burial labyrinths with their underground chambers, which are connected by passages with blocking, stairways, and corridors. While behind both these structures there lies the belief that matter gets its substance from the flux, but here it does not get its burial significance. It is just standing alone, without the significance of the factors relating to the dead person and his inheritance. Burials are about transmissibility according to established rules of descent, which here is missing due to the evident lack of coffins or other indicative signs.

Instead, a science appears here, concerning the flux and the soul, a perverse knowledge about their corresponding masses in the pressured wave patterns of the air, one for one – in the way that flux makes matter filtered with its own substance, with the soul, with the specific wave patterns of its faculties. This kind of thinking about the practical graspability of the soul is identical to Socrates's fear about the Sophists: they only believe and trust in the graspable; for them the soul is a kind of matter, separable from the body.[15] For Protagoras nothing is, but is always becoming (Plato, *Theaetetus*, 157A–C), as nothing exists in itself, but this nothing arises out of motion, in-between objects (which is fundamentally and exclusively a troglodyte experience and practice). Indeed, in this region of Cappadocia (see Göreme for instance) the landscapes have the same soul-as-matter-responding-to-nature character as the one we described about Tassili, with its lunar landscape having a correspondence with its machinators (Horvath and Szakolczai 2018a: 127–130). However, behind the flux, in reality there is a second layer, the enduring, unchanging pattern of the principle of good, the sense of the world, which gives to every living a potential to live its form to the full, without the material graspability of wave patterns, rather as capacities, strength and potentials, the integrity of living from what one inherited, and progressing towards the heirs, something not seen and not experienced in Kaymakli, as those who dag it out were not interested in it.

The idea of gestation-factory is further reinforced by Kaymakli's seven rounded millstone forms, and the seven seats in the main 'operational theatre', that must owe something to the cosmological tradition of the seven planets that survived in the Sumerian and Egyptian cultures, and continued in the ideas of Thales or Pythagoras about the sacred numbers of nature. As the constellations move gradually across the hemisphere and reappear in the same regular successions, the pattern of the troglodyte activities must have been varied and regulated. The varying speed of the planets across the constellations as a kind of nerve bundle again constitutes a different move, which should have been modelled underground in a way or another, if the structure indeed happened to model the matrix (generative model) of the universe. Such indications are few, but they are present there in Kaymakli: in the seven millstone gates, in the circling passage ways and the chambers which – together with the shafts – are perhaps miming the gestation of the universe for every living. In this andesite egg-form stone on the third floor of the Kaymakli (see Figure 7.3), with its 57 hollows dug out, like rings forming the circles of the cosmos, even their number being close to the number of constellations, in various traditions. We moderns know 88 constellations, 52 in the Northern and 36 in the Southern hemisphere, while in the *Almagest* of Ptolemy, written in 150 AD, there are 48 constellations. Their first, poetic description was given by the Greek poet Aratus in his poem *Phaenomena*, written about 270 BC, on the basis of Sumerian, Babylonian and Egyptian knowledge. It followed the same rolling model, suggesting a matrix where everything is in a circular movement of birth and death, included a rounded cosmos and circular movements inside it that recurred in cyclical manner:[16] 'All these constellations thou canst mark as the seasons pass, each returning at its appointed time: for all are unchangingly and firmly fixed in the heavens to be the ornaments of the passing night' (Aratus, line 451). In this dark, damp dig-out in Kaymakli the constellations reappear, and with a mind working behind them, providing man-made models for the energy/flux manifestations of the Tartarus. The motion of the planets and the constellations is not and was never a matter known by many, and their cycles were not easily modelled and structured, but in an environment where no disturbing factors frustrated one's work, this could have been done after some initiation into the matter by a learned one.

Yet, this is still not the full story. Of course the constant efficiency of the process is highly questionable, it is influenced by a number of factors, the constellations are just a minor one. Its *vagus nerve* is the troglodyte's mind-set, its stubborn joyless will to get in contact with the Tartarus's fluxes. Their underground system is a sensual mine-field, developing enough sensuals to get in motion the whole system, for which strangely enough their pure will was sufficient. However, it needed constant input from various sensing, sensational offerings, sacrifices, pain and pleasure, as only these wild reflexes – should we say, the perverted Eros? – could regulate and sustain the flow of fluxes. Perhaps with increased pressure and stretch on victims it could be maintained for a while – but not forever; the whole system become dehydrated and died out. When and how, we do not know.

In Kaymakli the artery of the passages has a soul receptacle in the middle, on the ground, as seen in Figure 7.3. Perhaps this is the scope of the whole factory, as the Troglodytes must allow air fluxes of sensuals to pass in both directions in order to produce a density difference; a one-way passage of only denser-than-average flux from level to level will cause pressure to develop, resulting in higher or lower density than it was before. Their dig-out passages multiplied in every possible corner of the underground system, extending to long kilometres. For instance in Derinkuyu deep down, at the bottom of the shaft tunnel the last chamber is a movingly simple retreat, with painstakingly carved arches and niches in the central space for volatilising the flux and reinvesting its vital energy in the matter, as in a preparation for gestation, where it is possible for the soul to become slower or quicker, or gaining or losing density. During this transformation process the major part of the density of the soul is converted during the actual transformation by exploiting the properties of the pressed soul in a move that is gathering and adjusting souls in the 'gaping urns' of the central receptacle for a new usage, for new versions.

But how to direct the accumulation of fluxes into new creations? The text of Theophrastos is clear enough about the usage of different air densities, 'to bear away the dragon' from water to the air, from the cold to the warm, from the moist to the dry. The simplest example for this artifice is the pistol, which operates the air density difference with such intensity that it is able to generate a killing energy. The two systems operate in identical manner. For revolvers, there are cartridges placed into several chambers, each of which can be positioned as a tube in front of the pistol barrel, very much like the shafts function in the troglodyte system. A hammer, like the troglodyte dig-out gate is positioned on each side of the tube. The basic idea in both is to pull the gate (hammer) back, preparing a delayed (steretic) act, setting off an action that differs from the previous one, by lining up the next tube (as if a shaft) after the gate and then to release the functioning of a new gate (which functions as a hammer). In this way the compressed air explodes by pulling the trigger, which charges the compressed air to dispense the contents of the tube when the pressure is released, thus driving the bullet down the tube of the pistol. What gives stability to this process is the spiralling grooves inside the tubes. Extending the tube increases the speed of the compressed air, since its pressure accelerates the whole process, both in the gun and in the dig-outs. In any case, just to pull the gate before each tunnel tubes and then to pull the circuit to release the gate gives the engine its functioning mode, as simply pulling the circuit will force the gate backward and then release it. The air pressure, the simple accumulation of fluxes pushes the gate backward. With this play of air depression and condensation one can release a large volume of energy, which in the case of the pistol is for firing the bullet, while in the case of troglodytes' dig-outs can presumably serve to animate objects. Obviously, a pistol is easier to use than the troglodyte re-animation system, as in the former one only needs to pull the trigger in order to fire, yet there is a certain simplicity in the functioning of the latter as well. It can easily fit together by dig-out designs, with its gates and shafts for changing the flux's density, which results in a simple and affordable engine-weapon. Fluctuating pressure into the tubes, chambers, shafts is like arterial blood, which is manifesting itself in bodies and keeping itself alive in bodies.

An *aurea praxis* was needed for pulling up the souls from the Tartarus, to become as fluxes for the transformative agents for bringing forth. The souls of Tartarus were infinite, never dying out, cool supercilious (this is why the titan name, for the buried energy in Tartarus), without measure and limit, but abundant (note the myth about the guarded golden apple in its depths), but also 'the joyless land, where are Death and Wrath and troops of Dooms besides; and parching Plagues and Rottennesses and Floods roam in darkness over the meadow of Ate' (Empedocles, fragm. 121). However, one must be careful, as this is a mutual act, a merchant activity, as the troglodytes pay back for the flux gained from Tartarus by feeding it with a supposed equivalent of the stolen souls, what they gained from the living, while making them dead and changing their forms, covering them with alien flesh.

The Titans' deprivation, dumbness and vainness is confirmed in their pathos, following on their sensuals, that was recorded in the same style, always in a sad, suffering tone, smiling over life and death, fraught with intolerance, full of grabbing aggressiveness. Their face shows of being true, sincere and pure, evoking a sympathetic, I-am-always-with-you feeling: they are subverted and yet frivolous in subservience, helpless victims, the living dead. This predisposition was expressed by Empedocles (fragm. 124) in the following manner: 'Alas, O wretched race of mortals, sore unblessed: such are the strifes and groanings from which ye have been born!'. The set of connected fragments by Empedocles in which this description was contained is introduced by the following passage: '120 roofed-in cave'; while he captured their activities in a precise way: 'from living creatures he made them dead. changing their forms', while 'clothing them with a strange garment of flesh' (fragm. 125–126).

The dwellers of this joyless land were lonely and exploited, yet prosperous in energy for hunting down souls. The deep force of such poignancy was a correspondence between effluences, all that could be moved, pushed and forced into the shafts of the underground. Idle sensuals and idle troglodytes abounded in pitifulness, embracing each other, as if in mutual commiseration was the root of an exquisitely truthful companionship. Their misery thus led them to a lecherous, aggressive and intolerant dumbness, always being insulted and always wanting to insult, a life that is visibly nothing but a collection of vices, given that they considered themselves as absolved of all responsibility. Consumed by lasting sorrow and profound hopelessness, their tired apathy displayed an uncompromising zeal for catching others into their own misery.

Effluences are fluxing toward contacts, in particular to contacts similar to them in sensuals, but where are the bodies in this process? Souls as transformative agents must be sealed, otherwise they escape. This is well known in alchemy as a way to capture Mercury so that it would operate, together with Saturn in the transformation processes, producing soft, effeminate, pertinacious objects, subverted by the alchemist operator, but channelled through the body of the alchemist. The internet functions in the same way, as the algorithms incorporate the sensuals of the viewers into the process. As Empedocles reveals, and again connected to caves, that for effluences to unite, they must share sympathy (fragm. 89–94). The troglodytes operated by catering for and abusing sympathetic feelings. They were not dead, but living people who went down, first into the caves that were there, and then the structures they themselves dag out. The reason for such activities was likely their searching for mercenary contacts with the dead. Why would someone dig channels tens and tens of metres under the ground if not driven by special interests?

The troglodytes were tricksters among the people, and there was nobody who could not feel them out to be magicians. People were not always deceived, either by their 'sagacity' or their winking-blinking merriness, by their smiling cheek villain injuriousness for captivating minds.[17] But they had reputation for being monstrous and horrific, who were creeping beneath the surface with their hideous-looking appearance, like slimy, loathsome reptiles, in search of victims for a bargain, a selling or perhaps a killing, that suited them so badly – all this debauchery, dissipation, and the rest of it, for promptly feeding their Tartarus demons with the dissolute impulses of robbed souls.

Abyss was coming upon them. When their souls had sickened and grown strange, they could only be soothed by more lust and wantonness, by a cunning mesmeriser villain, often pictured as the jester or as the soul-snatcher trickster.[18] While they are bitter towards those who have led them deep into the iron grasp of the abyss, from where is no escape, still tricksters feels some relaxing liberation by not withdrawing themselves from this bad association. The trickster might have nabbed itself in liminality with the constant urge to increase its influence by innocent souls, so its main concern is what new power can it acquire to cajole its victims into a sympathetic relation. How to liberate their sensuals and make them to resonate with its own one? If ever anyone wittingly deceived and corrupted the souls,[19] then one is maximalising the probability for the growth of impulses, and so the resulting absorption of effluences: the very probability of payment for the demons.

Such thinking is fertile in expedients, and here the trickster overlaps with the figure of the jester, both in pursuing self-interest rather than following principles, and in efficiency for accomplishing a purpose in a guileful way. The jester, like all other tricksters, is merely an expedient for protecting its own type, and never to overcome it. It can only get out of the liminal trap it got itself into by substituting itself by others, which is a typical substitutive sacrifice. Its ill-nature is compromising its own neck by keeping the networks of influences within their due bounds, without ever considering the possibility of alterating its own liminal situation. Whether the trickster or the jester imitates a personality, invents an expedient, or finds the issue of a complicated situation, it is always and ever in the abyss of liminality, unable to restore the person in itself, as it was irretrievably lost. They are types rather than persons; never born and never dying, never in progress and never arriving, rather in a constant eternity of infinite unchangeability.

This circularity is secured by the technique of delayed (steretic) action. The trickster heavily invests in recruiting, for a flow of new souls is constantly needed to pay off effluences of sensuals.[20] Tricksters have their eyes close upon others, especially upon young and gentle souls, slowly but irresistibly instilling into them the poison of impropriety and limitlessness, blackening their intentions and changing their inner power into a lack of restraint, or indulgence. The healthy normality of others is hedged round and round, until reaching the state where nobody could help oneself anymore, thus fall into the numberless intricate labyrinths of impulses, which is the lowest order of anything: liminality, realm of the mime.

A most common expedient of tricksters is to excuse themselves for their lack of sense through asceticism, practicing self-denial and thus catering for pity and sympathy in the feelings of others, bringing some improvements in this way which have been granted to them, thus gaining the supply of new and more numerous souls, which then supersede both the earlier and ruder system, and also the ephemeral and elusive improvements they produced. This expedient even gives them an aura of superiority over normality, keeping a narrow watch upon reality which of course abhors liminality.

Tricksters are soul-devouring provokers of sensuals, duplicitous poisoners who are traversing borders in order to accumulate the sensuals of existing things, just as the flux or surface integral of vector fields,[21] which is known to us by means of the sympathetic feelings given off by them, which we receive. They impose themselves on others by making them feel that they are at one with them in desperateness, making them believe they belong together, thus rendering them reluctant cooperators in their libertinism, following the maxim that whoever is down is entitled to do anything, without responsibility. As the fury of kidnapped, pitiful, sympathetic souls liberates the flux, now the villain can play on its own ground by accumulating resonances, emotional vibrations, thus canalising the souls out of their forms, profiting from self-neglect. The trickster is an evil agency, plotting against the souls, which – once liberated, or detached from the body – become discharged into a liquid mass, in a process similar to the formation of crowds, as it was described in classic works of mass psychology (e.g. Le Bon, Tarde, Michels or Canetti).

The Kaymakli mechanism creates an action/energy potential. This energy is the result of the movement of the fluxed souls into and out of the underground chambers, passages, gates and shafts where, as a second step, an energy potential was sustained that sufficiently spread into matter, into the revitalisation of the dead, transforming the dead into living again: manipulating life. As Toulmin and Goodfield noted, the manipulators of nature were kept at a careful distance in Antique Greece: 'critical speculation about the powers of nature was in fact an unpopular minority activity even in Athens' (Toulmin and Goodfield 1961: 63).

Troglodytes remained, as they ever were, otherworldly, hollowed-eyed demonic men who are dampening the human spirit of normality and absorbing energies from the living. They were considered as tricksters who were changing people's mental health to depression and suicidal self-harm, who can stole human capacity and creativity and leave loneliness and pain instead, who are poking into men's desires and making these addictive to them, keeping men swiping and intoxicated, desiring desire. The troglodytes' unpleasant and grimly world was too monstrous and disagreeable to be taken as the subject of query in the Antiquity, beside their secrecy that made it difficult to discover the nature of their activity. Unless it infiltrated through science, as it happened from the 16th century onwards, and so became a visible, accepted and established practice in modernity, as modern alchemy (Morrisson 2007).

The opinion about them as heartless magicians, reckless impostors, cold manipulators, who believe in nothing and are only set in advancing themselves was never altered, though their tight numbness and their monotonous, convict-like appearance made them endurable. Endurance was achieved probably several times, especially when it paired with fortune seeking, as we now will illustrate this point in the next chapter through the case Najera, northern Spain.

Notes

1. Kant was reputed not to let the sun enter his bedroom, allegedly because the sun helps insects to grow.
2. 'Most scholars, indeed, derive the name "Erembian" from *eran embainein*, a name which later peoples changed to "Troglodytes" for the sake of greater clearness. Now these Troglodytes are that tribe of Arabians who live on the side of the Arabian Gulf next to Egypt and Ethiopia' (Strabo 1.2.34).
3. When Hephaestus was born, he was thrown down by Hera. In revenge he sent as a gift a golden chair with invisible fetters. When Hera sat down she was held fast, and Hephaestus refused to listen to any other of the gods except Dionysus – in him he reposed the fullest trust – and after making him drunk Dionysus brought him to heaven (Pausanias, 1.20.3). See also the mystery cult of the Kabeiroi, who were also called the Hephaistoi, 'the Hephaestus-men' (Kerényi 1991: 57).
4. Sensuals are resonances to phenomena whereby an oscillating system, such as a swing, will oscillate more strongly when it is exposed to a periodic force that is applied with the same frequency as that of the oscillating system. For example, a swing will swing to greater heights if each consecutive push on it is timed to be in rhythm with the initial swing.
5. Shafts are tubes in form of a voided arrow that rotates and transmits power, as the drive shaft of an engine. Could be an axis of a movement, could be imitated as columns, between the capital and the base: connecting the sky with the earth, bringing down the rays of light and penetrating the Earth from the sky. It forms a movement and transmits motion in any rate, even if a sinister or a cheated one: 'the shafted one' for the harsh or treacherous manner of the trickster. The shaft as the revolving rod that transmits power or motion, we will discuss later in this chapter.
6. Square root of two is the irrational number, the famous 'incommensurability' of the Greeks, that can only be expressed by an endless, infinite decimal: 1.4142 … Here the rock cut down so far as 80 metres is the irrational incommensurability with the purpose to challenge infinity. If the whole rational world conformed with rational principles, then the irrationality of the troglodyte square root shook this, threatening its measure, form and harmony. As an example see the Dénezé-sous-Doué la cave aux scuptures, the 16th-century upside-down parody of reality. In doing this, the sculptures are echoing the establishment in trickster mode, shattering its measures.
7. One of the most famous frescoes of Çatalhöyük is thought to depict this volcano.
8. See also Pindar, as discussed in Wolpert (2002: 77).
9. Shafts, more than just a vertical space, are present in Atapuerca, where the *Homo antecessor* were found at two sites in northern Spain dated in the Lower Palaeolithic, in the Rising Star Cave (South Africa), where the human fossils discovered are 335,000 and 236,000 old and in the Upper Palaeolithic Lascaux Shaft Scene (France) indicates a trigger function to the shaft. For more about shaft as revolving, transmitting rod, see Horvath (2013).

The troglodytes 141

10 In our reading the famous *clinamen* of Lucretius should also be situated here. Note also that here the two rather different senses of the word 'spin', to weave, but also to twist around, are joined. It is thus not surprising that the modern media-driven 'spin doctors' are so similar to the Zande spider 'witch doctors'.
11 Millstone is a fantasy name given by the tourist industry, according to a cliché. These rounded forms are at every level, often in the middle of the path randomly.
12 Both in the sense that this was 'taken down', under the ground, and that it was an 'undertaking', or an 'enterprise' – this word having the 'in between' inside. Old English *underniman* even had the meaning of 'entrap'.
13 About the effect of the sun, see Aristotle's *Meteorology*; see also Yates (1964: 251) about Bruno's turn to understand Aristotle, also about 'Man as Magus' (28).
14 All sensitive beings are alike in possessing a soul, according to Aristotle.
15 We are aware that the problem of separation is much older than Plato's thought, and continued to infiltrate philosophy and religion by the Stoics until nowadays. But the Greeks, especially Aristotle, did not accord too much importance to this matter. They did not see an absolute distinction between animated or inanimate matter.
16 While the spherical universe was widely accepted in Antiquity, where the heavenly bodies move along a circular path (here the earth as well circular, spherical like the sun, moon and the planets) the Babylonian view about the earth was more like a rectangular box. The Pythagoreans located the centre in Fire (the sun itself is moving around this central Fire) and not in the Earth itself. But Plato and Aristotle adhered to a firm geocentric position.
17 'Smiling cheek' was used by Shakespeare in *The Merchant of Venice* (act 1, scene 3) for the villain indicating that the evil mind could use artful tricks quoting scripture and misinterpreting it in ways that render his wicked acts reasonable; warrant or substantiate.
18 The jester is the one who is ignorant enough to go against the tides of hierarchy, while also a maniac who single-mindedly tries to restore his reputation. There are political jesters, economic jesters, scientific jesters, religious jesters and jesters of art.
19 The phrase 'they wittingly deceived and corrupted the youth' refers to the Sophists in Plato, *Meno*, 92A.
20 Plato (*Meno*, 76C) calls the flux resonance or effluence (*aporrhoé*), referring to Empedocles.
21 Its meaning is that when you integrate over the surface then you get a new value, you create or matrix into existence a new form. But this convergence or transformation is a nonlinear integrable system, and not the authentic matrix's linear transformability.

8 Monsters
Creatures of the flux

Monsters: creatures of the flux

> Believe that nothing is impossible for you. Think yourself immoral and capable of understanding all, all arts, all sciences, the nature of every living being. Mount higher than the highest height; descend lower than the lowest depth.
>
> Giordano Bruno (in Yates 1964: 198)

In anthropological accounts the trickster appears as a jolly good fellow, cracking jokes and telling tales. On a more remote and mythological level it is considered a second founder of the world, thus even a presumed benefit bringer of mankind – though in order to re-build, something must first be destroyed, and the trickster is indeed a creator-destroyer, practicing the ambivalent craft of creative destruction, so question marks are growing about him. So it is not surprising that even at the level of stories the jolly outsider soon turns out a ruthless machinator, dividing communities, sowing discord, if not outright wringing necks. Once becoming established, the clown turns demonic. Mythological accounts also move in this direction, where the old prankster starts not just guide but steal souls, being soon engaged in even more obscure and sinister operations, secretive machinations with demons and monsters. Thus, complementing the Homeric hymn 'To Hermes' with the works of Hesiod, we gained a fuller vision of the trickster, showing its truly evil face, aligned with the powers of Tartarus, or Hell.

We need to specify more clearly the trickster's links with demons and monsters. The distinction that demons are two-legged human creatures that have some animalesque features, while a monster is a four-legged or bird-like animal with some human features is a helpful idea, but only a first approximation. We need to move further, using the classical accounts mentioned before, but also Milton and Goethe, here especially the last pages of *Poetry and Truth*, conclusion to his life-long ponderings about the demonic/daimonic, published just before he died, but also films, like Murnau's *Nosferatu*, and its remake by Werner Herzog, or Tarkovsky's *Stalker*. Demons are external forces, spirits – or, as we used throughout the book, fluxes – associated with the underground, who need mediators towards the world above.

These mediators or agents are men, the foolish minded (a type described by Plato). They are not yet tricksters – how could a living man be a spirit – but as they offered their body to be filled and their soul in exchange for the fluxes, they managed to get in contact with the demons, becoming – now as living dead – their servants in deprivation; while the monsters are their artificial creatures, most frequently embodied in artistic objects, but – as the accumulation of fluxes can produce new entities – at the limit can become self-moving, even living, like Golem or Frankenstein, or the moving statues evoked by alchemic and hermetic treatises, or even in Shakespeare's last works, both prominently discussed by Yates (1964, 1975b), not to mention the recent web-slaves and their so to speak demonic possessions.

Depicting demons and monsters was always the prerogative of artists, but to consider such works of arts as mere expressions of creative playfulness would be as naïve as to consider the trickster simply a jolly good fellow. Alfred Gell (1998), in the most fascinating work on the anthropology of art ever written, argues that art, technology and magic form a single nexus, and the aim of such depictions is to have an impact on their viewers by enchanting them thus taking away their power of reason, succumbing to the creators and operators of such images, or other works of art.

Such images have close affinity with the grotesque, even in name, as grotesque literally means 'cave-like'. The term is from the mid-15th century, connected to the Renaissance excavation of Nero's *Domus Aurea*. While the images discovered there, in the underground parts of the building go back to Roman times, the association of such images with caves is much older. They can be traced as far back as the 'Room of Monsters' in Pergouset cave, dated to 33,000 years ago. The room that can only be accessed by crawling almost 100 metres, mostly through extremely narrow and muddy channels, contains a number of composite beings, considered by Michel Lorblanchet, the archaeologist exploring it for over four decades as a world creation mythology. The other rooms on the way contain a series of vulvas, evidently engraved in different periods.

The presence of such images is always associated with liminal times and places: periods of accelerated change, or roads and other points of traffic, especially their points of intersections. Crucial chronotopes include Mesolithic-Neolithic Tassili, various renaissances, or the Silk Road. While this name is only a few thousand years old, the road is much older, and was for timeless times the main channel of communication between East and West, and also the South. The images preserved in the monasteries of Tibet, a passage between India and China, but also – due to its height – a remote place offers precious insights. In one, the altar is surrounded by 'faces [that] are grinning from the silks beside it' (Thubron 2012: 173); in another, the walls are filled with 'the demon counterparts of kindlier gods ... wrathful deities [that] infiltrate the Tibetan pantheon with terror'. Presumably, some are genuine evil monsters, while others are representations of kindlier deities who only 'don awesome forms to fight ignorance and evil', but these claims are just as ambivalent, to say the least, as the activities of the Greek benefit-bringer tricksters, Prometheus and Hermes. Thubron traces the origins of such figures to India (65–67).

An important and recent study, aiming to be comprehensive, is offered by David Wengrow, an archaeologist, in a lecture series devoted to Michael Rostovtzeff, a well-known historian who wrote classic works about the history of the connections between Russia and Iran, focusing on the links between such images and commerce. Rostovtzeff's work prepared studies about the invasion of classical Greek culture with images of monsters from the East through the mediation of the Russian steppes and Iranian highlands (Wengrow 2013: 13).[1] However, the work of Wengrow has some limitations. While the connection between monsters and composite images is indeed tight, to idea to replace the word 'monster' by 'composite image' (1) smacks from the Enlightenment downplaying of the seriousness of such mental games, recalling the ignoring of the serious destructive threat behind the apparently innocuous plays of the trickster. In fact Wengrow (25–31), while evoking the shape-shifting of tricksters and shamans, explicitly denies that such images imply threats, claiming that they rather generate empathy with the animal world, which is the same innocent naiveté as to call the Magi images of 'open females' as gynaecological position, celebrating the fertility of women.[2] Wengrow also downplays the importance of such images in prehistory, while Pergouset cave and the Tassili Desert Mountains, two of the most amazing locations for such images are seemingly unknown for him. However, the emphasis he places on Mesopotamia and the Bronze Age, and the combination of urban culture and commerce being central for the radiation or emanation of such images is certainly well-taken (59ff), and the singling out of the Iranian plateau and Syria, so central for the Silk Road (just as for the magi and rituals of sacrifice), as hotbed for such composite images and their role in a 'construction of the unreal' is particularly important (64–65). Wengrow also mentions the ideas of Wittkower, who traces such imagery to Sanskrit fables and later the courts of Persia and India (108).

Such images, frequent in seals used by Mesopotamian and Babylonian scribes, encapsulate well the 'bureaucratic imperative to confront the world' (71–73); or, in Nietzsche-Weberian terms, the life-hostile and world-rejecting, nihilist character of such activities. Babylonian monster images, like those of Humbaba, were oscillating between masking and depiction (77). According to Jean-Pierre Vernant, such disrupting faces produce the effect of strangeness, 'oscillating between two extreme: the horror of the terrifying and the hilarity of the grotesque' (77). Concerning the technological background for the dissemination of such images, Wengrow places the emphasis on Mycenaean late Bronze Age civilisation, emphasising the foundational myth of Argos, and connecting this to the building of polygonal walls, mythically by the giant Cyclopses (78–79).

In our civilisation similar images were present in medieval churches, around gates, or in the underground crypt of temples and cathedrals, continuing the troglodyte logic. Their role was interpreted as apotropaic, chasing away evil spirits, treating the like with like. Most often such creatures were wild beasts, rarely monsters and especially demons proper. A genuine pullulating of monsters and demons took place towards the end of the Renaissance, culminating in images of saints assailed by demons, favourite themes of the first printed engravings, by Martin Schongauer, obsessing in particular Leonardo and Michelangelo (Szakolczai 2007a). In his classic study the Lithuanian Jurgis Baltrušaitis (1981: 237–238) argues that, beyond the rediscovery of Antiquity, the most important source for the frightening viciousness of such images was the Far East. The first representations of holy men attacked by demons appeared in Japan, mid-14th century, as part of a Buddhist dream-imagery. Compared to medieval monsters and bestiaries, they were animated by a 'new spirit' (246), in particular the 'spectre of death that haunted Buddhist Asia' (265). The novelty in Renaissance West was that such images were combined with dances of death, performed by actors (265) – where we see the hand of Byzantine mimes, escaped to the West around the fall of Byzantium.

Still, these Renaissance images offer more than testimony of oriental intrusion, as they suggest an antidote, as mindful thinking then was still strong enough to handle the onslaught of the demonic. This is discussed in the magisterial work of Enrico Castelli (1900–1977), on the demonic in art. The demonic not only terrifies or entertains, but also seduces, the biggest seduction being to become like a god (Castelli 1952: 11). The demonic, or the devil, has no being, as is in eternal becoming, the flux itself (11–12). Whether by evoking the fantastic or tormenting through open threats, its aim is to constrain the beholder to escape the world (21–26). The solution is not to take up this suggestion, but neither to fight, rather to pray, and most importantly to remain still, immovable (26, 34–36), the only way to get outside the flux, especially when it threatens to become permanent. The ultimate, paradoxical solution is to get rid of all artificial images (27), as 'salvation is conditioned by the refusal to consider a dissolute world as an existence' (35).

The cumulative impact on our culture of demonic and monstrous images was enormous, as 'an enlivening breath (*soufflé vivifiant*) was spread by these effluences (*afflux*), a pulsation in the mountains and in the rocks, the magic of crystal and of flower chalices. These are no longer agreements and curiosities, rather a dramaturgy and dazzling glare (*éblouissements*)' (Baltrušaitis 1981: 296). Such impact became particularly strong when, from around the 1520s, it became joined to an increasingly realistic depiction of nudity, sexuality, and violence, at first disguised under the cloak of mythological imagery. This prepared the ground for the rise to dominance of the sublime, also retrieved from classical Antiquity through their preservation in Byzantine undercurrents associated with alchemy, and which over the modern centuries step by step replaced and destroyed the Platonic culture of beauty and grace that until the Enlightenment ruled Europe (Szakolczai 2016: 67–93).

Monsters and demons are figures of formlessness, of emptiness, but it is not sufficient to state that emptiness is outside reason, as there might be a sensual behind that emptiness. We can only understand the nothing if we can get the idea of nothing, or the void, by getting shocked and terrorised into it. The void might have a content that makes us echoes. Death is a joyless, sad state, yet we are born with it as a destiny, so it is part of ourselves during our life.

The 'geometric joy' of emptiness

This idea is illuminated through a poem by Emily Dickinson:

> A Prison gets to be a friend—
> Between its Ponderous face
> And Ours—a Kinsmanship express—
> And in its narrow Eyes—
>
> We come to look with gratitude
> For the appointed Beam
> It deal us—stated as our food—
> And hungered for—the same—
>
> We learn to know the Planks—
> That answer to Our feet—
> So miserable a sound—at first—
> Nor ever now—so sweet—
>
> As plashing in the Pools—
> When Memory was a Boy—
> But a Demurer Circuit—
> A Geometric Joy—
>
> The Posture of the Key
> That interrupt the Day
> To Our Endeavor—Not so real
> The Check of Liberty—
>
> As this Phantasm Steel—
> Whose features—Day and Night—
> Are present to us—as Our Own—
> And as escapeless—quite—
>
> The narrow Round—the Stint—
> The slow exchange of Hope—
> For something passover—Content
> Too steep for looking up—
>
> The Liberty we knew
> Avoided—like a Dream—

Too wide for any Night but Heaven—
If That—indeed—redeem—
   (Emily Dickinson, poem no. 652)

The American poetess states that while the nothing imprisons us into itself, this can only happen because we have a kinship with it. While it can be the product of a state of mind, it is not a pure invention, rather a heavy burden that we all bear. And we may agree with her that once we accepted the notion that man has a nothingness inside, it is natural to ask where this nothing comes from, and natural to answer that it comes from the great pit of void, which we called, after the Greeks, as Tartarus. There is a good indication in Dickinson's poem concerning how the phantasm of nothingness can gain features as something existent, a steely existence so strongly felt that no escapes are possible from it; even more, it can be eroticised, not only endured:

And in its narrow Eyes –
We come to look with gratitude

Why was this emptiness so attractive to build a whole system around it? Does it give comfort and pleasure? Dickinson says yes, the denial of ourselves into nothing, or circuits, gives rise to ease and a kind of Eros, 'A Geometric Joy'. We doubt, however, if mindfulness could be adopted on the grounds of nothingness; probably not. What the poetess was inspired by and impressed by was the pleasure of carelessness inside an automaton working mechanism – so close to the genuine joy of self-forgetfulness, due to companionship. Here poetic art probably played a part, that initially was challenging and finally became blocking, as the nothing is indeed a perfect circle: the zero, '0', where initial and endpoint are sewed together, as if in a net, there is no inner progress possible, only endurance, a heavy suffocating longing for union. It is so well described by Plato as Eros in his *Symposium* (191D): 'Love, reassembler of our ancient nature, who tries to make one out of two'.

The interest of Eros is unchanging: it is a sensual for possessing, for union, but just as soul-snatching is painful today, prisoning the soul was terroristic for all times: even more, perverted Eros as a circle was a sign of magic, the sterile hunger for sensuals, when someone is grabbed and pulled into a perverted existence of utter boredom. Eros has a phantom existence, amusing itself with life, without feeling its risks and limits. It creates monsters, which can be considered as a post-mortem punishment Eros. Monsters became part of pure construction, as if following mathematical rules; a parcel, a piece of a solid mechanical circling of nothing, with eventless faces living on the compost of an erotic past, where nothing is born, just multiples unite with tangled limbs. Monsters are sterile, though they are creative, even excessively so, constructing and multiplying objects, ideas, and images constantly, in the line of incommensurability, that share no common unit with the measure of reality, where everything is comprehended within itself. The monster, rather, is the living dead, co-dweller of the troglodytes in this line of incommensurability: unreal, unformed and measureless, voided beings. Due to their continuous lying and fake self-presentations, both the troglodyte and the monster destroy carefulness: what they raise is a nil amount of value, that only causes a rumble. They operate with the scale of nothingness, the zero, that they hold as the highest distinguishing sign of union, having no concern for the good, for temperance and justice, which has the greatest power among both men and gods.

Nothing could more perfectly demonstrate the unreasoned nature of the nothing that a troglodyte is completely glad and pleased by its crooked state (see Giordano Bruno's[3] words in the motto). It does not want to demonstrate or prove and arrive or aim at anything else than this union: abolishing the being of others and make them equal with this gladness in its union with perverted Eros,[4] bringing oblivion. Beneath the mask of this evil mind, as it aspires to become established as a merry-good fellow, its existence is revulsive. Its life is the life of nightwalkers,[5] but loaded with energy, until the point of its ability of snatching souls. It is filled by the void, thus became immortal, infinite and powerfully advancing in the transformation of others but never able to transform its very self. In that mutated form of the living dead the transformative processes are always and continuously maintained, so the circular movements are starting to gain physical shape on the surface of the earth in long walls. They are sneaking all around the Mediterranean and the Atlantic, mirroring their underground structures as complicated horizontal spinning-tops with steady, regular and continuous circular motion, grown out from troglodyte dig-outs. The favourite places of troglodytes are those similar to Cappadocia, where calc-alkaline volcanic sediments developed over the former Neo-Tethys sea bed, like Hal Saflieni in Malta, where three superimposed levels of chambers were cut into limestone. A similar Y shape like in Kaymakli, and a reduced well-like shaft indicates the carrier of transformation, just as a rich ornamental design of trilithons, spirals, and imitated corbelled masonry.[6] Other examples include Orvieto, a very old city (this is even the etymological origin of the city name, *Urbs vetus*), at the liminal point in between Tuscany, Lazio and Umbria, or the contemporary regions associated with the three prehistoric tribes that founded Rome, where an underground network hosts thousands of tuff chambers, shafts linked by tunnels that lie beneath the city, webbed together by escape tunnels and grown into a creature separate from the city, with its vitality and reason.

The volume of such networks might be larger or smaller, depending on cases. Such structure appears in a miniature form again in San Salvatore Abbey (in Mount Amiata, the largest mountain in Tuscany, a compound lava dome), with uterus and cave motives in the crypt. Similar structures include the Monastery complex of Fruška Gora, on the border between Croatia and Serbia, or the Sassi di Matera in Basilicata, Italy. It has an autonomous movement like a kind of animal, sneaking, swelling out from the underground into dry-stone walls all around the Mediterranean, where it manifests like an organically grown monstrosity, eager to occupy and dissolve. Its power can be liberated anytime if warmed up to a boiling point and fed properly by sensuals. At any rate, there was something inside these structures that connected them to the mysteries of exchange and circulation, and several groups of people appointed themselves to keep them alive by feeding them.

When we look at the troglodyte dig outs, we can see them how they animated a whole world underneath, mirroring the organic world, but placing themselves into the centre – as if they were authentic parts of Eros, and not just parasitic abusers of its emanations. Obviously as the troglodytes could see only an inverted image of themselves in them, it was vain, dull and full of vengeance. Their crookedness was first to be caged and hid deeply by bends and curves, and then it became visible without changing its tortuous and twisted shape. Their position in the exchange networks they participated in – as their underground dwellings were always situated near roads and other centres of exchange – was distinguished by their quality of being deceitful and dishonest.

The discussion so far can be resumed in four points. The first concerns the substance of troglodytes, outsiderness, as they are not part of life, only identify with one aspect of it, Eros, and furthermore its bad part. They are thus twice removed from reality. The second point concerns their model, which they derive from the isolated organism, but conceiving the body as a tomb, thus remaining true to themselves and continuing twice removed from life, and orienting where the flux of Tartarus is manifesting. The third point is that they are continuously in movement (flux circles of souls, nothing is linear and inherited, nothing is permanently stable), while the fourth concerns to catch and imprison, to isolate, seal and divide the flux for the work of the transformation process for the countless embodiment of the corrupted forms, each derived from the previous cleavage, multiplying and repeating themselves, dying and resurrecting into infinity through the matrix container, which crowns the moist underground. With these four points we arrived at the Gnostic world-view that was most probably formulated in this way by the troglodytes.

The flux is also named as Mercury in alchemy, who would like to escape from the transformative process, so it must be sealed, isolated and eventually divided for the work of the transformation machine by Saturn, who is the drier-fixer of the soul into a new body, the carrier of the living dead. More significantly, later the whole process of transformation would be subordinated to Hermes/Mercury as an authority, who grew into the role of the founder of alchemy, gaining a trickster god stature that has continued to grow until now, culminating in modern technologised science. While the most enduring contribution of Hermes/Mercury is the Mercury-Saturn link, both concerning the planets and the metals (probably a Sumerian derivation), it is, we presume, a fundamentally troglodyte perception about the condensation of dry and wet emanations of the earth into the bodies of different objects, like stones and minerals, in correspondence with the organic world evolving life into continuous bringing forth.[7]

However, as with every process, there are several logics and reasoning underneath. One is the production process: absorbing and dividing the flux; another is the influence of people's will on the earth: until they have started to pay back the absorbed energies by offering their souls for union with marrying bad Eros (in a forced or involuntary way; see in particular the grotesque vulgarity of *hieros gamos* rituals). This is where Hermes the thief and guide of souls has a mythological voice, and a trickster one. The model works, just like in the case of contemporary internet technology: the more you invest into changing people's minds, the more you harvest in sensuals, which you reinvest into the frequencies of the flux, as if paying for its services, the biggest business of the contemporary. With this perfect circularity we reach nothing and will arrive nowhere, only to our destruction, until the complete eradication and devastation of the fabric of human life – tearing it up from its natural roots.

The flux volume is the void – this is why there is absolutely nothing underneath in Kaymakli. The chambers are empty, ornamentation is minimal, the atmosphere is haunted. When emitting and smothering all-enveloping threads of hypnotisation by sensuals, the alienation from life serves as an useful instrument. But it is also inevitable to pay for the flux manifestation service by earthly objects, with sacrifices, as without a hypnotic spell nobody is giving up the dearest and most unique reality for nothing. Still, it is also necessary to obtain the consent of the victim, as nobody can be made unchaste against her will (Euripides, *Bacchae*, 313–316). So we have a give-and take merchandise: as a compensation for giving up oneself, one's virtuous existence, it receives extra fluxes in sensuals, which recalls the technique of divinisation. The troglodyte shafts are hollow and round, like a pillar directed to the middle of the earth, connecting sky and underground water, entrapping the flux that is arriving if evoked to life, as an air energy vibration, pushing the flux down into the deepest recesses, and then gradually allowing to climb higher and higher, as the rounded doors opened one-by-one from the inside, leaving the high and low flux densities confronting each other. This insideness is significant. The manipulator, Maxwell's demon is always inside, and never outside. By taking the principle out of compound bodies (chastity), through isolation, attack and digestion, and so transformation, it gains actual substances. It is easy to decompose matter, just as to liberate the soul: there are no substances that are able to resist painful pressures. The outcome of this are the living dead, who have nothing to do with virtue, moral and good feelings, courage and bravery. They are the product of pressed influences, a new, hybrid material substance, with the new identity of a composite being. Monsters represent something close to commixture processes that are coagulated into living substances. In a similar laboratory set-up belongs the alchemist's claim about the homunculus, returning dead matter to a sort of life, as for Paracelsus in his *On the Nature of Things* (as in Principe 2013: 132), whose liberation was hastened by cunningly evil art.[8]

Monsters, the composite beings of demons, men and animals are frequenting the nothing, accepting that they are despised and feared at the same time. They are supercilious subhumans driving for annihilation and ruin in the cloak of an anthropomorphic system of social intercourses of reasoning and understanding. They are living by refashioning us, transforming our understanding and drives into something else than the one we had before. They embody a new order, where Oedipus must answer for the riddles of the Sphinx and not the other way around, first by abrogating the right to ask questions, and then by fitting the answers into a system, making everyone forgot what were the questions, who asked them and why – meaning in what concrete context. They provoke fear, not only because they present a brute force (dragons), but they represent an enemy against which there is no defence (the hydra has ever new growing heads, the medusa kills with her glance, the three-headed Chimaera's breath is raging with fire). They are furious, ugly, filthy, unpredictable and intensely violent, frighteningly imposing their will to abase humans, to crush their soul. The fifty-headed Cerberus eats raw flesh, with a taint of carnality so typical for the living dead as well – ever hungry and uncontrollable. They are like the monsters seen by the alchemist George Ripley (1415–1490), described in his letter-poem to King Edward IV:

> The third day again to Life he shall uprise,
> And devour Birds, and Beasts of the Wilderness,
> Crowes, Popingayes, Pyes, Peacocks, and Mavies;
> The Phoenix, the Eagle white, the Griffon of fearfulness,
> The Greene Lyon and the Red Dragon he shall distress;
> The white Dragon also, the Antelope, Unicorn Panther,
> With other Birds, and Beasts both more and less;
> The Basilisk also which almost eche one does fear.
> (Ripley undated)[9]

They are immune to attack, immortal, and only immortals can eliminate them, like Heracles. Due to their formlessness no earthly weapons can harm them, as such weapons are designed for forms (bodies). But as monsters are unreal, their form is nothing, though they exist; even kingdoms could grow out of them, as it happened in Najera in 1044, through their recognition. We will see in the following that the need for recognising such mysteries was implicit from the very first in powerful kingdom building. The original living dead mindset, however, gave it a particular direction.

The Santa María la Real Monastery of Nájera

Najera is on the Camino de Santiago, between Logroño and Santo Domingo de la Calzada,[10] in the Rioja area, less than a hundred km-s from Atapuerca cave, one of the most important Palaeolithic sites. The Monastery was founded by King García of Nájera in 1044, on a cave into which a hawk he was chasing flew in, but when he entered the place he found an image of the Virgin instead of the hawk. His fight against the Islam thus received a good omen, and he initiated the building of the Monastery. At the entrance of the cave there still is the Royal Pantheon of the Monarchs from Navarre, hosting the Royal dynasties, including the founder king García. And so the heroic kingdom of Nájera-Pamplona in northern Spain is based on two foundational myths at the same time, the hawk and the virgin or – better to say – their composition into one good omen, the hawk as the volatile element, the escaping Mercury, and the dry and serious Saturn in the image of the Virgin.

152 *Tracking trickster traces*

But the cave of the Monastery is not alone. The whole of Najera is a troglodyte dig-out. The Castle hill itself is the copy of the Kaymakli structure, and Las Siete Cuevas ('The Seven Caves') were also dug out by hand, just like the underground structures of Cappadocia, layered in several floors, with Y forms, repeated seven times under the ground. So city and monastery both were grown out of caves, like the giants Obriareus, Cottus and Gyes, whose father, Zeus, bound them to live underneath in anguish and grief, but brought them up again to the light, saying: 'for remember our friendly kindness, and from what sufferings you are come back to the light from your cruel bondage under misty gloom through our counsels' (Hesiod, *Theogony*, 651–653).

The three giants of Tartarus, as we saw in Chapter 7, added their power to that of Zeus in his dreadful strife and fight against the Titans. Here, in the foundational story of Najera monastery, among the good omens there was the hawk, the god of the sky in Egypt as Horus, the protection and royal power from gods, the solar gift together with the mother, the figure of the cool and serious Virgin, they overlapped with each other, from the hero point of view they were a very satisfactory device for victory. Hagiography then might do their task, but there was something intrinsically unreal about them.[11]

Whatever is the case, in due course the inheritors of the kingdom founded by the King García of Nájera made this unreality the starting point for their renovation of the Monastery. This was instigated by Rodrigo Borgia, former abbot of the Monastery, and completed 1493–1495, thus after he was elected as Pope Alexander VI in 1492, securing irresistible power to carry out his decoration plans. He is reputed as the most vicious of the many infamous Renaissance Popes, and his activities greatly contributed to provoking the events that eventually led to the Reformation and the schism of Europe. The most famous element of this renovation is the choir stalls. The work has been attributed to the Amutio brothers, locals from the village of Cardenas, and if it is so, then by troglodyte craftsmen. They evidently vehemently craved their state of mind into the chestnut wood, producing a monstrous vulgarity hidden behind a falsified state of grace. They shared the exuberance that hooked the earlier troglodytes when they brought forth in profusion all the monsters and composite beings their imagination could conjure up. Overflowing with eager enjoyment to show the upside down, the caricature, the abnormal, the incommensurable, gave a sprightly animation for the awful, rabidly filling the space given to them in order to hurt and disfigure. Everything responsible for sheer energy became sickeningly fixed by their vigour, carving penises, deformations, and profuse ugliness, inducing the spectators to search for correspondences (see Figure 8.1).

Here in this liminal image, as being on the side of the entrance to the Choir, we have all the attributes of the trickster as a jester, except its phallic appearance, so visible in prehistoric trickster images. However, on a closer look, a gap between his legs becomes visible, a later date censure, as its phallus was definitely scratched away. However, a number of phallic images are still present, in the flute form between his lips (the air-bag of the flute having the form of a

Figure 8.1 The entrance to the Choir of the Monastery in Najera.
Source: authors

testicle), in the pompon ending the ribbon of his out-of-ordinary cloths, in the standing animal ears of his head-dress, but even more definitely on the two phallic handles on the two sides of the stairs, most important liminal and also explicitly hermetic (Herma-like) material symbols, as without grabbing them one could not enter into the choir (not visible in the image). One can imagine what a remarkable experience this could have been, in the last years of the 15th century, to gain access to the choir of the church by taking into one's hand a male member. The jester speaks freely about the folly of the church,[12] of any genuine devotion, conveying his disappointment to us, mocking the ceremony, the words, the songs that were sung in the choir. The two dogs on the jester's right and left side recalls the Tartarus monsters, but just as Zagreus, the hunter (an ancient version of Dionysus) and his dogs, captured in the constellations Orion and Sirius.[13] Their motive was also present in the Palaeolithic engravings, in particular with monstrous composite images with humans. Fools have their own history, their time and place, but with their eccentric hats that furthermore have antenna-like erections, alertly searching for connections, they do not belong to a holy environment, being rather entertainers at the banquets of rich households. But other recurring figures of the trickster are also present: profusion, swelling, effervescence, multiplication, leaping of the dancer that is somehow diluted in the underground chambers and thus confounds the jester with the sacred.

Apart for showing monsters, the carvings are executed in an explicitly blasphemous way. Jesus is shown with the satyr features of snub nose and thick lips, while the Virgin is depicted in a humiliating pose, giving the atmosphere of vulgarity, recalling the words Euripides about Dionysus, the Asian god of ecstasy, the Roaring God who was born with garlands of serpents and reputedly came to Thebes from Sardis, the city of metallurgy, promising to the subverted unity with itself and a total release from restrain by his sorcery, thus conjuring up foolish thinking and knavish cleverness in mischief:

> I have come to this Hellene city first, having already set those other lands to dance and established my mysteries there, so that I might be a deity manifest among men. In this land of Hellas, I have first excited Thebes to my cry, fitting a fawn-skin to my body and taking a thyrsos in my hand, a weapon of ivy.
>
> (Euripides, *Bacchae*, 20–27)

Even king Pentheus couldn't stop the contagious spread of unreason, rather had to see his own people and relatives, grandmother and mother devoid of sense, witnessing the introduction of wicked, unhealthy rites (248–262), even acting foolishly and become mad himself in the general atmosphere of bewitchment and defilement, when he became dazed and confused, seeing double. So finally the god, also called Zagreus or 'the hunter', tricked him and exacted his vengeance on the king, leading him towards disaster. In the words of Dionysus:

> Let us punish him. First drive him out of his wits, send upon him a dizzying madness, since if he is of sound mind he will not consent to wear women's clothing, but driven out of his senses he will put it on. I want him to be a source of laughter to the Thebans, led through the city in women's guise after making such terrible threats in the past. But now I will go to fit on Pentheus the dress he will wear to the house of Hades, slaughtered by his mother's hands.
>
> (Euripides, *Bacchae*, 849–861)

Such escalating madness, recalling fleets of hounds, when people are snatched out of their houses, turned out of their wits, hunted down and plundered, can only happen in a state of possession: 'not without the help of some god' (765). This impossibility of measuring up, the lack of a common quality on which to make a comparison is the work of the incommensurable, which contaminates by contact, spreading like a forest fire,[14] and progressing first through the most vulnerable and then through everybody, proving that its *dynamis* is irresistible, recalls the behaviour of fluids, not of solids, so belongs more to the physics of Lucretius than Aristotle.

The vision of nature by Lucretius[15] is based on the behaviour of fluids, on their irreducible pattern of falling downwards and then circling up, producing turbulences in the stream, like the circularity of the wavelength:

> How sweet it is, when whirlwind roil great oceans ...
> Brings great enjoyment, but the sweetness lies
> In watching evils you yourself are free from.
> (Lucretius 2.1–10)[16]

This is not the closed, composed, finite and measured world of Aristotle or Plato, but the unpredictable and overwhelming incommensurable infinite. It is random and turbulent, fluid, like a 'whirlwind roil[ing] great oceans', the flux, where man starts to negotiate the selling and buying of entities that are equal with the flux, namely souls. Dionysus who often turns feral and evil becomes furious towards those who do not want their souls to be liberated by his cult, evolving into ecstasy and bypassing the toilsome reality. The wonder-making King García of Nájera, who idolised his person and defeated his enemies, making his kingdom to grow, at least for a time, was driven by an irrational *dynamis*, an irresistible force.

What is the original source of all this wicked dynamism? Could it be that King García is justified by his faith to such an extent as to gain prominence by drawing upon mysterious powers? If so, then his strength was based on the same incapability of judging, measuring, or considering in any other way than through the incommensurable. And, just as the strength of the monsters, it was incommensurable with any reality, even though they became recognised as success stories, unique sources of faith and wealth. In one way or another, the incommensurable made its presence felt in almost every segment of his success, and this is quite crucial to its main progress, where characters move in a void and the space is infinite, where there is no bottom of the universe and no place for entities to rest, but things move by their own weight and never stop their course or refrain from movements in an unlimited way.

Hence we are now confronted with the U-form structure of the choir, familiar from Kaymakli, with obscene carvings in the courtyard as well, with the cosmology of the circular forms and symbols, we see that deeply buried force of giving forth, create a new, shown by monsters that erupts in this different space and allocation like a catholic church. What makes the uterus motive spread? What drives the incommensurable flow to cover every segments of reality? What is the nature of its dynamics, responsible both for the appearance of the frenzied jester trickster in the choir door and the tearing of every measure in the form of monkey-dog-human composites and other monsters on the choir stalls? With every standard these are brutally unmeasured, incommensurable; they are hideous and dreadful, repulsive and wicked, just to further unlimit the unlimited, as if liberating the spirit from the bottle. Their deformity is filthy like Tartarus itself, source of these eruptions that reach beyond all bounds, in all directions without any rest, as coming from and through the void, driven in various ways, and rebounding in monstrous forms through the various turbulences of whirls: getting into the world by rebirth. They are new enactments for the energies of the abysses of Tartarus.

In order to have a full answer to these questions we must recall the Platonian explanation of nature, and leave apart – or, better, completely forget – the cosmological theories initiated by Bruno about cosmic pluralities, the infinite universe and the cosmos having no centre.[17] If the moving earth is not the centre of our world, and the whole universe is not a finite entity, with its every part connected to each other, then we remain without an answer concerning how Tartarus could set itself upon existence, which from the idea of organic correspondences, initiated and practiced by the troglodytes, lead headlong into the incommensurable. Such dynamism originated from underneath, a setting chosen by the troglodytes and amplified by their dig-outs. It was hidden and almost forgotten, its features were blurred, but correspondences in nature did their work. It acted by causing Tartarus to erupt, first inside their manipulators, and then in everyone that came into contact with the flux, just like wine appeared in Dionysus's protean and fluid pots, as through an automaton:

> Between the market-place and the Menios in the city of Elis is an old theatre and a shrine of Dionysus. The image is the work of Praxiteles. Of the gods the Eleans worship Dionysus with the greatest reverence, and they assert that the god attends their festival, the Thuia. The place where they hold the festival they name the Thuia is about eight stades from the city. Three pots are brought into the building by the priests and set down empty in the presence of the citizens and of any strangers who may chance to be in the country. The doors of the building are sealed by the priests themselves and by any others who may be so inclined. On the morrow they are allowed to examine the seals, and on going into the building they find the pots filled with wine. I did not myself arrive at the time of the festival, but the most respected Elean citizens, and with them strangers also, swore that what I have said is the truth.
> (Pausanias, *Description of Greece*, 6.26.1–2)

If this is so, then mythological foundations had their correspondence in monsters, composite beings, living dead, which explain their success and energy. But this need not greatly surprise to us: the foundations of Rome, or the Sumerian tales about the Ubaid monsters (Collins 2001: 41), similarly evoke how buried energies can be brought forth out of the house of the dead, the Tartaros, with ever new thoughts concerning how to pay for some successes and secure further successes by transporting souls there. Here souls had to follow their own course, getting into the net of vibrations,[18] similarly to the troglodyte dig outs where the network was divided into sections by the millstone gates. In the case of Kaymakli there are seven such millstones, dividing the network into seven portions by their holes. By opening and closing the millstones the troglodytes allowed the swifter, lighter souls pass from lower level to the higher, while the slower, dense souls to pass from back from the higher to the lower. In this way the troglodytes could accelerate, without too much fatigue, the density of the soul's flux, accumulate the density in one level and soften, lower in other. The millstones served as trapdoors between the two parts of the receptacle system, the higher and lower level of soul density, thus dividing the souls by temperature, density and mass, and could transform them, altering their velocity, by placing them next to each other. The density of the souls decreased in one level and increased in the next one, but both moving out of the range that corresponds to normal air density. This is the crucial point, density difference, and the tension inside souls can be seen in the hit or beaten cup forms all around the walls, ceilings and the floors of troglodyte dig-outs that we called receptacles, as presumably they were receptacles of soul manifestations in things.[19] Were they the cradle of monsters? The soul's inner tensions were converted by the mechanical energy of transformation, which can be used to do the mechanical work of transformation by the simple engine of density difference. It does this by bringing the soul from a higher density state to a lower density state. This transformation of the soul generates frequencies in the whole body of the troglodyte dig-out, while transporting higher density to the lesser one, until it reaches again the average density once its manifestations in objects are deposited, like when the wine became materialised in the pots in Pausanias's tale.

Notes

1 Wengrow (2013: 90–91) locates this in 7th-century BC Iron Age Archaic Greece, when such images suddenly intruded from the East, disrupting the aristocratic order through trade.
2 For such images in Wengrow's book, see Wengrow (2013: 75–76).
3 Bruno, who was tried and condemned for theological heresy and for dealing in magic, died in Rome's Campo de' Fiori in 1600.
4 In Agrippa's words, 'no one has such powers but he who has cohabited with the elements, vanquished nature, mounted higher than the heavens, elevating himself above the angels to the archetype itself, with whom he then becomes co-operator and can do all things' (as in Yates 1964: 240).
5 'Nightwalkers, Magi, Bacchoi, Lenai, and the initiated', Heraclitus fragment B14. This is the earliest appearance of the word *Magi* in Greek texts (Bremmer 1999: 2–3).
6 Prehistoric art objects in Malta recall Tassili, the Balearic islands (place of important Kabeiroi coins) and Arslantepe (the first great Bronze metallurgy centre), thus serves as if a link between them.
7 This is discussed in particular by Presocratics. For details, see Horvath (2019b).
8 The homunculus, just as the stealing of the soul, is among the many features of *Faust* in which Goethe intuited the core of modernity.

158 *Tracking trickster traces*

9 Spelling was modernised as much as possible.
10 The cock story of Santo Domingo de la Calzada, among the most absurd medieval miracles, is still alive in the cathedral, where a pair of real cockerel and hen sings during mass celebrations. It is possibly from the same troglodyte mind-set as the choir of Najera, to be analysed soon.
11 For a similar example, more or less from the same time and place, see King Alfonso X of Castille (1221–1284), 'may be the first Enlightenment hero', who asserted that 'if [he] had been of God's counsel at the Creation, many things would have been ordered better'. As Susan Neiman adds, such a claim is 'less harmless than we think' (Neiman 2002: 14–17).
12 These images were made just about a decade before the praise of folly by Erasmus.
13 Dogs have a reputation of being connected to the dead, among others as scavengers. Hekate, a goddess close to Hermes was associated with dogs, while Hades was guarded by Cerberus.
14 We should note that in classical accounts the origins of metallurgy were traced to forest fire.
15 Titus Lucretius Carus (99–55 BC) was a Roman poet, follower of Epicurus.
16 We should mention Leonardo's similar fascination with whirling water, returning in his apocalyptic 'Deluge' drawings, possibly provoked by his reading of Lucretius, as the text was then recently (in 1411) discovered by Poggio Bracciolini.
17 Just to restate the obvious, our world does have a centre, everyone is a centre in and for itself, just as every well-ordered community, promoting the good life, no matter how small it be. It is only the chaos which does not have a centre.
18 We should recall that spiders perceive that they captured victims by the vibrations of the net. Prehistoric and non-modern people had extremely acute knowledge about the activities of the animal world of their surroundings, going into minute details.
19 Frances Yates uses the example of astral magic for the conjuring of celestial gods into temple statues by invocations: '[s]o it would become a legitimate practice ... to "draw down the life of heaven" by sympathetic astral magic' (Yates 1964: 41).

9 Evil alchemy
The incommensurable

> But not all bodily matter is tight packed / By nature's law, for there's a void in things
>
> Lucretius, *The Way Things Are*, Book 1

> Primum non nocere / First, to do no harm
>
> Hippocrates

A central argument of this book is that such a joint treatment of the philosophical problem of evil, and the anthropologically based concept of the trickster, gives a unique access to the heart of our reality. This can be seen particularly well through the paradoxical and joint ignorance of both the question of evil, and the figure of the trickster, in modern rational thinking, while one of the main special features of classical and Hellenistic Greek concerns exactly the very particular significance attributed to a certain modality of evil, and the trickster, in thought. This concerns, on the one hand, the problem of the devil, in its various forms (Satan, Lucifer, etc.); and the existence and importance of a series of Greek trickster figures, like Dionysus, Heracles, in particular Prometheus, but most importantly Hermes, discussed in Chapter 3.

With the rise of Enlightenment thought, the figure of the devil, omnipresent in the medieval imagery, became an impossibility for serious thinking, a mere figure of prejudice and ignorance; so much so that for a long time even the very idea of evil became unthinkable, a mere consequence of ignorance. However, the presumption that this was something inevitable, a necessary consequence of rationality, is refuted by the fact that two of the most canonical pieces of modern literature, Goethe's *Faust* and Milton's *Paradise Lost* are centrally devoted not simply to the problem of evil, but the question of the devil. This active ignorance of the devil has a parallel with the passive refusal of the figure of the trickster, as a central, similarly constitutive character of our understanding. What this means, to begin with, is that, on the one hand the characteristics of the trickster capture with a striking completeness the main features of modernity – exchange, production, interaction, growth, destruction, dissolution, substitution, subversion, or new versions – so much so

160 *Tracking trickster traces*

that the trickster could be outright considered as the deity of modernity. Yet, while several authors of anthropology, literature or philosophy wrote about the trickster parasite in this sense – Thomas Mann, Károly Kerényi, Carl Jung, Michel Serres – this never became an accepted piece of knowledge. However, our argument is even stronger, as we claim that the specific way in which the trickster mobilised, how the extremely expansive trickster figure became in the centre of the procedurality of production has a lot to do with the special, unique aspect of our culture, that led to, we are sad to say so, the well-known technological miracle, which then became one of the cornerstones of European culture – in a strange relationship with the philosophical problematic of Eros, grown into the destructive global war against all chastity in life.

That this aspect has not received much attention so far is largely due to the marginalisation of the problem of the liminal incommensurable – a trope that was for long ignored even in philosophical thinking, as it was incompatible with the basic principles of neo-Kantian thinking; and which even now is not taken seriously in the social and political sciences: the dynamics of the form decomposition. However, such an ignorance of the irrational incommensurable in general, and the figure of the evil in particular, is a tremendous liability of modern rationalism, as the figure renders it evident that the modern, rationalistic effort to attain a pure transparency of commerce, health or communication is an illusion, and a very particular one, as such modalities of purism themselves absolutise evil – as a series of contemporary thinkers as different as Pietro Citati, Foucault, Deleuze or Jean Baudrillard recognised this.

A generalised depravity is engulfing on every body, undermining their mindfulness, an evil lethargy that has combinations and dissolutions, fillings and emptying, pleasures and pains, increases and diminutions, but is always separate from reality in an unchanged, uncaused, unreasoned manner. Of course this is not the freedom from pain, that ignores the power of pleasures, but an imitation of every feelings by an extreme decomposition of the original, an abstract general substrate that works on imagined chunks of bodies and their souls into an universalisation. We became raw material in the pit of desires, bodies in imitation of others' souls, desires, substances, except thinking for good as it is ignored as quality. In the incommensurable everything is considered as a pure dynamism for itself, an abstraction, the vision of a picture in two dimensions, without the depth of reality. Reality became encoded into the incommensurable, good crafts, feelings and thought are transformed into a general, abstract substrate in order to emphasise the vibration of the sensuals for union. A strange, cool and deadly algorithm – scripted in advance – is moving in tectonically formed, enchanted rings over our heads, taking apart our independence, the 'Geometric Joy' of Dickinson's poem. This mode of acting has a distinct alchemic favour as it has a predilection for opening up bodies joint by joint, dissecting their mind and soul and taking away both into another entity.

If this happens, then forces start to act at a distance that have no sources anymore, while events become abstractions, papier-mâché reductions of the original ones. In this wasteland space and time have lost their material, finite meaning and come to exist without any cause or purpose. Unfounded emotions are stirring the bottomless pit of the sensuals, where they become mere commodities, spinning a commodity exchange between the two sides of the square, alongside the irrational shortcut diagonal. In this intellectual liminary that is inflicting pain and suffering and is consuming the fallen one, gaining energy when the previous one died – the incommensurable has been growing silently and sleeplessly, working without any pause, in an eminently conscious and constructed way, an invisible system that was purposefully moulded into place, until everyone was caught and digested, that extends to scapegoating and the mechanism of sacrifice. For setting up of this system, none of the weird changes were missing, cross-dressing, undressing, trans-racing, trans-sexing, and other weird changes, fixing the populace into the position of being interested in nothing else than temporariness. The blatant abuses of people and their heritage became mere slogans in confusing transitions, without realising that the issue is quite different. This merciless energy and passion for perpetual change, always singling out and attacking the line of least resistance, ruthlessly producing results for feeding Tartarus with souls, an irrational, monstrous, operational machine of destruction and generation was working in accord with some very ancient system. The Greeks were the first to observe the incommensurable in contrast to the commensurable, the world as a rational, measured and proportioned one in contrast to the unmeasured, but mechanised and regulated. It was often said that after they had been influenced by the dim remoteness of oriental cosmology, and been informed of the interconnections in nature, they developed the idea of a unique principle, soon made their own: to distinguish between the world, which always is solid and stable, apprehended by reason and reflection, and an another one, which is enigmatic, always repeating itself in mechanical transformation, but never real, though sensually conceived as an existence. It is ill disposition in thinking that is evil, not the incommensurable, the mindlessness that is gained by hermeneutic error, a kind of understanding which is hateful to every Greek but happens in Alchemy.[1]

Turning their attention to forms and matter, the Greeks saw a meaningful world. From their perspective the soul was associated with mindfulness – the divinity has no wants and to have few wants is the neatest approach: it is caring for good will. By projecting forward this image they discovered the universe complete with the earth and with every living being as a finite and unique phenomenon. But maybe their most interesting idea was the infinite soul, revolving around it in various densities,[2] and cohesion between them in benevolence. The idea is unique in itself, as it emphasises the generative and not the destructive side of movement. Here was an object, different from other matters, around which everything rotated, and from which everything was derived,[3] the soul, as while it is an empty vessel, the receptacle matrix

162 Tracking trickster traces

which keeps the universe moving and living, it nevertheless obeys the laws of nature and the loving qualities of divine character, never losing self-control or being intoxicated by sensuals. However, it exists, it is like the incommensurable flux, which produces all those things which we call self-existent: hearing, seeing, sensations, materialisations. It exists besides the real, only in feelings, unformed, invisible. It is a third element of nature, this incommensurable that is in between the finite and infinite, as the diagonal between the two sides of the square.[4]

The incommensurable is a separate entity from the finite as well from the infinite, an unproportional unreality, an eternity that has neither birth and nor death, no parents, only offspring. It does not act, though gives rise to both pain and pleasure, though somehow is intelligent, invisibly existing in a mute way, which goes on forever. The Greeks always asserted the unity of the world,[5] were devotees of the beauty of forms and completeness,[6] and not the division of nature, as everything can be identified through reason. Such reason circulates everywhere, it will never cease to work, it will never die or grow old, and nothing that belongs to reason will perish as such. The Greeks were delighted in reason; they have found a treasure of wisdom in it. For them it was part of the joy of living, an enthusiasm that filled their life – that there is this one idea in everything, living or not. This, however, did not bother the operational mind who was feeding and exploiting this feeling machine, the incommensurable, with the fluxities of the soul. Oriental thinking was always tortured by its own vision of impersonality, its lack of respect for nature, a wastefulness present in its meaningless destruction of life, and its waste of energy on projects that turned out to be completely useless; a vision of the world as senselessness, the utter unimportance of integrity.

While the link between the rise of philosophy and the actions against Plato's main spokesperson 'Socrates' may never be fully resolved, the problematic discovery of some irrational notions certainly played a role in it. Would it be possible that there is a third thing, different from pleasure, goodness, wisdom, reason that perfected the Greeks' life, in existence beyond it, is there anything unknown beyond the desire that every Greek pursues, wishes to catch and get possession of it, and has no interest in anything in which this good is included? Is there a deprivation of all these goods, an emptiness beyond existence, an another sort of being that is utterly unaffected by reality, a nonsense, a muteness – note that irrational numbers are also called as surds, *surdo*, the mute one – they have not been acquainted with so far? Socrates ended his days in voluntary death after being excluded by his own community for the improper, destructive thinking of negativity,[7] as if emphasising the dramatic effect of this difference from the Greek way of thinking. Beyond the commensurable which for Greek understanding meant an end to differences between opposites, creating harmony, the dark negativity of indifference emerged in their thought through the incommensurable, which at the beginning they did not comprehend very well, as the words of Protarchus in Plato's *Philebus* (26C) illustrates: 'Yes, I

Evil alchemy 163

believe I understand; I think you mean that the infinite is one class and the finite is another class among existing things; but what you wish to designate as the third class, I do not comprehend very well.'

This unreasoned, uncaused, disproportional unreality that always existed and never dies but eternally arises, out of sensuals, of pain and pleasure, neither good nor bad in itself, but resulting in oblivion, this emptiness sounded impious for the Greeks, a state of puzzling in-betweenness, and was not something acceptable for their frame of mind.[8] Mistaken pleasures or false opinions due to misdirected perception or a lack of memory that produce a failure to unite with the senses is the incommensurable, but is not yet the evil. The incommensurable implies a lack of ability to behold right ideas, thinking instead in pictures, but due to this one does not steal souls, does not want to occupy other personalities, does not enter a mode of operation to set up a system that destroys reality, dislocating it out of its ordered borders. Its agents are those, and only those, who stepped over this border and set up for themselves the task of creating new identities, thus saturating everything with a suffocating odour of evil. Evil is unable to learn the connection between Eros and good thinking and consequently the beauty of laws, sciences and institutions that are all one in kindred, virtuous thinking. Evil may become a majority,[9] and when such evil submits the minority that remained good, the state of human life becomes worse than ever: life would be dominated with anger and fears, would release diseases and wars and poverty and all that is ignoble with merciless energy and passion, pouncing on and destroying good intentions and virtue.

Trickster knowledge as a hermeneutical error occurs when presuppositions spread about knowledge that ignore the noble patterns of nature. It is a way to render chronic the disease of injustice, which then becomes the incurable cancer of existence. Alchemy appears to be a major source of all the errors of the intellect. It is only interested in producing results, waging wars against reality with the overall effects of utter devastation, best illustrated by the alchemical methods used to debase the appearances and the virtue of objects beyond recognition. Perhaps at the beginning it was an airy thing, winged and divinised, and it was not able to make a transformation until it received inspiration, as designed by the neo-Platonists. However, it eventually grew into a mechanised enterprise of transformation, named as (al)chemistry, then became a natural science, bringing about unprecedented technological changes, animated by merciless energy and passion with which it broke down any object, all the more so as its agents were convinced of promoting truth and well-being. As an example, we should mention Ptolemy (c.85–150 AD), the first known author of an alchemical writing, who is explicit about the schism between man and cosmos. Space and time were thrown here and there, and now man is the one who can make a profit out of it. Ptolemy gained such ideas by standing back and looking at the facts with the eyes of cool observers, from the safe distance of his Alexandrian studies, initiating changes in an oriental manner, thrusting the incommensurable into action. It revealed a particularly complicated division between man and nature,[10] and Ptolemy gave himself the assignment of clarifying the nature of this division as the first step towards neutral knowledge. He eventually managed to show, and before him already Lucretius, that a useful fit could be obtained by cutting things into two, like the universe into the earth and the cosmos, while overemphasising the political significance of the latter on earthly matters. This also assumed a constant flow in a natural circular motion, where the new is just the transformation of the old. While Ptolemy took a seemingly Aristotelian position, his wedding of astrology with astronomy can be traced back rather to Stoicism, to a kind of religious enthusiasm, alien to Aristotle, but familiar to oriental thinking. Not only his smooth-sounding, uncommitted phrases, but their combination with distant practicalities concerning how to gain favour from gods with proper predictions, like forecasting planetary movements, as if practitioners of alchemy were themselves gods, resembled the old Babylonian astronomical practices of divinisation, which aimed at drawing down the gods, or the 'forces of attraction' (Toulmin and Goodfield 1961: 45).

The logic of alchemy as if puts things under a spell, as it never stops moving, promising immortality, as in a way it itself is an eternal, ceaseless activity, as there is always a thing which is not yet split and transformed. Like Proteus, it continuously transforms itself, but also and at the same time transforms things, everything around itself. Trickster-alchemists always change their shape, yet they always remain the same, as they cannot abandon themselves, cannot regain the form they have lost, but are sources of deprivation and first causes of transformation for all other living things, as they are revitalising beings that died. Alchemy mobilises everything that ceased to move but can be stimulated to become alive again. Since alchemy is something that does not come into being by a normal way, through a mindful desire for virtue, it must also be something that does not perish either. All that comes into being should come into being from a principle of bettering itself, according to Aristotle. If this principle is destroyed, then whatever comes into being remains in liminal prematurity, which means that it does neither perish nor is born, it has only offspring, but not *filii*, in the sense of filiation, with resemblance to parents. It is in this way, then, that the evil trickster becomes the creator of unreal things that never die and never disappear. Deprivation is the essence and definition of alchemy, which offered a reckless way to evil, to a mindless existence, losing forever the good and beneficent. Note that once such trickster logic is set into motion, it will no longer need special operators, or evil tricksters, as it will spread automatically by the fooled ones.

Alchemists can flag and advance alchemical thinking by cutting up bodies and letting them fall, like in shafts.[11] They insinuate themselves as correctors of a corrupted world, thus benefit-bringers to mankind.[12] The affinity between alchemy and money/ the economy was always tight, as alchemists always justified their operations by the presumed need to eliminate poverty forever. As Pseudo-Democritus expressed it, in his treatise on dyeing, such transformative activity 'frees us from poverty, the incurable disease' (as in Martelli 2017: S151). Needless to add, real poverty or deprivation is not a fact of nature, to be mended by operators, but almost always the direct outcome of such manipulations. The fragmenting and fracturing acts of operators are injuries, an aggression committed with a fierce and frightening, deadly power for the acquisition of the souls of decomposed bodies, deploying the apparently inexhaustible resources at their disposal, destroying everything that they needed and what they did not need: entities, authorities, sensuals, impulses. The reason for this is that alchemist tricksters have to acquire souls in order to sell them to the flux, paying for the services the flux offered them. While these are blatant abuses, for the tricksters these are just matters of transportation from one shape to another, and after all we all die.[13] But for us this is our only and single life, in this earth, unique and unrepeatable, so we would like to live it ourselves, without their assistance.

In terms of the deprivation and schism of the matter, and following Lucretius,[14] as he followed Democritus, matter can be described as a loosely packed entity containing void and following a mechanical growth 'by no tool of Gods' (Lucretius I: 158–159). Thus, any object might take its origin from anything and could spring from any kind of other matter. It does not require direct filiation, anything grows by chance, from any stock or limb – without divine will.

This thinking is remarkable for two reasons. First, the reasoning that 'if things come from nothing, all things could produce all kinds of things' (Lucretius I: 160–161) is one which will be repeated infinitely, until this day. It can be followed using any materials, and it gives a wholly adequate result in production with ingredients that are passing into each other in an infinite circle. Once things do not come into being after their kind, after filiation, after the *eidos* of the forms, nobody can trace any substance to its source anymore – so any variety is possible, as nothing can disintegrate entirely into nothing. The second remarkable point in the logic is that, as matter is indestructible, things are held together – out of any death a new life is born, so every annihilation produces a new entity to be born. For a straightforward technological recipe for production it is enough to follow and acknowledge this logic of the void, inside the matter and in-between things, as the void is a space of relationships.[15] The significance of the void is that while any state of action or passion implies a previous action or passion, the void does not. It does not become because it is becoming itself, but it is in a state of becoming because it becomes, it is liminal forever. Similarly, it is not real, because it is in permanent movement, fluid, yet, it has a form and so it exists, but it still suffers from a lack of birth and death.

The logic of Lucretius lays down the steps to be followed, taking up the 'hard task' of explaining in Latin the 'dark discoveries' of the Greeks (I.136), so that the reader could see the heart of 'hidden things' (I.145), but confident that the procedure specified will lead to the desired result. Thus, if there is a void in things, if any void is a vacant and empty space and things move in that, and if the void is the motive for any impulse, then everything in nature is dual (I.419–420): not consisting of matter and form in an inseparable unity, as Plato and Aristotle claimed, rather matter and void in their schism. The void does exist, and it moves only to annihilate the matter, but this is their connection as well: so things are schismatic and antagonistic, anyone and anything only lives at the price of the life of another, without the assistance of their own mindfulness.[16] Furthermore, in void where things exist, no rest is allowed to bodies, but they are in unceasing motion (II.95–98). Wondering through the great void is something like an originary, primordial experience (II.105).

The same is true for technology, where a simple human intervention of cutting the matter and liberating its void substance is itself enough for its rebirth and eventually multiplication. As the void exists, every matter contains a void within it, and due to that void things can be cut up, crushed or broken almost infinitely, and made to adapt new forms by imitation.[17] This simple rule is true for water, air, earth; they are what they are since the void is in them, in a lighter or denser combinations.[18] They share the technological truth of Lucretius: as the void reaches the incommensurable, the universe is viewed as something infinite and decentred, eternally divisible by imitation. However, after Lucretius, the logic of the incommensurable was left behind, as a contrasting idea was taken up the Church, which became the dominant view until about the 17th century. However, the alchemic recipes for practical transformation survived in the Orient, in Byzantine Sophistic, and in various occult doctrines, until their revival with Copernicus and Newton, which eventually gained unchallenged dominance in our technologised world.

As Aristotelian thinking was the leading scientific doctrine of the Church, Gnostic divinisation and similar oriental ideas spread inside alchemy, the archetypal proto-science of imitation. We see this alchemic logic behind the idea of Ptolemy. While he pretended to continue the old, Euclidian thinking, he in fact based his system on the incommensurable, half way back to oriental thinking: that we are only methodological observers and not participants anymore in the universal circular move. There is something up-side-down here, even in this kind of evolutionary innocence, which is rather an introductory step towards the wasteland of alchemy. In this way the original idea of the Greeks to explain the universe with terms familiar for us on Earth became abandoned: Earth and the universe became two different entities, and the task of man on Earth is to learn how to catch and bring down cosmic powers for his own uses by divinisation, by the union: 'using it as a model for their own behaviour, assimilating – as it were – the powers of the soul of it' (Ptolemy, as in Toulmin and Goodfield 1961: 157).

The Greeks rejected the reality of the incommensurable, as with it it was impossible to finish anything. Once we incorporate the incommensurable in our world, it is always possible to create something new, outside measure, by division or decomposition, producing something that is indeterminate. In this way division becomes an infinite series, existing in its incompleteness, as an outcast, out of the class of real existence, something without proportion (proportion can be obtained only through homology, between quantities of like kind), but with an interconvertibility between entities. The Greeks stopped fiddling with the idea of interconvertibility around the time of Hesiod and Pindar, first with their views on the divine world, emphasising the self-support of man, the light-heartedness in living, and then with the possibility of living life to the full within the borders of one's reality and not extending it further on, as that only brings the lost, dark, wondering existence of fluids, resulting in a vain growth of wealth.

In reality, the form of the good is the last thing to be seen, and it is reached only by mindfulness. However, once one has understood it, one must conclude that it is the cause of reality: correct, ordered and beautiful. But insensible merging with evil makes a black hole in reality with stamped, masked people, who are bewildered. They are the keepers of a huge monster of sensuals, and they have the knowledge what it desires, how this monster has to be approached and handled by sensuals, strong and mild, fed by souls, which makes it smooth to handle. The troglodytes have spent enough time in the Tartarus to acquire all this knowledge, though erratic, and they started to spread it even in the form of alchemy, which in fact was only a way of excess, resulting in slavery to demons.

The difference between mindfulness and mindlessness might be a trivial concern, as everything could be imitated or learned, but in really important matters miming becomes of all ugliness the most hateful. It is a parasitic method, as instead of relying on one's own forces, it looks always to the outside about what to do. It is useless for a proper living, only serves to manipulate others for promoting one's own interests. Thus, the efforts of alchemist tricksters were of no avail, they could not have a good grasp on reality, rather ruined it with their sick, constant pursuit of change and transformation. They had no beneficial effects, they could not gift the blessing of light-heartedness, rather brought despair and uncertainty with their vain actions, just as all their flirting word-plays were unprofitable. All their transformative undertakings were dirty and violated the intactness of matter, taking away their souls, whether it concerned the artificial craft of metal making and dying, or glass working, which comprised the sequence extraction-distillation-sublimation with the aim of imitating forms, and so drowsing them down. A particularly filthy example concerns the embryo offering in glass working, using a sympathy between the embryos and the transformation of silicon into glass, paralleling the seven metals with the planets, as if these were gigantic uterus (Toulmin and Goodfield 1982: 37–38). A more consolidated example is the use of particular correspondences between earthly objects and their imitative celestial counterparts in the ziggurat buildings for creating scales in being. Out of all this comes the increased possibility of imitating the cosmic void as a transformative (matrixing) vessel, imitating the number of planets, including the sun and the moon, and further on, the imitation of the basic metals and their correspondences with the human bodies and the seven magic squares, interpreting the universe as a subject of operation, division, multiplication, and alteration by the soul, a basic and fundamental use of incommensurability. The incommensurable has dynamism, its use is easy and simple: it is at hand by the simple multiplication of forms. Anyone can gain its power, but not reality, as the incommensurable is not part of it, though it exists.

The existence of tricksters is not the result of filiation, or formed by bringing together equal partners, but only of imitation, by multiplying a greater by a less or a less by a greater, and is therefore always contained in unequal sides. We can represent it by the shape of hybrids or monsters, the incommensurable results. They are not commensurable with the others in their form, but only in the areas of the planes in which they have the power to form, this is their relationality – the sparks on the jester's cap in the choir. Their dynamism does not have the meaning that we give in general to 'power,' namely the result of resistance and inner strength, but a deadly absorption of others as a kind of fluid mechanism of invasion. Filiation catches the absorbing, digesting substance by transmitting graceful characters, fine and stately appearances, while substitution by imitation results in an all-become-one monstrous disgrace of ugliness.

If one follows Herodotus's *Histories*, the difference between the neighbours of the Greeks, who are barbarous and arbitrary, imitating Greek customs but living in tyranny, without self-command and behaving like ill-willed family slaves, a very clear distinction emerges between those with a reasoning mind and the incommensurable without a centre. For Pindar a life should not be oriented to poor substances, but keep as close as possible thinking good and doing good with a gentle mind: 'having the sun always in equal nights and equal days, the good receive a life free from toil, not scraping with the strength of their arms the earth, nor the water of the sea, ... Since the sand of the shore is beyond all counting, who could number all the joys that Theron has' (Pindar, *Olympian 2*, 62–5, 99–101). The Greek vision of the world, which is centred, benevolent and keeping one strong, gave them powerful and magnificent features, they became one of the most beautiful people of their time, a small enclave among the mass of stateless, rootless and reasonless, irregular and unpredictable, who seemed to belong to another world, and this is the crucial fact to recognise about alchemy, that its faculties were derived wholly out of Greece. The Greeks focused on solids, as resumed by Plato, while oriental alchemic thinking derived elements from the incommensurable, and had no better arguments than the attraction between masses, claiming that nothing is concrete but subject to the ever-present desire for catching a form, and so desire is the cause that repeats cause in an infinite way. Alchemy was used to find a simple and more conceptual description of motion, realising that apparent movements could be easily explained by disintegrated arrangements in an infinite and multi-centred environment, where everything is in flow in the void. Following this suggestion much later on modern natural science occasionally recalls a tenuous Buddhist speculation.

What do you see from life if it becomes a delirious turbulence? It reveals two, once rivalling schools now in one embrace. One is the Epicurean, to which the godless materialist Lucretius belonged, while the other is the divinising Stoic school, which combined secular materialism with a unity with the

Evil alchemy 169

deity. This added a new version to classical natural philosophy. The latter started from a fixed configuration of matter and form, from solidity, the Platonic solids,[19] that followed as explanatory model the geometrical ideas of Theaetetus, and also Aristotle's classificatory schemes, assuming a constant natural order of properties. The new, second view starts with a set of more or less irregularly moving bodies, without a fixed space and time, out of which a flux is growing, just as the force of gravity or mutual desire which leads to production, and the transformation of properties. Lucretius postulates the same infinity as Archimedes, a kind of fluid mechanics of infinite production. This became a science, a modern one, which are strewn with incommensurable flows and cutting up species, where everything is in a continuous transition, in contrast to ponderability.

The first view corresponds to the way we had virtually everything in the past: clean air, landscapes, transparent sea and rivers, singing birds and wild animals, all that characterised reality in the past and that by now has all but been lost. The new existence in which we all live is essentially open in form, fluid and transformed, dynamic in intention, seeks to disguise its mass, form, density and ponderability. A ponderable world has been transformed into a leaking pot. What for us now appears as static and turgid is already the result of previous alchemic transformation, created out of something destroyed. What we now have has sprang out of a turbulent desire to express lust by digesting forms and proportion, out of a constant turbulence which, as the world proceeded, was gradually transformed into a hectic war against any measure, generating a world that consequently seems lifeless, and thus helps to justify further and ever more dogged, as if possessed, fury of destruction. It no longer conforms to the five regular polyhedrons solids, discovered by Theaetetus and described by Plato (in the *Timaeus*), but is preceded and accompanied by catalytic substances; making use of catalytic properties in order to increase the speed of alchemical reactions. As a contemporary example the modern media does have a fatal, catalytic role in orchestrating such transformative operations, assist substantial change in other substances, without itself ever undergoing any permanent change, remaining evil, non-being, non-real but existent, becoming infinite like any god (the one who gives, multiplies), thus becoming our god, an incommensurable (when the incommensurable becomes the bringing forth). It has an explosive dynamism to propagate itself and exterminate others. It is needless to point out that unreal objects, produced by alchemical technology, usually have a marked visual difference from other, real objects; and even when they look the same, they behave differently, and have different effects. To give a trivial example, stones on the surface of the Earth do not get rusty, and do not contaminate anything, in contrast to metals, especially those that were merged with each other.

It is a matter of debate how and why this transition in interpretation took place, in Antiquity as well as in modernity. A frequently cited factor is the discovery of the incommensurable. The early Pythagoreans held that all things are number. They are rational, and so are real. A simple recognition of ratio permitted the Greeks to interpret reality as something measured, whole and proportioned. All Greek temples were built on the basis of such ratio, including the number, shape and size of columns. This assumption rhymed with a life in which nothing broke down the lines of harmony, this is why the discovery of the incommensurable in the diagonal of the square created such a shock. This means that there is no size that could serve as a common unit of measure for the body and the soul. They can only be properly related through education and conditioning. But alchemy operated through the incommensurable, in darkness, without responsibility, producing impossible conformities, communications, links, relations, building infinite connections using the flux. For them bodies are just conjunctions, this is the way how a relation can be established, but souls are fluid, can be made to participate in an unending flow of transformations, while the universe is a complex vortex to be caught and pulled down, treating the soul as just a material medium to be liberated from the prison of the body.

Harmonious ratio breaks down for the lines that form the side and diagonal of the square. For example, if it is supposed that the ratio between the side and diagonal may be expressed as the ratio of two whole numbers, it can be shown that both of these numbers must be even. This is impossible, since every fraction may be expressed as a ratio of two whole numbers having no common factors. Geometrically, this means that there is no length that could serve as a unit of measure of both the side and diagonal; that is, the side and diagonal cannot gain the same length multiplied by a different whole number. Accordingly, the Greeks called such pairs of lengths 'incommensurable'. In modern terminology, the term 'number' is applied to such quantities as the square root of ($\sqrt{2}$), but they are called irrational. For the Greeks, an 'irrational (*alogos*) number', like 'political economy', was an expression that had no sense, as no numbers could exist that does not express logos, measure, and limit, while latter confused the political community (*polis*) and the household (*oikos*).[20] The incommensurable remained a perplexing phenomenon for the Greeks.

This result was already well known at the time of Plato and the irrational, as we have discussed in Chapter 4, may well have been discovered within the school of Pythagoras in the 5th century BC.[21] But one can only discover the incommensurable irrational if one knows what is rational, measured and proportioned. We need the notion of unity, which is possessed by an individuum's *eidos*, or entities that can be counted but cannot be divided.[22] They could constitute a multitude, but only as a unity of indivisible entities (Dodds 1951), as part of a filiation when as a heritage the past is preserved in the present. Incommensurability, on the other hand, is a multitude without authentic proportionality, a merely arranged one, a mere convention that can again and again to be renewed, as it has no inherent measure. This became a problem later for Aristotle in his *Physics*. He was also perplexed about the relations between different quantities and the accepted incommensurability of money:

Evil alchemy 171

> That it is demand which, by serving as a single standard, holds such an association together, is shown by the fact that, when there is no demand for mutual service on the part of both or at least of one of the parties, no exchange takes place between them [as when someone needs something that one has oneself, for instance the state offering a license to export corn in exchange for wine]. This inequality of demand has therefore to be equalized. Now money serves us as a guarantor of exchange in the future: supposing we need nothing at the moment, it ensures that exchange shall be possible when a need arises, for it meets the requirement of something we can produce in payment so as to obtain the thing we need. Money, it is true, is liable to the same fluctuation of demand as other commodities, for its purchasing power varies at different times; but it tends to be comparatively constant. Hence the proper thing is for all commodities to have their prices fixed; this will ensure that exchange, and consequently association, shall always be possible. Money then serves as a measure which makes things commensurable and so reduces them to equality. If there were no exchange there would be no association, and there can be no exchange without equality, and no equality without commensurability. Though therefore it is impossible for things so different to become commensurable in the strict sense, our demand furnishes a sufficiently accurate common measure for practical purposes. [15] There must therefore be some one standard, and this accepted by agreement (which is why it is called nomisma, customary currency); for such a standard makes all things commensurable, since all things can be measured by money
>
> (Aristotle, *Nicomachean Ethics*, 5.5.13–15)

Greek intellect was perplexed about incommensurability, as it was incompatible with partnership in virtue and the nobility of the goodness of the soul (Plato, *Meno*, 88D–89A).[23]

While the soul itself is irrational, as part of the flux, its incommensurability needs mindful control to fix its measure, its bodily limits. However, merchant mentality can dissolve such limits, in an attempt to promote acquisitive purposes. Through Fibonacci and his nil, and through other proportion-violating enterprises like alchemy, through Byzantine or Arabic channels it eventually transformed medieval Europe. In this perspective the 'one', the number of unity for the Greeks, was handled as another number, carrying out operations between unity and unlike things, and also started to introduce the 'nil' as a 'placeholder', a thinking impossible for the Greeks – a number without identity is no number, so they did not recognise it, not in the sense of being ignorant, but rather refusing to grant 'legitimacy' or 'rights' – as it violated the nature of both numbers and mathematical operations themselves. But now the heirs of troglodytes started to consider incommensurability as a useful velocity magnitude in commerce and similar partnerships, violating homology itself, the dearest for the Greeks, and bringing instead the affront of trickery, an illusory image-magic, spreading imitation, jumping from persons to representatives, from characters to masses, where multiples have no common denominators, just as in the underground hollows of the troglodytes.

The Greeks discovered the incommensurable as something substance free and imitative, thus having very little matter in it, but a sea of sensual activity. The incommensurable is filled with virtual particles, which are always there, keeping sensuals smoothly or not in the flow. As all those who are dealing with it found it almost completely undetectable – unless, as it was discovered by them, the incommensurable has an incredibly powerful copying potential:

> So likewise it is right that the substance which is to be fitted to receive frequently over its whole extent the copies of all things intelligible and eternal should itself, of its own nature, be void of all the forms. Wherefore, let us not speak of her that is the Mother and Receptacle of this generated world, which is perceptible by sight and all the senses, by the name of earth or air or fire or water, or any aggregates or constituents thereof: rather, if we describe her as a Kind invisible and unshaped, all-receptive, and in some most perplexing and most baffling way partaking of the intelligible, we shall describe her truly.
>
> (Plato, *Timaeus*, 51A–B)

This invisible and formless being, the receptacle receives all things and in some sensual way partakes in the intelligible, yet it is most incomprehensible, as Plato stated it. Its sensuality is the tangibility that is in the soul, the dynamism that accelerates the expansion of the cosmos, and is full of virtual particles that are used by alchemy as fluxes.

The alchemy of the sensuals

The incommensurable, which is baffling and obscure, is a receptacle-like from where elements are passing into each other in eternal transformative repetition. Fire, water, air, earth are all coming into being from one another. Each of them exists potentially in each, and they correspond to one another in relations in the universe, even with a certain continuity as Aristotle stated (*On Corruption and Generation*, 339a11–339b2).

However, manipulation of nature exerted by operators was a disgust, not just for the beauty-lover Greeks, but also for the sober Romans, shown in the anger with which Pliny (30.5) wrote against magic: that activities 'so utterly incredible, so utterly revolting' were accepted by humans and transmitted from time immemorial is a most extraordinary phenomenon of history.[24] Pliny wrote in the 1st century AD, during the reign of the last Claudius emperor, Nero, accusing the materialist Democritus that he instilled into men's minds a sweet enthusiasm regarding the tricks of alchemists about the conquest of nature, as the fluidity of all things stimulated easy irresponsibility.[25] The art of transformation and the traditions connected with it survived for so long ages, as there always remained a continuous succession of adepts to ensure their transmission. It held a supreme domination over people's mind. Whether disguised as religion or appearing as astrology, it infiltrated politics, science and everyday life, from Mesopotamia through Assyria to Persia, as a sheer mania of chimerical illusions about commanding nature at the expense of a suffering world, with the result that our abodes became peopled with ghostly imitations. The written documents we have from the first centuries AD, from Alexandrian and later Byzantine sources, are well documented by Frances Yates (1964) and Brian Copenhaver (1992). Main sources include the alchemical Leyden and Stockholm Papyruses, that offer some hints about the earliest origins of transformative operations: the salt of Cappadocia for silver and the stones of Phrygia for dying (see Linden 2003: 48). The neo-Platonic Emerald Tablet is an important document demonstrating a syncretism of Greek thought with oriental ideas, resulting non simply in the intermixture of religious ideas but of world views, even states of mind, visible for example in the conflation of Hermes and Egyptian Thot. In this way in decadent Hellenism Hermes became a creator god, the source of all knowledge on cosmography, astronomy, geography, and religion, with all its forms and rites, and in particular on medicine.

All these subjects are discussed in the spirit of oriental godlings in a remarkable manner of cutting into pieces and turning upside down the world: 'That which is below is like that which is above, and that which is above is like that which is below, to accomplish the miracle of One Thing ... thus was the world created' (Hermes Trismegistus 2003, II, XI). Jung in his *Alchemical Studies* (Jung 1967: 57–108) presented Zosimos of Panopolis (*c.*300 AD) as the arch-alchemist, who is envisioning torture and violence in his studies of transformation. Thus, when on a bowl-shaped altar survivors are crying from pain, vomiting up blood and their own flesh, the author is asking: '[f]or how does the nature learn to give and to receive' (Zosimos, Lesson 1, as in Linden, 2003: 51).

As we argued in our *Modernism and Charisma*, a suspicious trickster logic results in renovation, for recreation of matter from the dead, an art of transformation that uses as transformative substance pain and pleasure. The extraction of the soul of the matter, described as skinning, scalping, torture is something essential in the alchemical process, when a vessel is provided, the receptacle uterus for the one, who must be immersed and reborn from it. Alchemists take a concrete body obtained by some trick, imprison it in their vessel, destroy and torture it until it changes into something that is in their view indestructible and unalterable. For them torture does not need any other justification than perfecting the matter. They even torture the soul until it escapes from body, as the body 'must be tormented with the most subtle spiritual thing' (as in Jung 1967: 330), akin to the soul. Alchemy must reach every segment of life, as it is an alien substance; objects are obstacles, they must be eliminated, punished and changed. The annihilation of any form and every living matter dazzles the mind with unlimited questions about not only the Gnostic influence on alchemy but, in a much wider sense, the impact of the incommensurable on reality, the triumph of the

174 *Tracking trickster traces*

placeholder on the holders of place, spreading disease, sickness, depression and sadness on the forms, bodies, and things that are present on Earth.

In Byzantium, the Sophists, who in the meantime had grown, in two steps, into establishment positions in the Empire, advocated the idea of alchemy, and were able even to criticise those opponents who complained about their transformative diligence:

> How then can those vile critics censure us,
> They who in secret learning are inept,
> And who in sophic wisdom have no share?
> How can they say we sophists speak untruths
> With their own minds so pitifully maimed
> They give no thought or care to things divine?
> They ask how gold is ever to be made,
> How that can change which has a nature fixed,
> Placed there of old by God the demiurge,
> Who formed its substance never to be moved
> From that position which from early time
> Was its abode and destined resting place;
> They say gold thus abides, nor suffers change,
> For naught can be transmuted from the class
> Or species where its origin took place.
> They who speak thus but trifle with their minds
> And nothing say that bears the stamp of truth.
>   (Browne 1920: 196)

Proud of their craft, in the name of all Sophists Theophrastos celebrates the importance of the Sophist skills in transformation, operating on the bodies and the souls:

> We sophists, and the rhetoricians too,
> Are fortunate and lead a life most wise;
> We know the nature of created things,
> The kinds of elements, and understand
> How, by close union each to each, they tend
> To one new form, most fair and wholly strange,
> With brilliant splendor filled, its make-up such
> That it bestoweth wealth and great reward.
>   (Browne 1920: 194)

Their transformative ambition is unlimited, until 'All mortals to be taught and disciplined' how all things interconnected and transformed by the assistance of knowing minds, like they succeeded to prove it in Astrology, medicine, metallurgy, minerology and plants, biology, and the likes: 'We teach mankind their natures, good and bad' (195), as '[t]he transformations of sophistic art' (197).

However, the practical execution of this design in our view is to be traced back to the troglodytes, in particular their greatest ally, the erotic Echidna monster – the snake with human head – of the Tartarus. They call it the dragon, symbol of transformative change from the earliest days of alchemy, who devours its tail and bears the alchemical motto of three words and seven letters, meaning 'all is one', or that which is above is like that which is below, that everything is interconnected, there is no separation, there are no distinct qualities, no possibility for independent existence, everything is corresponding and fluctuating with each other, universalised and equalised into a common sensual, of course denying their original, concrete, fixed bodies. Bodies are obstacles, they must be given up for the sake of the flux. The Ouroboros symbol was used by Alexandrian alchemists to typify the unity of matter into a mass of vibrating sensuals, as its substance and meaning is eternally one and the same. This was revealed to the Alchemists, together with its economic uses. Their heating and liquidising operations promoted material changes by dissolving the form-matter composition, first killing it, thus eliminating the body, and in a second step channelling the escaping soul into a new, selected matter. Their intermediary action, which shared the qualities of the two elements or substances, was the union, which also much occupied the ziggurat architects, mentioned above.[26]

This is the moment of the void, whose sign is itself the same Ouroboros snake circle, the 0. It takes over place, time, matter, ultimately destroying the body of the world. It becomes incorporeal by means of fake, imitative, copied forms and reasoning, a complete fulfilment of the Gnostic dream (Voegelin 2000).

This part of the voiding process is described by Theophrastos as the second slaying of the dragon, after the first one presented above, with a repeated operation of rhythmic dipping, until the dragon releases its soul to those humans who have been enriched by alchemy; as the following lines say:

> And slaying him again with knife of fire
> Draw all his blood which gushes blazing hot
> And red as shining flame when it ignites.
> Then dip the dragon's skin into the blood
> Which issued from his belly's gory wound
> (As thou wouldst dip a whitened robe in dye
> Of murex purple); so wilt thou obtain
> A brilliant glory, shining as the sun,
> Of goodly form and gladdening the heart
> Of mortals who behold its excellence.
> (Browne 1920: 208)

Their appreciation of transformation is echoed again in gorgeous rhetoric asking forgiveness for killing ('Forgiveness asking for our trespasses', 213), with the ever ready justification: 'And bringing gain and wealth to mortal men' (212).

These are cruel and clear words. There are no illusions anymore concerning moral admonitions of purifications, or the ecclesiastical bettering of the corrupted, until finally in the 17th century the English Alchemist Robert Boyle (1627–1691) stated the obvious reason beyond all these covering processes, multiplication: 'who will have the virtue of their Stone increased in such proportion?' (Boyle 1998). While Boyle was still preoccupied by the absence of virtue in such processes, once alchemy transmogrified itself into natural science, such worries were increasingly swept aside as obstacles in the progress of science.

Even before Boyle, Avicenna (c.980–1037), on the basis of Aristotle, made a similar observation in his commentary upon alchemy that there is no way of splitting up one combination of species into another one, as it was supposed to be the core secret technique of alchemy; that such operation is ultimately meaningless: 'As the claim of the alchemists, it must be clearly understood that it is not in their power to bring about any true changes of species. They can however, produce excellent imitations, dying the red (metal) white so that is closely resembles silver, or dying it yellow, so that it closely resembles gold. They can, too, dye the white (metal) with any colour they desire, until it bears a close resemblance to gold or copper; and they can free the leads from most of their defects and impurities. Yet in these (dyed metals) the essential nature remains unchanged; they are merely so dominated by induced qualities that errors may be made concerning them, just as happens that men are deceived by salt' (Avicenna 1991: 5). This is an abrupt rejection of the possibility of transformation on a factual basis. What such operations gain is nothing else than a mere copy, an imitative process of the authentic one. Things exist as self-subsisting entities, in their goodness and cooperation, while monstrosity is just an unreality.

Nevertheless, as the mystical doctrines of the Alchemists gained ground, the transformation of metals into gold to be regarded as an imitation of the transformation of the lower man into the virtuous higher one, started with the Alexandrian Neoplatonists, began to fade away. All such idealism ended with the 17th-century rationalism. However, even before, the matrix logic never evaporated in the hinterland. It received a full-length exposition in the Islamic period. As the alchemist identified with Khalid ibn Yazid (635–704) writes in his *Secreta Alchimia*: 'Also you must consider, what is groundwork and beginning of the Magistery; which is as Seed and Womb to the Generation of Living Creatures, which are shaped in the Womb, and therein Fabrick, Increase, and Nourishment' (Khalid ibn Yazid 1968: 62).

All the fundamental ideas of alchemy, that all matter should be turned into something better than it was before, perfecting itself, that the soul which is nourishing the body, can be grasped and caged, was the working of nature's bastard child, the troglodyte, whose ambition was to accelerate transformation, tearing the souls from their matter and readjusting them into other forms. The aim of their trickery was to achieve on objects by pairing or coupling them, by creation what nature achieves by filiation. This was done by first dissecting them and then incubating them until rebirth. Such theories branched into ever new

Evil alchemy 177

directions, regaining speed after the four hundred years of interruption by the Greeks, who in 700–300 BC, or between Homer, Pindar and Hesiod and the Alexandrians of Hellenism, reasserted the idea of the limit, the solidity of forms and the finite character of our world. When Philippe II of Macedon in 338 BC occupied Athens, all their ideas were taken up by minds who effectively synthetised the oriental and Greek heritage.[27] As time went on, the general framework of Greek thinking became part of the religious world view, while those who eventually came to be called scientists concentrated on practical accomplishments by their techniques, animated by an impossible, mechanical rationality, where in the incommensurable, as John Donne (1572–1631) wrote in 'An Anatomy of the World' (1611), at the moment when the marginal position of Theophrastos was already destined to become the mainstream:

> The sun is lost, and th' earth, and no man's wit
> Can well direct him where to look for it.
> And freely men confess that this world's spent,
> When in the planets, and the firmament
> They seek so many new; they see that this
> Is crumbled out again to his atomies.
> 'Tis all in pieces, all coherence gone,
> All just supply, and all relation.
> Prince, subject, father, son, are things forgot,
> For every man alone thinks he hath got
> To be a phœnix, and that then can be
> None of that kind of which he is, but he.
> (Donne 1896: 207–218)

Notes

1 This chapter relies on Horvath (2013, 2015a).
2 Plato discusses the density of souls in the *Laws* and in the *Republic*. Due to the presence of the divine spirit, it is dense in philosopher-kings. The soul of ordinary people is low density, but could be solidified by education.
3 The universe is a self-moving soul. Planets and the hemispheres are souls in movements in a transformative vessel with the moving circles of the flux as a transporting energy. They are related to the human soul with their perfect relations and periods. This relation is given to everybody, but not everybody is able to live with it (Plato, *Timaeus*, 43E–44D).
4 The Hungarian term for diagonal (*átló*) is particularly interesting, as is derived from the same root as *megátalkodott*, 'arrogant'. In Hungarian, not only infinity but even irrational numbers are connected to hubris.
5 Behind the flux Plato gave voice to the eternal, permanent principles of good will, as good will is the nature of things, it lies beyond the matrix, it is the bringing forth beyond everything really existent.
6 Souls have to be attuned to a paradigmatic form of good will that exists both separately and inside of us. This is the only way to have good feelings and good will and cooperation with others, because it is the manifestations of all forms, so

178 Tracking trickster traces

our reality depends on our ability to participate in good will: this life is the happiest and the more reasoned (see Aristotle, *Nicomachean Ethics*, 1177b27–1178a4).
7 Negativity was the accusation against the Cynics as well. They negated the values of the polis and propagated a self-sufficiency that was independent from social institutions, pursing perfection, an oriental idea. The founder of the Stoic school, Zeno (c.334–c.262), started as a Cynic and attempted the ascent of the soul to the divinity by self-divinisation, by a unity with the god-head, an alchemical idea.
8 This state of in-betweenness, between fullness and emptiness as falsehood, as generating pain both in the body and the soul, between true and false affections and expectations was brilliantly described Plato, as if capturing modern symptoms of schizophrenia: '[b]ecause of his condition, he is suffering, but he remembers the pleasures the coming of which would bring him an end of his pain; as yet, however, he does not possess them' (*Philebus* 36A).
9 See the ideas of Tocqueville, the most important modern political philosopher, about the tyranny of the majority.
10 One must be divided before to be united, as only what is taken apart can be united.
11 The famous 'swerve' (*clinamen*) of Lucretius (II.216–93) might have been the outcome of such experiments.
12 We have seen in Chapter 3 that such pretence was central for Hermes; and that the 'Homeric Hymn to Hermes' used a hapax to express this – a word that cannot be found in any other surviving classical Greek text.
13 As Keynes (1964: xx) famously exposed the life-hostile logic of neoclassical economics, 'In the long run we are all dead'.
14 Until Lucretius there was no complete statement of atomism. The atomist Leukippos's and Democritos's views were only known from secondhand fragments.
15 The problematic character of mere relationality was brought out by Michel Serres (1982: 21–23).
16 In neoclassical economics, this logic is present in the idea of opportunity cost, which Alfred Gell (1992: 206–220) identified as the animating centre of this mode of thinking.
17 An interesting example about both cutting up and imitation is the offering of embryo during glass making, burying them in the furnace (Toulmin and Goodfield 1982: 37).
18 Density, also technically as 'specific weight', is a central term for Lucretius, and recalls the Kaymakli mechanism.
19 Everything has a limited number of definite shapes, things are not immutable, and could change only by way of filiation, that could be related back to their geometrical composition. This is how they can create units. The five solids can be built up from two simple triangles, they have volume and the volume must be bounded: material substances are always homogenous with their properties and constitutions, which works together to fulfil its proper from, appropriate for their function.
20 The term 'political economy' was coined in France, in the first years of the 17th century, in a few treatises associated with the Huguenots.
21 'The Pythagoreans were the first to make inquiry into commensurability, having first discovered it as a result of their study of numbers. There is a legend that the first Pythagorean who made public such matters perished in a shipwreck' (Heath 1939: 215).
22 In fact, already such counting is problematic, as it implies the power of size, through large numbers, basis of Neolithic warfare ('Silver Age'), before Bronze Age warfare based on metallurgy.
23 See also Aristotle (*Politics*, 1252a).
24 According to Pliny (30.9) Democritus, supposed author of alchemic and magical treatises, even entered various tombs to find the books of hidden Eastern wisdom (see also Martelli 2017: S32–6, S69–73).

25 'Casting your light upon the elements', in the *Alchemical Dialogue of Cleopatra and the Philosophers* (as in Taylor 1951: 57), indicating the corrupt state of elements in nature, waiting in dark imprisonment for salvation by the Alchemist, when they will appear as the 'babe from the tomb' (59). The phrase 'nature conquers [or masters] nature' was the expression of the alchemist Pseudo-Democritus (1st to 2nd centuries AD), used as an incantation (as in Linden 2003: 39; see also Martelli 2017: S153, 155, 159, 165, 167, 171). Note that the expression, just as similar rhetorical verbal flowers like 'nature is delighted by nature', or 'nature is satisfied with nature', simply makes no sense, just impersonating nature and being anyway tautologies, versions of the infinite Ouroboros symbol, and yet, in the form of the 'conquest of nature', became the catchword of modern technologised science. The work was supposedly derived from the Persian *magus* Ostanes.
26 About imitation in the case of Ancient Babylonian ziggurats, see Toulmin and Goodfield (1982: 37): 'these giant temples each comprised seven superimposed platforms, with areas corresponding to one of the seven colours, and one of the seven metals'.
27 As often argued, the real predecessor of modernity was not Classical Greece or Republican Rome, but Hellenism. We heard this first from Alessandro Pizzorno.

Concluding comments
On methodology in tricksterology

> For it is the law of fate that evil can never be a friend to evil, and that good must always be friend to good.
>
> Plato, *Phaedrus*, 255B

This book can be read as a guide in trickster destiny, concerned with method-related considerations. Talking about the methodology of this book, in a strict sense, is of course an impossibility, as the refusal of conventional methodology is at the centre of this work. Yet, this book is a trove of reflections on methods, in the sense of ways of doing things.

Our method, to begin with, is a way of doing *political anthropology*, as we always deemed ourselves. This was certainly not the neo-Kantian sense of a particular discipline, limited to a set of objects, and not even a discourse that belongs to a particular field. For us it must have something to do with real fields, or areas of the real world, and cannot be reduced to mental games, or a kind of thinking about the rules and modalities of thinking. Rather, it has to do with many fields, in so far as it is concerned with connecting them. Thus, political anthropology is close to sociology – at least to the Weberian sense of sociology, also as a reflection on the rise and dynamics of modern world. It is close to the sociology and anthropology of Bruno Latour, developed in the footsteps of Gabriel Tarde and Michel Serres. It also has particular affinities with the work of Gregory Bateson, offering a version of the pattern that connects, which was at the centre of Bateson's undertakings.

But our way of doing political anthropology also implies something else, something fundamental, and even – in the strictest sense – foundational for thinking, in the original sense of philosophy. We keep forgetting, or consider it as an accident of origins, that Plato named philosophy as a form of love: it is not wisdom itself, nor its pretence, that is a form of Sophistry, rather the love of wisdom. Focusing on the specific features of Eros, just as keeping in mind the broader questions of love, is a central part of our method; in fact, any form of knowledge that is not inspired by and oriented toward love is not worth the trouble. To love is not an individual option, but our '*maximal obligation*' in this global world, and it lies even beyond 'mere' morality (Serres, 1995a: 204, the last paragraph in this book of conversations with

Bruno Latour). Without faithful dedication, there are no proper relations – thus mindfulness is a central concern in dealing with Eros. But, even more importantly, love is fundamentally concerned with reality, as the outcome of things that were done following good Eros is the only reality. It incorporates understanding, cooperation and considerations, thus goes beyond parasitism, so well known as trickery.

The methodological guiding principle of good Eros is to be complemented, still following the spirit of Plato's work, with a series of similar principles. These include, and prominently, beauty, a central and by no means marginal issue for Plato. Beauty is a central concern even for science and mathematics, which cannot work without having an eye on harmony, or on reality – we would add, in the absence of a technological messing up. As one knows, the ugliest animals are the abandoned varieties of domestic animals, just as the only ugly part of the landscape is one which was previously cultivated but by now became abandoned – not carefully loved anymore – left to the incommensurable, the irrational dynamism of decomposition.

Still, as just as another reminder about the meaning of political anthropology, we can add that central to all this is nothing else but goodness. Without it, men are worse than all the demons conceived in the imagination of artists. Goodness, of course, is a very broad term, and yet its basic coordinates are clear enough. Its characteristics were discussed throughout the book, especially in the chapters of the second part and indeed the entire book. For the conclusion, let us say that this goodness stands on its own, it is *sui generis*, and does not require evil to become visible or assert itself. For the same reason it is also radically different from mere relationality and in-betweenness, thus from behaviour directed by interests, whether economic or not. Abundance and grace is only there where life is guided not by consciousness, interests, or calculation, but careful attention, mindfulness or *phronesis* for goodness.

Life is the perpetuation of giving and receiving in goodness. It is inherited, in us and in our planet, and is not up for domination and exploitation. Being concerned with reality, we have the alertness to assure that life continues. If the logic underlying Serres's *Natural Contract* and Latour's *Gaia* is right, then the reality of life must be re-asserted, against dominating machinations.

Still, the question of connection regards not just the integration of two different spheres, us and the world, but also extends beyond. The central reference points here again are Plato and Aristotle. For a return to reality we must follow their reasoning, the need to participate in the benevolence of stones, landscapes, images, animals, houses and cities, and us populating them, placing ourselves into the perspective of other living beings, even objects, as – far from a supposed striving for neutrality – this is the heart of science, as again Michel Serres argues. This is not a matter of minor importance, as only in this way, by returning to a proper, mindful understanding, can we approach with success the problems of our contemporary world, by managing to consider the world in its totality, in life and death.

To take into account life on its own right is what distinguishes us from demons. Demons cannot escape their relations, are forever tied to them. However, reality exists outside such relations, and through mindfulness we can move outside the relations encircling us, while we made ourselves 'troglodytes of our collectives', being enclosed in the caves of the media, or the caverns of politics, ignoring the world, history keeping us imprisoned behind our walls (Serres 1986: 170–171). We are capable of renewal through and with the help of thinking, but as members of a culture now dominated by a technologised science playing the game of dominating nature forever and decisively pretend to play the role of victim, but in fact, and for a long time, switched to that of the aggressor.

John Donne put down the words cited at the end of the last chapter in 1611. The year seems innocuous enough, in Europe or elsewhere: no wars or revolutions were taking place that time, there were no changes in kings or dynasties. Yet, something must have been in the air that inspired Donne to formulate with such striking terms a vision that literally encapsulated the trickster effect.

He was not alone. It was around that year that his contemporary, William Shakespeare, also wrote one of his most important and last, conclusive, testament-like plays, *The Tempest*, in which he explicitly bode farewell to the theatre which he came to populate by a series of trickster figures, including Richard III, Falstaff, Othello and Polonius, culminating here, in this play, with Puck and Caliban, among others, and formulated some of his most famous lines, including the words about the human condition that are cited so often that one is embarrassed to repeat them and yet it is impossible not to evoke them here: 'We are such stuff / As dreams are made on, and our little life / Is rounded with a sleep' (IV.i.156–8).

1611 was also the year in which a more irrelevant-looking book was published by the Huguenot writer Louis Turquet de Mayerne, who a couple of decades before published another treatise about the need to regulate fairs. This new book, with the peculiar but intriguing title 'Aristo-democratic Monarchy', was the first comprehensive work about police regulations, going into minute details about rules required to secure order. If this were not significant enough – a significance that was recognised Michel Foucault (1981) – this book was also the first that contained the expression 'political economy', an expression that made no sense for the Greeks, as it was already mentioned, but which would have quite a career in modernity, and not just in thinking, as by its ramifications and real effects it much defined our destiny. Permanent liminality, in all its version, is nothing but immersion in the flux; and the flip side of the permanent wars of the 20th century is economic globalisation, the hyper-modern version of empire building, conducted by businessmen and entrepreneurs, the 'captains of industry' (Veblen), modern equivalents of the mercenary condottieri, and masterminded by the high-priests of modernity, current versions of the Sophists, the economists, distant heirs and inheritors of the ideas pioneered by Turquet.

It is to this play by Shakespeare that W. H. Auden would return with his poem 'The Sea and the Mirror: A Commentary on Shakespeare's *The Tempest*', his most famous work, which performs in its own time and place much of what John Donne's poem did with his. The context in this case was evidently significant, as Auden wrote his poem at the height of the Second World War. The poem was not directly about the war; rather it recognised the affinities between Shakespeare's work and Auden's own tempestuous present. Most importantly, it is about the responsibility of artists for the effects of their creations, thus containing Auden's reflexions on his activity as a poet – including the Heideggerian sense of *poiesis*.

It concerns the relationship between the reality of existence and the nature of art; a relationship in which something has gone sour. Instead of a harmonious dialogue between the two, a strange dialectics developed between them. On the one hand, the 'real' somehow interfered with the 'poetic'. The word used is 'intrusion', implying forceful entry, while the 'intruder' is a stock trickster figure. Auden was aware of the anthropological figure of the 'flying trickster'. Yet, this intrusion, for all its violence, is just a 'bagatelle' as compared to the real problem, when the poetic manages to intrude upon the real. Auden should be read through Heidegger and Gell: the intrusion of the real is committed by the art/technology/magic nexus, which this book traced, through the evil trickster, to prehistoric caves and underground structures. We also found that the monsters and demons conjured up by artists indeed have counterparts in the very unreal reality of the living dead, which can be evoked especially by irresponsible plays with a limitless Eros. In-between beings are real unreality, outside our world; but their evocation is always due to human irresponsibility.

Such plays with Eros were also evoked by Michel Serres when he argued that Don Juan, another 'apparition of Hermes' (title of his chapter), a figure associated with unlimited erotic conquests, should be considered as 'the first hero of modernity'.

According to Serres, Don Juan is the first hero of modernity as a ladies' man, or a man of desire; as a man of ideas or discourse; and as a 'scientific observer of society', or a sociologist – a term explicitly used, even twice (Serres 1982: 43–44). The second time Don Juan is characterised as a hero of modernity, he is depicted as a 'sociologist in the act', depicting modern society 'as a bunch of primitives' (52). But the most important reason why Don Juan is the first hero of modernity is because he embodies limitlessness, or the liminal incommensurable. This is best revealed in Don Juan's self-characterisation in the second scene of the first act in Molière's play, betraying the sordid modality of his 'innocent' desires. For Don Juan beauty, love and nature are not characteristics of the surrounding world, but features of external objects to possess. These objects of desire must always be new, and his desire to possess them knows no limits. They must be conquered; and the most extreme pleasure is gained by plotting for destroying the happiness of others.

These modalities indeed set the agenda for hyper-modernity, including science and alchemic technology, the theatre-economics-exchange nexus, the theatre-politics-war nexus, but especially the question of limits and liminality, and thus the inherent destructiveness of modernity.

Starting on the traces of the trickster, we ended up investigating the knowledge, habitat and customs of evil. Tricksters move in circles, but evil implies a definite turn-around, leading to a world turned upside down and emptied of reality. In such a world only relations remain, as everything becomes voided, and the same system will be perpetually reproduced, without any meaningful substance, once the soul was separated from its original body, resulting in copies, living dead. The outcome of such a demonic turn is a genuine circularity of deprived relations. Such loss of reality is the worst thing that can happen: it destroys goodness and comprehension, but keeps the totalitarian relations, setting up a combination of brute, hierarchical strategic games with an all-pervasive theatricality that hide unreality under the veil or mask of legitimating ideologies, inevitably producing a claustrophobic and paranoid, walled society.

Still, while this book explored our trickster destiny, this is not the end of the story. Primacy, following Plato, should be attributed to goodness and not to the evil; so the central question is how the machinations of the trickster, perverting Eros from goodness into acquisition, in several waves, going back to prehistoric settings, can be reversed. This is the real sense of tricksterology, or trickster knowledge: helping to recognise the destructive character of technologised, alchemy-based sciences, while guiding towards a return to prudency. We must find the way back to live in harmony with the gifts we were given with life, which is short but just enough to establish faithful relations.

What then is evil? If after all giving and not taking, or even symmetrical reciprocity, is primordial, based on recognising that with life we have already been given, then can we reconsider, fully incorporating Plato, evil as an abuse of Eros – especially as exchange relations are themselves its abuses? Stations and roads, transits and transportation, or liminal spaces constitutionally render evil possible by accumulating and accelerating – also through interferences and intersections – its powers to new creations. This is further promoted by metallurgy or any other transformative activity, like wine making, dyeing, eunuch-making and alchemy, as modalities of interruptions. The fundamental relationality of evil – as no trickster can survive without transformation: being a parasite, if it does not find something to be transformed within a reasonable time, it dies – also implies that the terms can be turned around, which can again be connected to the metamorphosis associated with trickster animals, like the snake, the spider and the composite-form monsters, including the living dead example throughout the book.

So, if the evil is present everywhere, cannot be avoided, as cannot be easily recognised due to its continuous change of outlook, what we can do at all? Tricksters always come from the outside, as they never participate, never belong, but produce harm and dissolution through sensual upheavals, as they always take up middle, thus in a sense central positions, from where their penetration is helped by their mimetic abilities.

As we indicated at the start of the book, we cannot start with the simple distinction between good and evil, as this is only an alchemic technique for the better dissection of things. Instead, we suggested a method by proposing similarities and quasi similarities, through ways of imitation. Following this, the difference between modalities of Eros does not depend on a table of values, but implies a sustained deviation from its rootedness in the basic principles sustaining the continuity of life. Eros is the strongest sensual in the universe, which can only be separated from life through specific machinations, for which we used the term alchemy.

Alchemy is a proto-technique for approaching, miming, subverting, subjecting, dissecting, assimilating, and reconstructing. It is a technique for leaching the whole of Eros, splitting it into two and appropriating its destructive, acquisitive part for its own interests. The aim of alchemy, and its heir, technology, is to dissect ever more objects and thus to possess ever more souls, and Eros is the best means to reach such ends. So the trickster and evil are products of human machination, and by setting alchemy in motion manage to reduce the most wonderful generative force of nature, Eros, into a lie, an independent creature of destruction, which generalises, universalises, globalises everything, as it is possessive: it totalises substitution.

The trickster is unreality and absurdity itself, thus producing evil, whenever it is irresponsibly set in motion, whether by yielding to its incommensurable attraction or by resisting it. Instead of doing so, and following Plato, it can indeed become invisible in good thinking, losing its dynamism if it is left alone.

So it should not be disturbed.

Bibliography

Unless otherwise indicated, all classical authors are cited using the standard bilingual Loeb Library edition.

Agamben, Giorgio (1998) *Homo Sacer*, Stanford, CA: Stanford University Press.
Agnew, Jean-Christophe (1986) *Worlds Apart: The Market and the Theater in Anglo-American Thought, 1550–1750*, Cambridge: Cambridge University Press.
Alexander, Jeffrey (2003) 'A cultural sociology of evil', in J. Alexander, *The Meanings of Social Life: A Cultural Sociology*, Oxford: Oxford University Press.
Aratus (1921) in *Callimachus, Hymns and Epigrams. Lycophron. Aratus*, trans. A. W. Mair and G. R. Mair, Loeb Classical Library vol. 129, London: William Heinemann.
Avicenna (1991) 'De Congelatione', in W. Newman, *The Summa Perfectionis of Pseudo-Geber*, Leiden: Brill.
Baltrušaitis, Jurgis (1981) *Le Moyen Âge fantastique: antiquités et exotismes dans l'art gothique*, Paris: Flammarion.
Bateson, Gregory (1958) *Naven*, Stanford, CA: Stanford University Press. [1936]
Bateson, Gregory (2000) *Steps to an Ecology of Mind*, New York: Ballantine. [1972]
Bateson, Gregory (2002) *Mind and Nature: A Necessary Unity*, Cresshill, NJ: Hampton Press.
Bateson, Gregory (2005) *Angels Fear: Towards an Epistemology of the Sacred*, Cresshill, NJ: Hampton Press.
Baudrillard, Jean (1990) *La transparence du mal*, Paris: Galilée.
Baudrillard, Jean (2013) *The Intelligence of Evil: Or, the Lucidity Pact*, London: Bloomsbury.
Beekes, Robert (2010) *Etymological Dictionary of Greek*, Leiden: Brill.
Binswanger, Hans C. (1994) *Money and Magic: A Critique of the Modern Economy in the Light of Goethe's Faust*, Chicago, IL: University of Chicago Press.
Blakely, Sandra (1999) 'Smelting and sacrifice: comparative analysis of Greek and Near Eastern cult sites from the Late Bronze through the Classical periods', in S. M. Young, M. Pollard, P. Budd, and R. A. Ixer (eds), *Metals in Antiquity*, Oxford: Archaeopress.
Blakely, Sandra (2000) 'Madness in the body politic: Kouretes, Korybantes, and the politics of Shamanism', in J. Hubert (ed.), *The Archaeology and Anthropology of Madness, Disability and Social Exclusion*, London: Routledge.
Blakely, Sandra (2006) *Myth, Ritual, and Metallurgy in Ancient Greece and Recent Africa*, Cambridge: Cambridge University Press.

Blakely, Sandra (2012) 'Toward an archaeology of secrecy: power, paradox, and the Great Gods of Samothrace', *Archaeological Papers of the American Anthropology Association* 21(1): 49–71.
Boland, Tom (2008) 'Critique as imitative rivalry: George Orwell as political anthropologist', *International Political Anthropology* 1(1): 77–91.
Bowersock, Glen (2004) 'Artemidorus and the second sophistic', in B. Borg (ed.) *Paideia: The World of the Second Sophistic*, Berlin: Walter de Gruyter.
Bowman, Glenn (2019) 'Walling as encystation: a socio-historical inquiry', in A. Horvath, M. Benta and J. Davison (eds), *Walling, Boundaries and Liminality: A Political Anthropology of Transformations*, London: Routledge.
Boyle, Robert (1998) 'An historical account of a degradation of gold made by an antielixir: a strange chymical narrative', in L. M. Principe, *The Aspiring Adept: Robert Boyle and His Alchemical Quest*, Princeton, NJ: Princeton University Press.
Bremmer, Jan N. (1999) 'The birth of the term "magic"', *Zeitschrift für Papyrologie und Epigraphik* 126: 1–12.
Bright, William (1993) *A Coyote Reader*, Berkeley, CA: University of California Press.
Brown, Norman (1969) *Hermes the Thief*, New York: Vintage. [1947]
Browne, C. A. (1920) 'The poem of the philosopher Theophrastos upon the sacred art: a metrical translation with comments upon the history of alchemy', *The Scientific Monthly* 11(3): 193–214.
Burkert, Walter (1984) 'Sacrificio-sacrilegio: il Trickster fondatore', *Studi Storici* 25: 835–845.
Burkert, Walter (1987) *Ancient Mystery Cults*, Cambridge, MA: Harvard University Press.
Burnyeat, John (1990) *The Theaetetus of Plato*, Indianapolis, IN: Hackett.
Calasso, Roberto (1983) *La rovina di Kasch*, Milan: Adelphi.
Calasso, Roberto (1988) *Le nozze di Cadmo e Armonia*, Milan: Adelphi.
Calasso, Roberto (2010) *L'Ardore*, Milan: Adelphi.
Calasso, Roberto (2016) *Il cacciatore celeste*, Milan: Adelphi.
Calasso, Roberto (2017) *L'Innominabile attuale*, Milan: Adelphi.
Camus, Albert (1956) *La chute*, Paris: Gallimard.
Canguilhem, Georges (1978) *On the Normal and the Pathological*, Dordrecht: Reidel.
Castelli, Enrico (1952) *Il demoniaco nell'arte*, Milan: Electa.
Chappell, Sophie Grace (2013) 'Plato on knowledge in the Theaetetus', *The Stanford Encyclopedia of Philosophy* (Winter edition), Edward N. Zalta (ed.), retrieved from https://plato.stanford.edu/archives/win2013/entries/plato-theaetetus (accessed 4 April 2019).
Citati, Pietro (2000) *Il male assoluto nel cuore del romanzo dell'Ottocento*, Milan: Mondadori.
Clover, Carol J. and John Lindow (eds) (2005) *Old Norse-Icelandic Literature: A Critical Guide*, Toronto: University of Toronto Press.
Collins, Billie Jean (2001) *A History of the Animal World in the Ancient Near East*, Leiden: Brill.
Conrad, Joseph (1999) *Heart of Darkness*, Hertfordshire: Wordsworth.
Cooper, John M. (ed.) (1997) *Plato's Complete Works*, Indianapolis, IN: Hackett Publishing.
Copenhaver, Brian P. (1992) *Hermetica*, Cambridge: Cambridge University Press.
Détienne, Marcel (1989) *Dionysos at Large*, Cambridge, MA: Harvard University Press.
Détienne, Marcel (2007) *The Greeks and Us*, Cambridge: Polity Press.

Bibliography

Détienne, Marcel and Jean-Pierre Vernant (1978) *Cunning Intelligence in Greek Culture and Society*, Brighton: Harvester Press.
de Vaan, Michiel (2008) *Etymological Dictionary of Latin and the Other Italic Languages*, Leiden: Brill.
Dews, Peter (2008) *The Idea of Evil*, Oxford: Blackwell.
Dexter, Miriam R. and Victor H. Mair (2010) *Sacred Display: Divine and Magical Female Figures of Eurasia*, Amherst, NY: Cambria Press.
Dieterlen, Germaine (1989) 'Masks and mythology among the Dogon', *African Arts* 22(3): 34–43.
Diogenes Laertius (1925) *Lives of Eminent Philosophers*, Cambridge, MA: Harvard University Press.
Dodds, E. R. (1951) *The Greeks and the Irrational*, Berkeley, CA: University of California Press.
Dumézil, Georges (1986) *Loki*, Paris: Flammarion.
Euripides (1973) *Bacchae*, ed. E. R. Dodds, Oxford: Clarendon Press.
Evans-Pritchard, E. E. (ed.) (1967) *The Zande Trickster*, Oxford: Clarendon Press.
Evans-Pritchard, E. E. (1976) *Witchcraft, Oracles and Magic Among the Azande*, Oxford: Oxford University Press. [1937]
Foucault, Michel (1966) *Les mots et les choses*, Paris: Gallimard.
Foucault, Michel (1981) 'Omnes et Singulatim: Towards a Criticism of "Political Reason"', in S. M. McMurrin (ed.), *The Tanner Lectures on Human Values*, Salt Lake City, UT: University of Utah Press.
Gell, Alfred (1992) 'The technology of enchantment and the enchantment of technology', in J. Coote and A. Shelton (eds), *Anthropology, Art and Aesthetics*, Oxford: Clarendon.
Gell, Alfred (1998) *Art and Agency: An Anthropological Theory*, Oxford: Clarendon Press.
Germain, Gilbert (2019) 'Technology and the subversion of control', in A. Horvath, C. F. Roman and G. Germain (eds), *Divinization and Technology: The Political Anthropology of Subversion*, London: Routledge.
Gernet, Louis (2001) *Recherches sur le développement de la pensée juridique et morale en Grèce*, Paris: Albin Michel. [1917]
Gillies, Eva (1976) 'Introduction', in E. E. Evans-Pritchard, *Witchcraft, Oracles and Magic Among the Azande*, Oxford: Oxford University Press.
Girard, René (1961) *Mensonge romantique et vérité romanesque*, Paris: Grasset.
Goody, Jack (2012) *Metals, Culture and Capitalism: An Essay on the Origins of the Modern World*, Cambridge: Cambridge University Press.
Guenther, Mathias (1999) *Tricksters and Trancers: Bushman Religion and Society*, Bloomington, IN: Indiana University Press.
Head, Barclay V. (1964) *A Catalogue of Greek Coins in the British Museum*, Bologna: Forni.
Heath, Thomas L. (1939) *Greek Mathematics*, London: Heinemann.
Heidegger, Martin (2017) *Ponderings XII–XV: Black Notebooks, 1939–1941*, Bloomington, IN: Indiana University Press.
Hermes Trismegistus (2003) 'The emerald tablet', *Gurdjieff Electronic Publishing* 7: 1.
Hesiod (1977) *Hesiod, The Homeric Hymns and Homerica*, Cambridge, MA: Harvard University Press.
Horvath, Agnes (1998) 'Tricking into the position of the outcast', *Political Psychology* 19(3): 331–347.

Bibliography 189

Horvath, Agnes (2008) 'Mythology and the trickster: interpreting communism', in A. Wöll and H. Wydra (eds), *Democracy and Myth in Russia and Eastern Europe*, London: Routledge.

Horvath, Agnes (2010) 'Pulcinella, or the metaphysics of the Nulla: in between politics and theatre', *History of the Human Sciences* 23(2): 47–67.

Horvath, Agnes (2013) *Modernism and Charisma*, London: Palgrave.

Horvath, Agnes (2015a) 'The genealogy of political alchemy: the technological invention of identity change', in Agnes Horvath, Bjørn Thomassen and Harald Wydra (eds), *Breaking Boundaries: Varieties of Liminality*, Oxford: Berghahn.

Horvath, Agnes (2015b) 'Memories and the self in the desert paintings of Tassili: the anthropology of the past', *International Political Anthropology* 8(2): 7–24.

Horvath, Agnes (2019a) 'Walling Europe: The perverted linear transformation', in A. Horvath, M. Benţa and J. Davison (eds), *Walling, Boundaries and Liminality: A Political Anthropology of Transformations*, London: Routledge.

Horvath, Agnes (2019b) 'Charisma/Trickster: on the twofold nature of power', in Bjørn Thomassen and Harald Wydra (eds), *Handbook of Political Anthropology*, Cheltenham: Edward Elgar.

Horvath, Agnes (2019c) 'Stepping into sterility', in A. Horvath, C. F. Roman and G. Germain (eds), *Divinization and Technology: The Political Anthropology of Subversion*, London: Routledge.

Horvath, Agnes, Camil F. Roman and Gilbert Germain (eds) (2019) *Divinization and Technology: The Political Anthropology of Subversion*, London: Routledge.

Horvath, Agnes and Arpad Szakolczai (2018a) *Walking into the Void: A Historical Sociology and Political Anthropology of Walking*, London: Routledge.

Horvath, Agnes and Arpad Szakolczai (2018b) 'Political Anthropology', in S. Turner and W. Outhwaite (eds), *Sage Handbook of Political Sociology*, London: Sage.

Horvath, Agnes and Bjørn Thomassen (2008) 'Mimetic errors in liminal schismogenesis: on the political anthropology of the trickster', *International Political Anthropology* 1(1): 3–24.

Horvath, Agnes, Bjørn Thomassen and Harald Wydra (eds) (2015) *Breaking Boundaries: Varieties of Liminality*, Oxford: Berghahn.

Hyde, Lewis (1983) *The Gift*, New York: Vintage.

Hyde, Lewis (1999) *Trickster Makes this World*, New York: North Point.

Jonsen, Albert R. and Stephen Toulmin (1988) *The Abuse of Casuistry*, Berkeley, CA: University of California Press.

Jung, Carl G. (1967) *Alchemical Studies*, Princeton, NJ: Princeton University Press.

Kant, Immanuel (2018) *Religion within the Boundaries of Mere Reason*, Cambridge: Cambridge University Press.

Kerényi, Károly (1976) *Dionysos: Archetypal Image of Indestructible Life*, Princeton, NJ: Princeton University Press.

Kerényi, Károly (1980) *Miti e misteri*, Turin: Bollati Boringhieri. [1949]

Kerényi, Károly (1986) *Hermes, Guide of Souls: The Mythologem of the Masculine Source of Life*, New York: Spring Publications. [1943]

Kerényi, Károly (1991) *Prometheus: Archetypal Image of Human Existence*, Princeton, NJ: Princeton University Press. [1963]

Keynes, John Maynard (1964) *The General Theory of Employment, Interest, and Money*, New York: Harcourt Brace Jovanovich. [1936]

Khalid ibn Yazid (1968) '*Secreta Alchimia*', in E. J. Holmyard, *Alchemy*, Harmondsworth: Penguin.

Bibliography

Kierkegaard, Søren (1988) *Stages on Life's Way*, Princeton, NJ: Princeton University Press.
Koselleck, Reinhart (1988) *Critique and Crisis*, Oxford: Berg.
Layard, John W. (1930) 'Malekula: flying tricksters, ghosts, gods, and epileptics', *The Journal of the Royal Anthropological Institute of Great Britain and Ireland* 60: 501–524.
Lee, Mi-Kyoun (2005) *Epistemology After Protagoras*, Oxford: Oxford University Press.
Lhote, Henri (1959) *The Search for the Tassili Frescoes*, London: Hutchinson.
Liddell, Henry G. and Robert Scott (1951) *A Greek–English Lexicon*, Oxford: Clarendon.
Linden, Stanton J. (ed.) (2003) *The Alchemy Reader: From Hermes Trismegistus to Isaac Newton*, Cambridge: Cambridge University Press.
Lucretius, Titus Carus (1986) *De rerum natura*, C. Bailey (ed.), Oxford: Clarendon.
Lwoff, Stéphane (1941) 'Gravures à représentations d'humains du Magdalénien III. Fouilles de La Marche, commune de Lussac-les-Châteaux (Vienne)', *Bulletin de la Société préhistorique de France* 38(7–8): 145–161.
Lwoff, Stéphane (1943) 'La Marche, Commune de Lussac-les-Châteaux (Vienne)', *Bulletin de la Société préhistorique de France* 40(7–9): 166–180.
Mair, Victor H. (1990) 'Old Sinitic *Myag, Old Persian Maguš and English magician', *Early China* 15, 27–47.
Mair, Victor H. (2012) 'The earliest identifiable written Chinese character', in M. E. Huld, K. Jones-Bley and D. Miller (eds), *Archaeology and Language: Indo-European studies presented to James P. Mallory*, Washington, DC: Institute for the Study of Man.
Marshall, Emily Z. (2007) 'Liminal Anansi: symbol of order and chaos; an exploration of Anansi's roots amongst the Asante of Ghana', *Caribbean Quarterly* 53(3): 30–40.
Martelli, Matteo (2017) *The Four Books of Pseudo-Democritus*, London: Routledge.
Mauss, Marcel (1968) *Oeuvres I*, Paris: Minuit.
Mauss, Marcel (2003) *On Prayer*, Oxford: Berghahn.
McDowell, John (ed.) (1973) *Plato: Theaetetus*, Oxford: Clarendon Press.
Morrisson, Mark (2007) *Modern Alchemy*, Oxford: Oxford University Press.
Murphy, Howard (2003) 'Some concluding anthropological reflections', in M. Mauss, *On Prayer*, Oxford: Berghahn.
Neiman, Susan (2002) *Evil in Modern Thought: An Alternative History of Philosophy*, Princeton: Princeton University Press.
Onions, Charles Talbut (ed.) (1966) *The Oxford Dictionary of English Etymology*, Oxford: Clarendon Press.
Overing, Joanna (1985) 'There is no end to evil: the guilty innocents and their fallible god', in D. Parkin (ed.), *The Anthropology of Evil*, Oxford: Blackwell.
Patočka, Jan (1983) *Platon et l'Europe*, Paris: Verdier.
Pelton, Robert D. (1980) *The Trickster in West Africa*, Berkeley, CA: University of California Press.
Péricard, Léon, Stéphane Lwoff (1940) 'La Marche, commune de Lussac-les-Châteaux (Vienne): Premier atelier de Magdalénien III à dalles gravées mobiles (campagnes de fouilles 1937–1938)', *Bulletin de la Société préhistorique de France* 37(7–9): 155–180.
Pindar (1978) *The Odes of Pindar*, edited and translated by John Sandys, Cambridge, MA: Harvard University Press.

Pizzorno, Alessandro (2000) 'Risposte e proposte', in D. Della Porta, M. Greco and A. Szakolczai (eds), *Identità, riconoscimento e scambio: Saggi in onore di Alessandro Pizzorno*, Bari: Laterza.
Pizzorno, Alessandro (2007) *Il velo della diversità: Studi su razionalità e riconoscimento*, Milano: Feltrinelli.
Pizzorno, Alessandro (2008) 'Rationality and recognition', in D. della Porta and M. Keating (eds) *Approaches and Methodologies in the Social Sciences: A Pluralist Perspective*, Cambridge: Cambridge University Press.
Pizzorno, Alessandro (2010) 'The mask: an essay', *International Political Anthropology* 3(1): 5–28. [1960]
Powers, William K. (1986) *Sacred Language*, Norman, OK: Oklahoma University Press.
Principe, Lawrence M. (2013) *The Secrets of Alchemy*, Chicago, IL: University of Chicago Press.
Radin, Paul (1924) *Monotheism among Primitive Peoples*, London: Allen and Unwin.
Radin, Paul (1927) *Primitive Man as Philosopher*, London: D. Appleton.
Radin, Paul (1937) *Primitive Religion: Its nature and origin*, New York: The Viking Press.
Radin, Paul (1972) *The Trickster: A Study in American Indian Mythology*, with a commentary by Karl Kerényi and Carl G. Jung, New York: Schocken. [1954]
Rayor, Diane J. (ed.) (2004) *The Homeric Hymns*, Harmondsworth: Penguin.
Ricketts, M. L. (1965) 'The North American Indian trickster', *History of Religions* 5, 327–350.
Ripley, G. (Undated) *Alchemical Works: The Compound of Alchemy & al.*, retrieved from www.labirintoermetico.com/01alchimia/Ripley_G_Compound_of_Alchemy_et_al.pdf (accessed 24 April 2019).
Saint-Périer, R. de (1935) 'Quelques oeuvres d'art de la grotte d'Isturitz', *Bulletin de la Société préhistorique française* 32, 1: 64–77.
Sedley, David (2003) *Plato's Cratylus*, Cambridge: Cambridge University Press.
Sedley, David (2004) *The Midwife of Platonism: Text and subtext in Plato's Theaetetus*, Oxford: Clarendon Press.
Serres, Michel (1982) *Hermes: Science, Literature, Philosophy*, Baltimore, MD: Johns Hopkins University Press.
Serres, Michel (1986) *Détachement: Apologue*, Paris: Flammarion.
Serres, Michel (1992) *Le contrat naturel*, Paris: Flammarion.
Serres, Michel (1995a) *Conversations on Science, Culture, and Time*, with Bruno Latour, Ann Arbor, MI: University of Michigan Press.
Serres, Michel (1995b) *Genesis*, Ann Arbor, MI: University of Michigan Press.
Serres, Michel (2014) *Le Parasite*, Paris: Fayard. [1980]
Singer, André (1972) 'The trickster theme: Winnebago and Azande', in A. Singer and B. V. Street (eds), *Zande Themes: Essays Presented to Sir Edward Evans-Pritchard*, Oxford: Basil Blackwell.
Singer, André and Brian V. Street (eds), (1972) *Zande Themes: Essays Presented to Sir Edward Evans-Pritchard*, Oxford: Basil Blackwell.
Snodgrass, Anthony (1980) *Archaic Greece*, London: J. M. Dent.
Stephenson, Roger H. (2000) 'The political import of Goethe's *Reineke Fuchs*', in K. Varty (ed.), *Reynard the Fox*, New York: Berghahn Books.
Szakolczai, Arpad (2000) *Reflexive Historical Sociology*, London: Routledge.

Bibliography

Szakolczai, Arpad (2007a) *Sociology, Religion and Grace: A Quest for the Renaissance*, London: Routledge.
Szakolczai, Arpad (2007b) 'Image-magic in *A Midsummer Night's Dream*: power and modernity from Weber to Shakespeare', *History of the Human Sciences* 20(4): 1–26.
Szakolczai, Arpad (2009) 'Liminality and experience: structuring transitory situations and transformative events', *International Political Anthropology* 2(1): 141–172.
Szakolczai, Arpad (2013) *Comedy and the Public Sphere: The Re-birth of Theatre as Comedy and the Genealogy of the Modern Public Arena*, London: Routledge.
Szakolczai, Arpad (2016) *Novels and the Sociology of the Contemporary*, London: Routledge.
Szakolczai, Arpad (2017) *Permanent Liminality and Modernity: Analysing the Sacrificial Carnival through Novels*, London: Routledge.
Szakolczai, Arpad and Bjørn Thomassen (2019) *From Anthropology to Social Theory: Rethinking the Social Sciences*, Cambridge: Cambridge University Press.
Szlezák, Thomas A. (1999) *Reading Plato*, London: Routledge.
Taylor, F. Sherwood (1951) *The Alchemists: Founders of Modern Chemistry*, London: Heinemann.
Thubron, Colin (2012) *To a Mountain in Tibet*, London: Vintage.
Toulmin, Stephen and June Goodfield (1961) *The Fabric of the Heavens*, Harmondsworth: Penguin.
Toulmin, Stephen and June Goodfield (1982) *The Architecture of Matter*, Chicago, IL: University of Chicago Press.
Turville-Petre, E. O. G. (1964) *Myth and Religion of the North: The Religion of Ancient Scandinavia*, Westport, CT: Greenwood.
Unamuno, Miguel de (1968) *Our Lord Don Quixote, Selected Works of Miguel de Unamuno, Volume 3*, Princeton, NJ: Princeton University Press.
Voegelin, Eric (1974) *The Ecumenic Age*, vol. 4 of *Order and History*, Baton Rouge, LA: Louisiana State University Press.
Voegelin, Eric (1997) *The History of Political Ideas, Vol. 1*, Columbia, MO: University of Missouri Press.
Voegelin, Eric (2000) *Modernity Without Restraint*, Colombia, MO: University of Missouri Press.
Walker, James R. (1980) *Lakota Belief and Ritual*, edited by R. J. DeMallie and E. A. Jahner, London: University of Nebraska Press.
Walker, James R (2006) *Lakota Myth*, edited by R. J. DeMallie, London: University of Nebraska Press. [1983]
Weber, Max (1976) *The Protestant Ethic and the Spirit of Capitalism*, London: Allen.
Wengrow, David (2013) *The Origins of Monsters: Image and Cognition in the First Age of Mechanical Reproduction*, Princeton: Princeton University Press.
Wolpert, Lewis (2002) *Science and Mathematics in Ancient Greek Culture*, Oxford: Oxford University Press.
Yates, Frances (1964) *Giordano Bruno and the Hermetic Tradition*, London: Routledge.
Yates, Frances (1975a) *The Rosicrucian Enlightenment*, London: Paladine Books. [1972]
Yates, Frances (1975b) *Shakespeare's Last Plays*, London: Routledge.
Yates, Frances (1979) *The Occult Philosophy in the Elizabethan Age*, London: Routledge.
Yates, Frances (1992) *The Art of Memory*, London: Pimlico. [1966]
Zitkala-Sa (1901) *Old Indian Legends*, Boston, MA: Atheneum Press.

Name index

Aeschylus 52
Aesop 61
Agnew, Jean-Christophe 86, 95, 11
Agrippa, Heinrich Cornelius 156
Alberti, Leon B. xii, 18, 32
Alexander VI (pope) *see* Rodrigo Borgia
Alexander, Jeffrey 7–8, 9
Alfonso X of Castille (king) 158
Amutio brothers 152
Anaximander 50
Aratus 135
Archimedes 169
Aristotle xiv, 5, 27, 109, 110, 115, 132, 141, 155, 164, 165, 169, 170, 171, 172, 176, 178, 181
Artemidorus 58–9
Auden, W.H. 23, 182
Augustine, St. 6
Avicenna 176

Baltrušaitis, Jurgis 145
Bataille, Georges 7
Bateson, Gregory 5, 20, 41, 61, 89, 180
Baudelaire, Charles 116
Bauman, Zygmunt 7
Baudrillard, Jean 8–9, 42, 123, 160
Blakely, Sandra 19, 52, 53–4, 56, 57, 58, 63, 64, 123
Boas, Franz 2, 15, 16, 36
Bonaventure, St. 23
Borgia, Rodrigo 152
Bourbaki, Nicolas 98
Bourdieu, Pierre 16
Bowersock, Glen 58
Boyle, Robert 176
Brown, Norman 42, 51, 52, 63
Bruno, Giordano 141, 142, 148, 156, 157

Calasso, Roberto 5, 59–60, 61, 63, 64, 79–102
Calvin, Jean 6
Camus, Albert 7
Canetti, Elias 139
Castelli, Enrico 145
Catullus 84
Cicero 5
Citati, Pietro 9, 160
Conrad, Joseph 39
Copernicus 166
Courbet, Gustave 60
Cratylus 74

Dante Alighieri 6
Deleuze, Gilles 160
Democritus 165, 172, 178; *see also* Pseudo-Democritus
Détienne, Marcel 18, 19, 21, 44, 51, 109, 119
Dickens, Charles 2, 42, 119
Diderot, Denis 51
Dilthey, Wilhelm 85
Dodds, E.R. 170
Douglas, Mary 88
Donne, John 177, 182, 183
Dumézil, Georges 18, 19, 21, 22, 23
Durkheim, Émile 7, 9, 16, 25, 36

Empedocles 129, 136, 137, 141
Epicurus 158
Erasmus of Rotterdam 158
Eucleides 66
Euclid 78, 166
Euripides 150, 154
Evans-Pritchard, Edward 11, 23, 24–42

Name index

Fibonacci, Leonardo 170
Foucault, Michel 5, 7, 8, 9, 28, 68, 69, 78, 93, 105, 160, 182
Freud, Sigmund 9, 25, 58, 90, 91

García of Nájera (King) 151, 152, 155
Gell, Alfred 61, 120, 143, 178, 183
Gernet, Louis 1, 19, 54
Girard, René 5, 9, 55, 61, 62, 84, 88, 89, 91, 92, 95, 96, 97, 110
Goethe, Johann W. 6, 62, 86, 119, 142, 157, 159
Gyges 58

Habermas, Jürgen 7
Hegel, Georg W.F. 70, 74, 86, 98
Heidegger, Martin 33, 38, 123, 183
Hephaestus 57, 124, 140
Heraclitus 27, 70, 71, 73, 74, 75, 157
Herodotus 55, 57, 58, 63, 71, 79, 101, 168
Hesiod 5, 43, 124, 125, 126, 131, 142, 152, 167, 177
Hippasus of Metapontum 78
Hobbes, Thomas 5, 91
Homer 5, 43, 50, 63, 119, 177
Honneth, Axel 7
Hyde, Lewis 5, 61

Jean Paul 93
Jung, Carl G. 160, 173

Kant, Immanuel 6, 7, 8, 140
Kerényi, Károly 5, 21, 29, 47–51, 52, 57–8, 61, 63, 64, 140, 160
Keynes, John M. 178
Khalid ibn Yazid 176
Kierkegaard, Søren 7, 98
Koselleck, Reinhart 5, 52
Kroeber, Alfred 16
Kurzweil, Ray 97

Latour, Bruno 5, 180, 181
Layard, John W. 15, 16, 19, 21, 22, 23
Le Bon, Gustave 139
Leibniz, Gottfried 100
Leonardo da Vinci xii, 145, 158
Leukippos 178
Lévi, Sylvain 88
Lévi-Strauss, Claude 16, 36
Livy 5
Locke, John xii, 70
Lorblanchet, Michel 143
Löwith, Karl 27

Lucretius 141
Luther, Martin 6

Mair, Victor H. 55
Malinowski, Bronisław 16, 24, 25, 41
Mann, Thomas 61, 160
Marx, Karl 9, 25, 52
Mauss, Marcel 63, 83, 84, 87, 88, 123, 124
Meletus 66
Meuli, Karl 88
Michelangelo Buonarotti 145
Michels, Roberto 139
Milton, John 6, 142, 159
Moliére 62, 183

Nero 143
Newton, Isaac 5, 70, 166
Nietzsche, Friedrich 1, 5, 6, 7, 9, 38, 42, 51, 52, 60, 61, 68, 78, 81, 83, 84, 87, 91, 95, 97, 98, 101, 116, 144

Orwell, George 8
Ostanes 179
Otto, Rudolph 48, 49
Overing, Joanna 23
Ovid 113

Parmenides 29, 73, 75
Pascal, Blaise 117
Patočka, Jan 50
Paul, St. 6
Pausanias 57, 59, 96, 140, 156, 157
Philippe II of Macedon 177
Pindar 140, 167, 168, 177
Pizzorno, Alessandro 33, 78, 118, 179
Plato xiv, 5, 7, 9, 10, 11, 23, 27, 29, 50, 51, 54, 56, 58, 60, 63, 65–78, 90, 95, 96, 97, 100, 101, 106, 107, 110, 113, 117, 120, 122, 123, 134, 141, 143, 145, 147, 155, 156, 162–185 *passim*
Pliny the elder 42, 172, 178
Plutarch 60
Poggio Bracciolini 158
Pound, Ezra 61
Praxiteles 156
Protagoras xii, 70–1, 74, 78, 134
Pseudo-Democritus 164, 179
Ptolemy 135, 163, 164, 166

Radcliffe-Brown, A.R. 16, 25, 41
Radin, Paul 2, 15–31 *passim*, 109
Renou, Louis 99
Rostovtzeff, Michael 144

Name index 195

Schleiermacher, Friedrich 74
Schongauer, Martin 145
Schopenhauer, Arthur 98
Sedley, David 70, 71
Seligman, Charles G. 24
Seneca 78
Serres, Michel 1, 5, 46, 50, 61–2, 78, 86, 95, 100, 160, 178, 180–3 *passim*
Shakespeare, William 6, 119, 141, 143, 182–3
Singer, André 25–7
Snodgrass, Anthony 49, 50
Socrates 9, 66–70, 73–6, 78, 134, 162
Sophocles 57
Stendhal 9
Strabo 140

Tarde, Gabriel 139, 180
Thales 134
Theaetetus 66
Theophrastos 126, 136, 174–5, 177
Theognis of Megara 54
Thubron, Colin 143–4
Tocqueville, Alexis de 178
Tolkien, J.R.R. 23

Toulmin, Stephen 42, 139, 164, 166, 167, 178, 179
Turing, Alan 98
Turner, Victor 41, 88
Turquet de Mayerne, Louis 182

Unamuno, Miguel de 7

Veblen, Thorstein 182
Vernant, Jean-Pierre 18, 19, 21, 44, 109, 144
Virgil 5
Virgin Mary 151–2, 154
Voegelin, Eric 5, 52, 60, 82, 100, 175

Warburg, Aby 101
Weber, Max 5, 27, 38, 42, 55, 79, 80, 83, 96, 101, 144, 180
Weil, Simone 98
Wengrow, David 144, 157
Whitehead, Alfred 9
Wittkower, Rudolf 144

Yates, Frances 141

Zeno 54, 73, 178
Zosimos of Panopolis 173

Subject index

absence 7, 17, 18
absorption 109, 111–2, 138, 139, 149, 168
abyss 125, 138, 156
accumulation xii, 3, 87, 139, 184
acquisition 108
Africa 29, 30, 35, 39, 52, 54, 56; South 140; West 15, 21, 30
age(s): axial 81; Bronze 53, 60, 96, 144, 157, 178; Golden xi, 53, 81, 82, 96 (of metamorphosis 96); Iron 96, 157 (of modernity 96); Silver 178
agent(s) 15, 39, 130, 143, 163; transformative 136, 137; *see also* operators
agora 38, 67, 73
aksara 77; *see also* indestructible
Alchemical Studies (Jung) 173
alchemy 26, 29, 38, 51, 56, 62, 85, 86, 89, 98, 123, 126, 137, 145, 149, 159–79; god of (Hermes) 61, 63
Alcibiades (Plato) 107
alienation 129, 150
Alexandria 163, 173, 175, 176, 177
algorithm 26, 137, 160
Almagest (Ptolemy) 135
altar 128, 143, 173
alteration xii, 47, 78, 138, 167, 173
ambiguity 19, 21
ambivalence 15, 19, 20, 21, 30, 47, 50, 119, 122; of communication 122; of modernity 15; of trickster 20, 121
America: pre-Columbian 111; North 15, 30
Anansi 30, 35
'Anatomy of the World, An' (Donne) 177
Ankara 64
annihilation xiii, 4, 10, 95, 97, 109, 150, 165, 166, 173; *see also* voiding
Antiquity, classical 38, 57, 58, 60, 67, 72, 139, 141, 145, 169

anxiety 10, 87, 114
apathy 137
apeiron 50; *see also* liminality
Apollo 45–6, 51, 105, 124
apparition 44, 45; of Hermes 61, 183; sudden 18, 44, 48
appetite 19, 109, 112, 120; *see also* eagerness
Arabian 140, 171
archaeology 9, 11, 17, 53, 67, 84, 89, 105, 143, 144
Ardor (Calasso) 88
Argonauts 52
Argos 53, 54, 63, 144
arrheton 50, 53, 57–9, 64, 68, 72, 76, 78; *see also* unspeakable
arrogance xii, 19, 27, 52, 177; *see also* hubris
Arslantepe 157
Artemis 59
artificial intelligence 26, 99
ascetic priest (Nietzsche) 9, 38, 68, 80, 81
asceticism 27, 42, 139
Asclepius 63
Ashanti 30, 35
Asia 15, 55, 79, 145, 154; Minor 58, 64; South-east 15
Assyria 173
Atapuerca cave 140, 151
Athens 54, 63, 66, 122, 139, 177
Australia 123
authenticity 18, 97, 106, 113, 141, 148, 170, 176
automatism 16, 26, 41, 164
Azande 11, 24–42, 141

Baal 38, 55
Babylonia 135, 141, 144, 164, 179
Bacchae (Euripides) 150

Subject index 197

Balearic islands 57, 157
beady eyes 108, 112
bear 83, 84, 96
beauty 50, 60, 68, 77, 78, 82, 94, 96, 100, 106, 145, 162, 163, 172, 181, 183
becoming 22, 113, 134, 145, 165
benefit-bringing 46, 47, 142, 144, 164
benevolence 35, 161, 168, 181
Bes 56
best practices 26, 40, 42
bewilderment 167
Beyond Good and Evil (Nietzsche) 1
bifurcation 95, 115
bipolarity 20, 27, 35, 71, 72, 122
blacksmith *see* smith
blood 55, 59, 60, 87, 88, 107, 111, 117, 129, 136, 173, 175; *see also* sacrifice
Bogazkoy 56
Boiotia 53
boundaries 19, 21, 28, 47, 52, 115, 116
Brahman(s) 37, 80, 88, 89
breathing 60, 126, 130, 145, 151
bridge 98, 109
bringing forth 68, 124, 131, 136, 149, 169, 177
Buddhism 79, 85, 145, 168; Tibetan 55
bureaucratisation 27, 144
Bushman 21, 23
Byzantium 38, 55, 126, 145, 166, 171, 173, 174

Cadmos 63
Cambridge ritualists 110
Camino de Santiago 151
cap 168; pointed 111, 114; Phrygian 57, 58
capitalism 101, 123; irrational rationality 27
Cappadocia 3, 12, 124, 125, 128, 134, 148, 152, 173
'captains of industry' (Veblen) 182
care 1, 66, 75, 111; self- 10
Care of the Self (Foucault) 58
carefulness 10, 147
carelessness 116, 147
carnival 116
castration 107, 110
Çatalhöyük 9, 38, 68, 140
cave(s) 37, 67, 78, 111, 137, 143, 148, 151, 152; art 22, 82, 89; *see also* individual caves
CCTV 31
Central African Republic 30
charlatan(s) 37, 54, 56
Chauvet cave 85, 94

Cheyenne 30, 96
Chimaera 84, 151
China 55, 143
Christianity 23, 30, 79, 81, 132
chthonic 31
Church 166
circle/circularity 10, 28, 37, 38, 83, 85, 86, 87, 89, 115, 121, 123, 130, 135, 138, 141, 147, 148, 149, 150, 155, 164, 165, 166, 175, 177, 184; devil's 28; vicious 80, 92
circulation 8, 9, 125, 148; *see also* substitution
clinamen (Lucretius) 141, 178
clown 17, 116, 119, 142
coins, Greek 57
Commedia dell'Arte 11, 107
commerce 61, 144, 160, 171; god of (Hermes) 61
communication 36, 46, 59, 61, 62, 94, 100, 106, 143, 160, 170; ambivalence 122; god of (Hermes) 61; *see also* technology
community 2–5, 18, 20, 26, 27, 29, 33, 37, 38, 40, 52, 54, 83, 91, 99, 121, 142, 158, 162, 170
concreteness xi, xiv, xv, 2, 8, 26, 32, 34, 41, 45, 49, 61, 67, 83, 85, 86, 92, 97, 99, 106, 150–1, 168, 173, 175,
Congo 30
conquest 80; of nature 179
consciousness 1, 7, 25, 87, 88, 93, 101, 161, 181; bad 81; hypertrophy 85; self- 84, 87, 93–4, 102 (origins 84–5, 93); split 93–4
consent: manipulating 123; of victim 80, 83, 88, 150
constellation 134–5, 153
constructivism 8, 144, 147
contentment *see* fullness
contingency xii, 41
cooperation/ cooperativity 17, 18, 176, 177, 181
correspondence 21, 75, 85, 97, 98, 130, 133, 134, 137, 149, 152, 156, 167
corruptness/ corruption 6, 19, 71, 93, 117, 120, 121, 138, 141, 149, 164, 176, 179,
cosmos 135, 156, 163, 164, 172
courage 22, 69, 73, 150
coyote 16, 21
Cratylus (Plato) 70, 71, 72, 76
creation 27, 28, 42, 53, 90, 93, 176, 183, 184; artificial 111; new xii, 12, 136;

198 *Subject index*

second 21, 22; world 21, 90–1, 143, 158; *see also* creative destruction
creativity 27–8, 42, 90, 139, 143, 147
Crete 53
crisis 29, 53, 62, 106, 110, 117; *see also* liminality
Croesus 58
crookedness 16, 148, 149
cross potent sign 55
crowds 139
cruelty 114, 116, 124, 152, 176
'Cultural Sociology of Evil, A' (Alexander) 7–8
culture xi, 90; debt 81, 82, 83, 86; Egyptian 134; European 46; gift 81, 82; guilt 82, 83, 86; Greek (classical) 1, 11, 27, 43–78, 98, 99, 101, 109, 117, 119, 124, 129, 131, 140, 141, 144, 147, 161–3, 165, 166, 168, 170–2, 173, 177, 182; hero 15; Magi/Trickster 60; Natufian 34; origins of 93; Platonic 145; Roman 55; Sumerian 134; of vengeance 34; walking 67
cunning 16, 30, 44, 47, 50, 54, 107, 119, 130, 138, 150; intelligence 18, 44, 47, 72
Cyclops 144
Cyprus 67
Czuczor-Fogarasi Dictionary 7

daimon 11, 52–6, 59, 63, 142
dancing 51, 56, 60, 129, 145, 154; warrior 56
darkness 10, 29, 39, 57, 73, 124, 127, 129, 131, 132, 136, 170; *see also* night
death 4, 26, 32, 33, 34, 49, 56, 62, 80, 83, 86, 90, 91, 99, 105, 117, 125, 131, 145, 146, 162; dance of 145; god of 109; kiss of 84
debauchery 124, 130, 138
decadence 81, 173
deceit/deceiving/ deception 16, 17, 44, 46, 47, 48, 58, 97, 98, 106, 119, 124, 131, 138, 141, 149, 176
decision xii, 23, 40, 75–6, 85, 86
decomposition 10, 76, 90, 150, 160, 165, 166, 181
deformity 56, 57, 152, 156
deification *see* divinisation
deity(ies) 3, 16, 17, 42, 45, 48, 49, 51–4, 79, 89, 90, 99, 143, 154, 160, 161, 169; creator 17, 27; liminal 50; Olympic 57; trickster 23, 50; *see also* gods
'Deluge' drawings (Leonardo) 158

demon(s) 1, 17, 18, 28, 32, 52, 53, 56, 62, 119, 124, 131, 138, 139, 142–5, 150, 167, 181–4; Maxwell's 150
Dénezé-sous-Doué cave 140
density 135, 136, 157, 169, 177, 178; difference 135, 157; flux 129, 130, 136, 157
depravity 25, 117, 160
depression 136, 139, 174
deprivation 8, 84, 94, 130, 131, 137, 143, 162, 164, 165, 168, 184
Derinkuyu 135
despair 34, 96, 97, 117, 139, 167
destiny 9, 86, 89, 97, 107, 125, 146, 182; trickster 5, 43, 180, 184
destruction xii, 5, 11, 15, 30, 34, 39, 42, 50, 56, 58, 59, 61, 73, 76, 80, 84, 86, 87, 88, 92, 93, 101, 105, 115, 122, 123, 125, 130, 142, 144, 145, 150, 159–165, 169, 173, 175, 183–5; of carefulness 147; of the concrete 97; creative xii, 28, 62, 123, 125, 142; of reality 8
devastation 39, 123, 150, 153
devil 6, 17, 39, 145, 159
Dionysus 43, 51, 60, 123, 140, 153, 154, 155, 156, 159
disempowerment 37, 39, 48
dissolution xii, 159, 160, 184; of carefulness 10
distillation 129–30, 167
divination 38, 40, 41, 105
divinisation 38, 42, 84, 98, 99, 106, 145, 150, 163, 164, 166, 168; of man 42; self- 97, 99, 178
divinity(ies) *see* deity, god(s)
division xii, 76, 120, 122, 162–7 *passim*
dog 109, 111–3, 155
Don Juan 61, 183
Doric (Greek) 53, 54; farce 57, 66, 78, 107
double bind (Bateson) 35
doubt/ing 18, 40, 75–6, 93, 122; Cartesian 75–6, 100
dragon 1, 126–7, 136, 151, 175
dream(s) 2, 29, 44, 49, 58–9, 75, 91, 145, 146, 175, 182; -time 123
dualism 6, 7, 40, 93, 122
dwarf/ves 21, 31, 56–7, 58, 63, 123, 124
dynamis see power

eagerness 29, 109, 129, 148, 152
East 53–4, 144–5, 157, 166
Echidna 126, 175
Economic History (Weber) 96

Subject index 199

economics xii, 42, 62, 184; neoclassical 25, 27, 178; theory 76
economy: alchemic 62, 99, 164, 175, 184; political 170, 178, 182
Ecumene (Voegelin) 60
efficiency 88, 93, 98, 107, 135, 138
effluence 7, 10, 107, 129–30, 133, 137–8, 141, 146;
Egypt 56, 109, 124, 132, 134, 135, 140, 152, 173
eidos 165, 170
Eleatic: Palamedes 54; school 73; stranger 68, 73
Emerald Tablet 173
empire 27; building xi, 79, 182; Byzantine 55, 174; Hittite 56; Persian 79; Roman 41, 53
emptiness xii, xiii, 12, 145, 146–7, 162, 163, 178
energy 8, 135–7, 139, 148, 150, 152, 156, 157, 161–3, 177
Enlightenment xi, 5, 6, 7, 51, 52, 73, 92, 144, 145, 158, 159
emitting/ emission 33, 77, 126, 150
entrapping/ment 7, 10, 22, 28, 29, 31, 33, 37, 42, 52, 82, 83, 84, 85, 141, 150
enchanting/ment 36, 38, 39, 43, 51, 84, 120, 143, 160
encystation 10, 12
epidemics 8, 51, 62
epiphany 51
episteme (Foucault) 69
Eros 52, 53; oppressive (Plato) 106; perverted 106, 135
eroticism 53, 83, 108, 113, 115, 116, 147, 175, 183
Eshu 21
esoterism 98
esprit de corps 36
Etruscan 38, 132
eunuch 58, 109–10, 184
Europe 5, 55, 69, 119, 145, 152, 182
Euthypro (Plato) 66
experience 6, 20, 48, 85, 86, 87, 90–1, 94, 96, 106, 116, 134, 153; personal 39, 81; primordial 166
experiential basis 90, 91
exteriority 2, 120

fable: Aesop's 61; Sanskrit 144
fairground 99, 182
family 18, 62, 99, 131
Faust (Goethe) 6, 34, 62, 63, 157, 159
feasting 34, 45

fermentation 131
fertile/ity 55, 68, 144
filiation 18, 116, 164, 165, 168, 170, 176, 178
fire 23, 62, 141, 151, 172; Agni 90; forest 155, 158; invention 22, 54; stealing 22, 51
fixation 26, 28–9, 30, 96
flood 62
fluidity 8, 10, 21, 126, 128, 155, 156, 165, 167, 168, 169, 170, 172
flux xii, 4, 8, 9, 10, 11, 12, 20, 21, 22, 28, 58, 62, 69, 70, 74, 75, 76, 77, 78, 84, 101, 106, 116, 125, 129–30, 134, 135, 136, 137, 139, 141, 142, 143, 145, 149, 150, 155, 156, 157,162, 165, 169–72, 175, 177, 182; accumulation 4, 10, 37, 130, 136, 143, 157; density 130, 136, 157
folktales 2, 11, 15, 16, 21, 24, 25, 27, 29, 35, 37, 42, 119
fool 15, 17, 116, 153; *see also* jester
force(s) 10, 12, 32, 33, 35, 59, 60, 80, 115, 137, 140, 151, 155, 161, 164, 169; converting 78; driving 4 (of modernity 42); of Eros 116; external 30, 35, 48, 94, 142 (hostile, evil, dark 33, 34, 35, 131, 142); generative 185; indestructible 51; inner 7, 33, 39, 40, 51, 167; moving 106; irresistible 125, 155; invisible 33, 42, 94; of substitutability 86; *see also* power
formlessness xii, 145
forum 38; *see also* agora, public sphere
fox 16, 17, 21, 23, 96
Frankenstein 143
frequency 59, 77, 140, 150, 157
friendship 18, 106, 130
Fruška Gora 148
fullness 18, 178
functionalism 7, 8, 25
furnace 56, 178
fury 38, 62, 139; of destruction 169

Gaia (Latour) 181
Gay Science (Nietzsche) 78
Genealogy of Morals (Nietzsche) 42, 61, 83, 91, 101
'Geometric Joy, A' (Dickinson) 146–7, 160
geometry 50, 74, 76, 78, 111, 115, 125, 169, 170, 178
gestation 132–5
gesture 22, 87, 96, 111
giant 21, 126, 144, 152
gift 46, 82, 86, 87, 184; culture 81, 82; poisonous 47; relations (Mauss) 83, 87

Subject index

Gift, The (Hyde) 61
Gnas 32
Gnosticism 5, 6, 9, 21, 29, 32, 33, 40, 51, 55, 60, 63, 71, 77, 82, 83, 93–4, 99, 100, 166, 173, 175; *see also* world, vision
Göbekli Tepe 23
god(s) 12, 16, 17, 18, 21, 32, 45, 46, 48, 52, 56, 59, 82, 87, 92, 93, 98, 99, 105, 106, 124, 140, 143, 147, 152, 156, 158, 164, 165; *see also* deities, divinity
God 12, 48, 55, 82, 154
goés 54, 56, 63, 71, 95
Golem 16, 143
goodness 18, 83, 106, 162, 171, 176, 181, 184
Gourdan cave 113
grace 22, 30, 50, 60, 85, 100, 145, 152, 168, 181; divine 6
Great Goddess 17, 53, 56, 57–8, 60
Greece 15, 34, 50, 53, 54, 57, 63, 67, 79, 111, 119, 139, 154, 157, 168, 179; *see also* culture, Greek
Grimes Graves flint mine 11, 113
grotesque 58, 143, 144, 149
growth xii, 115, 122, 124, 138, 165, 167; demonic xii; infinite 15; trickster 122

Hades 109, 129, 154, 158
Hal Saflieni (Malta) 128, 148
harbour *see* port
hare 16, 22
harmony 24, 34, 74, 76, 77, 100, 106, 115, 135, 140, 162, 170, 181, 183, 184
hatred 34, 52
heart xiii, 20, 39, 44, 45, 93; principled 86; its reasons 117
Heart of Darkness (Conrad) 39
hedonistic calculus 49
Hekate 158
Hellenism 173, 177, 179
Hephaestus 57, 134, 140
Hera 140
Heracles 43, 151, 159
herald 63
Herma 23, 153
Hermes 11, 15, 21, 23, 29, 33, 43–54, 57, 59, 60, 63, 79, 105, 124, 142, 144, 149, 158, 159, 173, 178, 183; in modernity 61–2
Hermes I-V (Serres) 61
Hermes Trismegistos 53, 173
Hermetism 49, 51, 53, 62, 98, 123, 143, 153

Hierogamy *see* hieros gamos
hieros gamos 57, 59–60, 106, 149
Hinduism 111; Vedic 11, 63, 77, 78, 79–102
Histories (Herodotus) 55, 58, 168
History of Rome (Livy) 5
Homeric Hymns: To Apollo 45; To Aphrodite 45; To Demeter 43, 45; To Hermes 43–7, 54, 105, 124, 142, 178
homology 75, 166, 171
hook symbol *see* Y-shape
Horus 152
hostility 47, 73, 82, 83, 84, 93; to life 84, 144, 178; to world 32, 33, 82, 84, 94
hubris 1, 4, 19, 22, 52, 91, 177
Huguenots 178, 182
human nature 6, 29, 39, 92; dark 25, 26; evil (Kant) 6
Humbaba 144
hunchback 107, 109, 113, 114
hunting 16, 23, 30, 32, 36, 37, 83, 86, 89, 92, 100, 113, 124, 153, 154
hybridity 3, 16, 17, 18, 19, 28, 31, 84, 109–14, 150, 168

Iktomi 30–1
Iliad (Homer) 50, 63
image(s) 11, 12, 38, 57, 60, 64, 69, 82, 85, 86, 91, 94, 96, 102, 105, 107–15, 118, 130, 132, 143–5, 147, 151–3, 157, 161, 181; composite 96, 144; mental 84, 90, 95; open female 55, 56, 60, 144
image-magic 68, 171
imagery 144, 145, 159; Gnostic 6
imagination 6, 25, 28, 63, 91, 152, 181
Imbros 53, 57
imitation xii, 7, 15, 22, 26, 33, 36, 42, 59, 68, 72, 95–7, 99, 106, 110, 119, 121, 160, 166, 167, 168, 171, 176, 178, 179, 185
immortality 4, 45, 63, 129, 148, 151
impostor 109, 140
Inandik vase 64
in-betweenness 3, 4, 16, 17, 19, 53, 61, 105, 106, 107, 108, 117, 134, 163, 165, 178, 181, 183
incantation 63, 179
inclination 62, 110, 114, 117
incommensurability 8, 11, 12, 27, 34, 41, 48, 50, 76, 101, 140, 147, 155, 156, 159–73, 177, 181, 183, 185; *see also* liminality
incubation 132, 176
indestructible 8, 9, 51, 77–8, 100, 165, 173

Subject index 201

India 55; Vedic 23, 37, 55; *see also* Hinduism
infiltration xiii, 23, 87, 139, 141, 143, 173
initiation rites 3, 36, 53, 54, 58, 60, 71, 120, 135; *see also* rites of passage
innocence 25, 47, 50, 120, 138, 144, 166, 183
integral reality (Baudrillard) 123
integrity 73, 122, 134, 162, 167
interconvertibility *see* substitutability
interest 4; self- 7, 47, 138
interference 4, 16, 75, 96, 184
internet 30, 31, 137, 143, 149
'Interpretation of Dreams' (Artemidorus) 58
interruption (Serres) 184
intersection 108, 115, 143, 184
intoxication 8, 51, 101, 113, 139, 162
intrusion 4, 27, 93, 96, 145, 157, 183
invasion xiii, 35, 96, 108, 115, 144, 168
invisibility 31, 33, 42, 58, 59, 63, 65, 94, 123, 133, 140, 161, 162, 172, 185
Ion (Plato) 58, 110
Iran 79, 80, 144; *see also* Persia
Iranian plateau 100, 144
Ireland 15, 55
irrational/ity 27, 34, 41, 50, 76, 78, 101, 140, 156, 160, 161, 162, 170, 171, 181; numbers 27, 34, 78, 140, 162, 170, 177; *see also* incommensurable
irresponsibility 4, 25, 172, 183, 185
Islam 30, 79, 151, 176
Isturitz cave 108, 111

jester 116, 138, 141, 152–5, 168; *see also* fool
joke/ joking 22, 35, 72, 73, 120, 142
joyless/ness 136, 137, 146

Kabeiroi 52–5, 56–60, 63, 68, 71, 78, 79, 140, 157
Kabeiroi, The (Aeschylus) 52
Kaymakli 3, 56, 124, 125, 128, 131–5, 139, 148, 150, 152, 155, 157, 178
khóra (open space) 10
kidney 38
killing 21, 37, 45, 62, 81, 83, 87, 88, 89, 92, 93, 116 ,136, 175
knowledge 31, 39, 50, 51, 65–78; acquisition 67–8; dark 165; divine 105, 106; god of (Hermes) 61; in-between 106; infinite 105; its linguistic terminology 64, 69, 76; magical 54 (technological 62); men of 97, 100; neutral 164; perverse 134; possession 3, 67, 68; power 22, 39, 80; problematising 66; as salvation 100, 179; secret 9, 11, 15, 36, 54, 63, 68, 69, 70–8, 85, 122, 165, 174; as sense perception 70, 74, 75; trickster 3, 4, 11, 16, 20, 63, 72–3, 93, 94, 105, 106, 121, 122–3, 163 (self- 2); as understanding 77; universalistic xi, 52, 75–6, 122; unspeakable 11, 57, 68
ksara 77; *see also* flow

labyrinth 78, 128, 134, 138
Lajja Gauri (goddess) 55
Lakota 30–2
La Marche cave 112
Lascaux cave 38, 85, 91, 140
laughter 30, 35, 116, 154
Laws (Plato) 70, 72, 177
Lemnos 52, 53, 57
Lepinski Vir 114
leprechaun 15
Levant 53, 54
Levites 37, 55
light-heartedness 167
liminality 6, 7, 10, 15, 29, 30, 31, 33, 44, 46, 50, 51, 53, 55, 62, 65–7, 78, 79, 105, 106, 122, 138, 139, 143, 148, 152, 153, 160, 164, 165, 183, 184; deity of 49, 50; permanent 4, 30, 35, 49, 50, 182
limit xii, 19, 49, 74, 77, 99, 113, 129, 136, 170, 177; *see also* measure
limitlessness 1, 4, 8, 9, 19, 39, 47, 49, 60, 62, 67, 97, 101, 110, 129, 138, 155, 156, 173, 174, 183
linear transformation 110, 134; perverted 123
links: alchemy-economy-money 164; analogous-digital 98; asceticism-rationality 42; Asia-Europe 55; birth-death 10, 129, 135, 138, 162, 165; consciousness-unconsciousness 25; continuous-discrete 95, 98; cranes-Pygmies 63, 64; demons-monsters 142; divine-human 4, 51, 53, 59, 60, 105; East-West 53–4, 55, 143, 145; economy-technology-democracy 5, 99; ends-means 26, 27, 82, 121; Eros-death 117; exchange-sacrifice 61, 84, 85, 87; evil-hubris 52; facts-norms 25; finite-infinite 98, 162–3; flux-void 10, 62; gift-sacrifice 87; Hellenism-modernity 179; Hierogamy-sacrifice 59; imitation-metamorphosis 95–7, 99; imitation-rationality 42;

imitation-violence 97; infantile-senile 41; infinity-zero 122; irrationality-rationality 27, 41, 101; knowledge-belief 94, 99, 100; knowledge-recognition 76; life-death xii, 1, 49, 86, 130, 137, 162, 165, 181; limit-unlimited 77, 129; magic-art-technology (Gell) 120, 143, 183; metamorphosis-possession 96; metamorphosis-theatre 111; modern-savage 36, 183; mortals-immortals 46; nature-culture 82, 163-4; necessity-pleasure 82; object-subject 25, 96; open-secret 73, 122; pleasure-pain 83, 94, 135, 160, 162, 163, 178; priests-actors (Nietzsche) 87; priests-prophets (Weber) 55, 99, 101; reflexivity-performance 66; sacrifice-Eros 115-7; *savoir-connaissance* (Foucault) 68, 78; sex-marriage 27; substitutability-concreteness 86, 97, 99; substitution-sacrifice 61, 97, 98, 138; substitution-connection 95, 96, 99; theatre-economics-exchange 62; Vedic sacrifice-modern rationality 90; weave-wave 42

liquid(ity) 8, 62, 139, 175

literati (Weber) 38; *existentiell* (Heidegger) 38

living dead 4, 10, 16, 17, 84, 117, 125, 129, 130, 131, 137, 143-51, 156, 164, 183, 184

Loki 15, 30, 63

loneliness 2, 3, 16, 17, 90, 122, 137, 139; *see also* outsider

love 69, 106-7, 116, 147, 180-1, 183; *see also* Eros

Lydia 58

lyre 45, 46, 47

machination 9, 11, 12, 26, 27, 39, 81, 117, 119, 123, 142, 181, 184, 185

machinator *see* operator

madness 39, 52, 154; divine (Plato) 56

Magdalenian 108

Magi 33, 37, 42, 55, 56, 60, 63, 69, 80, 82, 84, 85, 100, 101, 144, 157; biblical 79; as people 55

magic xi, 11, 24-42, 54, 56, 58, 61-3, 96, 113, 120, 122, 123, 124, 129, 131, 143, 145, 147, 157, 158, 167, 172, 178, 183

magicians 11, 24-42, 54, 131, 138, 140; *see also* sorcerer, witch doctor

Maia (nymph) 44, 45, 46

Malta 128, 148, 157

Maltese cross 55

managerialism 41, 76

Manicheanism 6, 40

Marduk 55

mask 29, 36, 38, 63, 111, 112, 118

master-serf dialectic (Hegel) 86

mathematics 27, 34, 61, 97, 100, 101, 126, 140, 147, 170, 171, 181

matrix 10, 20, 56, 67, 111, 115, 125, 133, 134, 135, 141, 149, 161, 167, 176, 177; perverted 20, 110

Maxwell's demon 150

measure 19, 34, 49, 54, 74, 76, 77, 100, 101, 115, 136, 140, 147, 155, 161, 166, 169, 170, 171; right 2, 7, 27; man as 70; divine as 70; *see also* limit

media 4, 62, 141, 169, 182; as modern god 169

Median 55, 79; *see also* Magi, Persian

mediation 51, 69

Mediterranean 45, 60, 63, 67, 111, 148

Megara 54, 57, 66, 67, 78, 107; *see also* Doric

mechaniota (trickster) 45, 111

memory 30, 52, 54, 76, 82, 90, 95, 163; guardians 9, 38, 68

Meno (Plato) 71, 141, 171

mentality: exchange 49; Gnostic 93; merchant 171; primitive 33; sacrificial 88-9; Trickster 111; Vedic 86-7, 89, 90,

Mephistopheles 62

mercenary 137, 182

Merchant of Venice, The (Shakespeare) 141

Mercury 127, 137, 149, 151; *see also* Hermes

messenger (of gods) 59

Mesolithic 108, 114, 115

Mesopotamia 144, 173

metallurgy 11, 23, 52-4, 56, 57, 86, 89, 123, 154, 157, 158, 174, 178, 184

Metamorphoses (Ovid) 113

metamorphosis *see* transformation

Midas 58

Middle Ages 6, 171

midwife (Socrates) 67-8

'millstone' gate 128, 133, 141, 157

mime 11, 20, 66, 107, 110-5, 138

mimetic rivalry (Girard) 89, 85

mindfulness (*phronesis*) xii, 1, 15, 41, 72, 77, 86, 87, 106, 110, 111, 120, 122, 146, 147, 160, 161, 164, 166, 167, 171, 181, 182

mindlessness xi, 2, 4, 42, 161, 164, 167

mimicry xii, 111; *see also* imitation

Subject index

Minoan 38; *see also* Crete
misogyny 36, 55, 56
mistrust (of oneself) 85
mocking/ery 45, 111, 116, 153
modernity 26, 42, 43; ambivalence 15; first hero of (Don Juan 61, 183; Faust 62); god of (trickster) 160; hyper- 182, 184; as orientalisation 99; secrets 15; as trickster land 51;
Momus 43
Momus (Alberti) 18, 32
monastery/ies 143, 148; Najera 12, 151–3
money 86, 164, 170–1; *see also* substitution
monster(s) 3, 12, 18, 25, 31, 126, 142–58, 167, 168, 174, 175, 183, 184; *see also* demon(s); hybridity; Pergouset cave
Nosferatu (Murnau) 142
Nosferatu the Vampyre (Herzog) 142
muteness 107, 115, 125, 162; global 115
mutilation 107; self- 38
Mycenaean (civilisation) 144
mystery: cults 3, 53, 59, 60, 71, 78, 140, 154 (Eleusian 43, 60, 71); doctrine 70–1
myth(s) 25, 60, 136; of origin 90, 144
mythology 2, 4, 9, 17, 23, 25, 52, 57, 126, 142, 143, 145, 149, 156; Bushman 21; classical 12, ; comparative 1, 2, 4, 11, 119; European 15; Germanic 57; Greek 1, 11, 17, 33, 43, 50, 52, 53, 60, 79, 81, 89, 95, 111, 122; Indo-European 57; Lakota 30; Nordic 57; world creation 91, 143

Najera 12, 140, 151–3
nakedness 111, 113
naming 36, 76, 95
Natural Contract (Serres) 181
Neanderthal 94
negativity 121, 162, 178
negligible (Weil) 97–8, 99
neoliberalism 26
Neolithic 30, 53, 67, 108, 109, 113, 117, 143, 178
Neo-Tethys ocean 125, 148
net(s) 9, 16, 22, 24, 39, 147, 157, 158; *see also* web
Nicomachean Ethics (Aristotle) 171, 178
night 1, 29, 33, 44, 45, 46, 49, 51, 124, 125, 131, 135, 146
nightwalker 148
nihilism 81, 83, 84, 85, 144
nil *see* zero
non-being 68, 107, 122, 169

normality 3, 17, 26, 29, 30, 33, 35, 48, 49, 86, 117, 121, 122, 138, 139, 164
nose 109, 112, 113; beak-like 111; pointed 108, 109, 118; snub 154
nothingness xii, 16, 18, 39, 84, 101, 147

oblivion 59, 148, 163
obscenity 56, 57, 60, 155
obsession 4, 7, 8, 26, 40, 55, 83, 108, 145
obsidian 57, 125
occult 9, 12, 53, 59, 60, 166
octopus 44, 109
Odyssey (Homer) 49, 50
Oedipus 150
omnipresence 9, 51, 92, 159; evil 7; trickster 31
On the Nature of Things (Paracelsus) 150
On Corruption and Generation (Aristotle) 172
open female image *see* image(s)
operator(s) 12, 107, 117, 126, 129, 131, 134, 139, 142, 143, 164, 165, 172
opportunity cost 178
opposite(s) xii, 72, 78, 95, 117, 162
oracle 32, 40, 42
order 19, 22, 62, 74, 91, 98, 102, 111, 125, 150, 157, 182; collapse of 91; divine 17, 70; of life 26; of nature 22, 169; origins of 101; of reality 20, 60; of things xii; world 21, 47, 70, 111 (graceful 22)
Order of Things (Foucault) 28
Orient *see* East
'Origin of the World, The' (Courbet) 60
original sin 6, 17, 81
Ouroboros 42, 126, 175, 179
outcast 15, 17, 23, 26, 36, 91, 93, 108, 166
outsider 2, 3, 16, 26, 35, 54, 91, 93, 108, 122, 124, 142, 149; *see also* loneliness

Palaeolithic 3, 11, 18, 38, 67, 82, 84, 85, 88, 89, 90, 91, 96, 105–14, 117, 127, 140, 151, 153
Palamedes 54–5
Pandora 57
Panopticon 31
Paradise Lost (Milton) 159
parasite 30, 46, 61–2, 160, 184
Parasite, The (Serres) 61–2
Parmenides (Plato) 66, 73
participation 20, 88, 93, 117, 120, 121, 178, 181, 184
passage tombs 67
Pech-Merle cave 55

204 Subject index

Peiraeus 66
Pelasgians 53, 57
penetration 59, 115, 140, 185
Pentheus 154
performative speech act 28
performativity 38, 66; *see also* theatricality
Pergouset cave 9, 38, 55, 68, 84, 94, 144; Room of Monsters 55, 80, 84, 85, 91, 143
Persia 37, 55, 56, 63, 79, 144, 173, 179
Phaedo (Plato) 69, 71
Phaedrus (Plato) 54, 65, 66, 73, 107, 120, 180
Phaleron 66
phallic/phallus 107–11, 114–5, 152–3
Philebus (Plato) 73, 172, 178
philosophy 100; classical xiv, 5 (natural 169); Cynic 178; empirical 70; Epicurean 168; European 9; idealist 5 (German 74); hermeneutical 74; as love of wisdom 180; neo-Kantian 25, 26, 160, 180; neo-Platonic 51, 163, 173; modern 98, 110; Presocratic xiv, 42 (Eleatic school 73; Pythagorean school 50, 78); rationalist 61; Socratic (Megarean school 66); Stoic 54, 141, 168, 178; Vienna school 41
Physics (Aristotle) 170
Phoenicia 53, 55, 57, 63
Phlyakes actor 107
Phrygia 53, 54, 57, 58, 173
pity 115, 116, 139
planets 134, 135, 141, 149, 164, 167, 177
Platonic dialogues 9, 65–71, 73; early Socratic 63, 69, 73; late 66; meta-character 66; middle 66, 69; sequential ordering 65; transmission mechanism 66; *see also the individual titles*
plot/ting 26, 44, 72, 73, 74, 122, 139, 183
poiesis (Heidegger) 183
Poetics (Aristotle) 110
Poetry and Truth (Goethe) 142
police 182
policy 26
political anthropology xi, xiv, 5, 9, 180–1
Politics (Aristotle) 178
polygonal walls 28, 144
ponderability 169
Poros 52
port 66–7
Poseidon 125

possession 59–60, 96, 118, 120, 143, 154, 162; shamanic 56
poverty 163, 164–5
power(s) 2, 9, 22, 30, 31, 34, 35, 42, 47, 50, 58, 59, 63, 68, 85, 86, 96, 97, 107, 112, 130, 131, 138, 139, 140, 147, 148, 152, 157, 160, 165, 166, 168, 171, 176, 178; external 92 (evil, dark 129, 142, 184); generating 60; of imagination 91; inner 51, 75, 86, 138, 166; invisible 85; irresistible 152; of mind 16, 23, 85, 86; mysterious 155; priestly 55; of reason 86, 96, 143; visionary 51; *see also* force
Prajapati 90, 91, 94
prayer (Mauss) 63
prehistory 11, 17, 37, 38, 42, 54, 60, 83, 85, 91, 105–36
presence 3, 4, 7, 8, 31, 42, 83, 107, 109, 117, 124, 143, 155, 177
priestly people 55, 79
prison 71, 96, 146–7, 149, 170, 173, 179, 182
procedurality 41, 85, 88, 107, 160
professional group 36, 37, 42, 54, 56
progress 5, 6, 15, 41, 63, 176
Prometheus 1, 19, 43, 45, 46, 51–2, 57, 59, 60, 62, 144, 159
Prometheus Bound (Aeschylus) 52
Proteus 95, 111, 164
protuberance 107, 113
psychology 85; mass 139
public: rituals 28, 54; sphere 5, 8, 9, 38, 73, 87, 99, 122 (*see also* khóra)
Pulcinella 11, 107, 114
pulsation 145
Puritan 9, 102
Pygmies 56, 63, 64

rationalism xi, xii, 6, 7, 9, 39, 51, 61, 85, 89, 93, 98, 101, 160, 176; metaphysical (Heidegger) 39
rationality 1, 25, 38, 41, 42, 72, 98, 120, 121, 159; irrational (Weber) 27, 101; mechanical *see* trickster; trickster 27, 177
rebel 26
receptacle 67, 125, 128, 131–6, 157, 161, 172, 173
reciprocity 120, 184
recognition xv, 8, 26, 45, 50, 62, 67, 77, 78, 84, 94, 121, 151, 163, 169
reflexivity 18, 58, 66
Reformation 6, 152

Subject index 205

relationality 168, 182, 184; as evil 184; mere 111, 178, 181; as a problem (Serres) 178; as totalitarian 184
religion 21, 32, 33, 71, 79, 90, 141, 173
Renaissance 6, 143, 145, 152
representation 56, 64, 85, 143, 145; duplicated (Foucault) 28, 93
Republic (Plato) 58, 63, 65, 66, 68, 72, 73, 77, 78, 84, 110, 177
resentment 17, 20, 93, 108
residue 98; *see also* negligible
resignation 8, 48
resistance 2, 34, 49, 73, 161, 168, 185
resonance 133, 139, 140, 141
responsibility 27, 48, 49, 85, 137, 139, 170, 183
revolution 9, 182
ring 58
Rising Star cave (South Africa) 140
rites of passage 4, 15, 21, 54; *see also* initiations rites
ritual 26, 27, 38, 41, 52, 53, 55, 56, 60, 84, 87, 88, 106, 107, 111, 112, 116, 121, 123
'Ritual of the Serpent' (Warburg) 101
road *see* travel
rogue 45, 46, 109
Rome 132, 148, 156, 179

sacred 31, 48, 83, 154; fluid 127, 128; marriage 58 (*see also hieros gamos*); numbers 134; theatre 111; transformation 54
sacrifice 11, 21, 41, 50, 55, 59–60, 61, 80, 83, 86, 87–101, 106, 107, 110, 111, 135, 138, 144, 150; child 56 (embryo offering 167, 178); and Eros 115–7; horse 89, 101; invention 51; mechanism 62, 161; origins 84–5; self- 94
Sahara 30, 38
Samothrace 53, 58, 63
San Salvatore Abbey 148
Santa María la Real Monastery 151–6
Santo Domingo de la Calzada 151, 158
Sardis 154
Sassi di Matera 148
Satapatha Brahmana 79, 88
Saturn 137, 149, 151
Satyrs 57, 111, 154
Savage Mind, The (Lévi-Strauss) 36
scapegoating 161
schismogenesis 20, 27, 30, 33, 36, 39, 74
schizophrenia 93, 178

science 61, 90, 97, 98, 100, 101, 134, 139, 142, 163, 168, 169, 173, 176, 181, 184; modern technologised 5, 101, 149, 179, 182, 184; neutral 181; social 2, 5, 15, 16, 24, 69, 160
'Sea and the Mirror, The' (Auden) 182
second reality 48, 91
secrecy 3, 12, 15, 38, 53, 54, 57, 59, 60, 63, 122, 125, 131, 139, 142, 176
secret society 5, 36, 52, 54
seducing/ seduction 36, 115, 120, 121, 145
self-consciousness *see* consciousness
self-contemplation: Cartesian theatrical 93; sacrificial 84, 88, 93, 95
self-denial 115, 139, 147
self-forgetfulness 51, 147
self-interest 7, 47, 138
sensuals 106, 107, 115, 116, 117, 120, 124, 129–40, 145–50, 160–7, 172–5, 185
serpent *see* snake
sexual/ity 19, 49, 50, 53, 56, 58, 59, 60, 82, 83, 92, 106, 114, 145; liberation 8
shaft(s) 10, 124, 125, 126, 128, 130, 134–40, 148, 150, 164
Shaft Scene (Lascaux) 38, 80, 85, 91, 127, 140
shaman 23, 56, 144
shortcut(s) 25–7, 161
Siberia 54
Silk Road 55, 143, 144
simulation 98
smith(s) 23, 52, 54, 56, 123; god 57
snake 16, 21, 22, 23, 28, 42, 57, 101, 125, 126, 154, 175, 184
sociability 18
soma (drink) 101
Sophist(s) 7, 29, 30, 36, 38, 51, 55, 56, 58, 63, 70–8, 95, 100, 122, 134, 141; Byzantine 166, 174, 180, 182; Second 58
Sophist, The (Plato) 29, 63, 65, 68, 73
Sophronic mimes 66
sorcerer 29, 36, 38–9, 42; *see also* magician, witch doctor
'sorcerer's apprentice' (Goethe) 86
sorcery 24, 29, 32-40, 112, 154
soul(s) xiii, 17, 23, 29, 33–4, 42, 71, 75, 77, 100–1, 106, 107, 115, 123, 124, 127–39, 141, 143, 149, 150, 151, 155, 157, 160–2, 165, 166–7, 170–8, 184, 185; ascent 178; body as prison 71,

Subject index

149, 170; careful 77; density 177; educating 65; evil (Gnosticism) 100; guide of 62, 63, 142, 149; indestructible 77, 100; immortality 77; pact with devil 39; self-moving 177; stealing xiii, 33, 50, 62, 117, 124, 131, 137, 138, 142, 147, 148, 149, 157, 163; virtuous 101
spectacle 38, 41, 129
spectator 116, 120, 152
speed xi, 47, 61, 134, 136, 157, 169, 171; god of (Hermes) 61; of mind 47
Sphinx 150
spider 16, 17, 22, 23, 24–31, 35, 42, 99, 141, 158, 184
spin/ning 26, 28, 35, 66, 74, 127, 141, 148; doctors 141
spiral 51, 136, 148
spirits(s) 1, 34, 42, 124, 130, 142, 145; of the dead 21, 34; evil 34
spirituality xi, 33, 99, 122, 133, 173; oriental 33, 99
split self *see* schizophrenia
Stalker (Tarkovsky) 142
Statesman (Plato) 63, 65, 73, 123
steresis 110, 136, 136
sterility xii, 110, 117, 147
strategic games 184
stripes 109, 110 *see also* hybridity
sublime 145
substitutability 40, 61, 86, 87, 97, 111, 166–7
substitution 4, 16, 58, 81, 84, 85, 86, 94, 95–9, 111, 133, 138, 159, 168, 185
Sudan 30
suffering xi, 80, 81, 90, 92, 99, 100, 120, 137, 152, 161, 173, 178
super-reality 42, 48
syllable 69, 76–7, 78
symbolon 3, 24, 83
sympathy 85, 116, 120, 130, 137–9, 158, 167
Symposium (Plato) 63, 66, 68, 73, 100, 106, 147

tabula rasa xii
Tartarus 1, 105, 124–6, 129, 130, 135–8, 142, 147, 149, 152, 153, 156, 161, 167, 175
Tartuffe (Molière) 62
Tassili Desert Mountains 3, 9, 11, 38, 55, 68, 109, 118, 138, 143, 144, 157

technology 8, 15, 32, 36, 39, 42, 55, 61, 62, 82, 89, 93, 97, 98, 101, 110, 111, 120, 123, 143, 144, 160, 163, 165, 166, 181, 183, 184, 185; alchemic 99, 169, 184; communication 36, 41, 42, 149
Templars 55
Tempest, The (Shakespeare) 182, 183
terror 1, 6, 8, 99, 116, 117, 129, 143, 147
theatre 62, 88, 110, 117, 121, 182, 184; Greek 57, 125; 'operational' 128–9, 134; sacred 111
theatricality 29, 34, 38, 39, 40, 66, 69, 87, 93, 111, 184
Theaetetus (Plato) 9, 10, 11, 63, 65–78, 134
Thebes 53, 63, 154
theory of Forms (Plato) 68–9, 120
theosis see divinisation, self-
Thessaly 53, 67
thief 17, 44, 45, 51; of souls 62, 149
thinking xi, 1, 6, 9, 41, 47, 58, 61, 74, 75, 76, 77, 81, 86, 89, 93, 95, 98, 106, 134, 138, 145, 154, 156, 159, 160, 161, 162, 163, 168, 171, 178, 180, 182; abstract 50; alchemic 126, 164–5, 168; Gnostic 82; good 163, 185; Greek 11, 19, 89, 162, 165, 171, 173, 177; modern 6, 159; mystical 37; oriental 99, 162, 164; Plato's 66, 69, 171; rational 7, 26, 50, 85, 89, 97, 120, 121, 159 (as doubting 76, 93); trickster 110, 122; Vedic 82, 92, 94, 97
thought *see* thinking
Thot 173
Thracian(s) 63
Tibet 55, 143
Timaeus (Plato) 10, 77, 100, 169, 172, 177
Titan(s) 1, 4, 17, 19, 41, 45, 51, 57, 60, 63, 129, 136, 137, 152
transformation (metamorphosis) 3, 8, 10, 12, 16, 20, 21–2, 23, 28, 31, 36, 48, 50, 53, 54, 56, 62, 67, 89, 95–6, 99, 108–13, 115, 119, 123, 125, 127, 128, 130–2, 136, 137, 141, 148–9, 157, 161, 163, 164, 166, 167, 169, 170, 172–7, 184; bestial 62; self- 28, 96
transhumanism 99
transition 49–50, 66, 68, 69, 78, 110, 117, 161, 169
transparency 8, 9, 108, 160, 169
trick 2, 4, 32, 36, 37, 47, 48, 64, 72, 77, 83, 92, 97, 113, 119–22, 173

Subject index 207

trickster: characterisation (overall) 17–8, 25, 44, 109, 121–2, 130; destiny 5, 43, 180, 184; god 21, 149; knowledge 3, 4, 11, 16, 20, 63, 72–3, 93, 94, 105, 106, 121, 122–3, 163 (self- 2); logic 5, 11, 12, 26, 35, 40, 48, 60, 123, 164, 173; as transformer and fixer 25, 28–9
Trickster Makes This World, The (Hyde) 61
troglodytes 10, 12, 57, 117, 119–41, 147–50, 152, 156–7, 158, 167, 171, 172, 175, 176, 182; characterisation (overall) 149; logic 144
trust 18, 35, 41, 62, 76, 94, 134, 140
turbulence 62, 155, 156, 168, 169
Ture (Zande spider trickster) 24, 25–30, 37
Turkey 12, 53, 57, 125
Twilight of the Idols (Nietzsche) 42
Typhoeus 126
tyranny 108, 168; of the majority (Tocqueville) 178

Ulysses 44, 49
uncanniness 29
uncertainty 30, 33, 42, 86, 87, 114, 167
unconscious 25, 58
underground 10, 31, 117, 123, 124, 125, 129, 131, 134, 137, 142, 149, 150; cave 36, 124; dwelling 63, 123, 149; people 123–4; structures 3, 12, 57, 117, 124, 128, 130, 132, 134, 135, 139, 143, 144, 148, 152, 154, 172, 183
underworld 16, 31
union 97, 108, 116, 147–9, 160, 166, 174, 175
universal machine (Turing) 98
universalism xi, xv, 5, 7, 9, 26, 40, 41, 52, 76, 81, 97, 115, 122, 160, 166, 175, 185
unlimited *see* limitlessness
unreality 3, 4, 16, 30, 34, 39, 49, 54, 86, 87, 105, 117, 120, 123, 130, 144, 147, 151, 152, 162, 163, 164, 165, 169, 176, 183, 184, 185; super 4
unspeakable 11, 53, 57, 58, 59, 68, 101, 127; rituals 39, 59; *see also* arrheton
uterus *see* womb

values 8, 48, 92, 94, 178; evil 7–8; of modernity 43; revaluation (Nietzsche) 81, 91, 92, 93; universalistic xv, 7, 185
Vedas 77, 79, 99, 100
Vedic reasoning 81

velocity *see* speed
vengeance 34, 149, 154
vibration 37, 126, 129, 139, 150, 157, 158, 160, 175
victim 28, 33, 44, 51, 80, 98, 101, 109, 115, 116, 120, 127, 135, 137, 138, 150, 158, 182; sacrificial 87–8, 92, 97, 116; *see also* consent
violence xi, 8, 16, 27, 29, 33, 54, 57, 58, 60, 62, 80, 83, 92, 94, 95, 96, 97, 116, 129, 145, 151, 173, 183
virtuality xii, 172
virtue 54, 60, 69, 76, 87, 100–1, 106, 131, 150, 163, 164, 171, 176
void xii, 8, 9, 10, 29, 62, 114, 129, 1 33, 146, 147, 148, 150, 155, 156, 159, 165–8, 172, 175; logic of 165
vulgarity 57, 60, 67, 107, 149, 152, 154; evil 106
vulva 56

wall(s) 10, 125, 131, 132, 143, 148, 157, 182, 184; polygonal 28, 144
war(s)/ warfare xi, 29, 50, 53, 54, 60, 61, 63, 163, 169, 178, 184; all against all (Hobbes) 91; permanent 182; WWI 15; WWII 183–4
wave(s) 33, 77, 100, 134, 155, 184
wealth xii, 58, 127, 128, 155, 167, 174, 175
weaving 28, 82, 99, 141; *see also* net, spin, spider, web
web 28–9, 31, 42, 82, 126, 128, 148; *see also* net
will to power 51
Winnebago 18, 31
witchcraft 11, 24, 32–41, 42
witch doctor 11, 25, 33–7, 42, 141; *see also* magician, sorcerer
witches Sabbath 33
womb 56, 67, 107, 114, 115, 132, 148, 155, 167, 176; *see also* matrix
world: conflict-free 115; escaping 83, 84, 145; of Hermes 48; religious rejection of (Weber) 83; second founder of 15, 16, 17, 20, 21, 23, 91, 93, 94, 123, 142; trickster 29; upside down 22, 173, 184; vision 32 (Gnostic 55, 77–8, 91, 100, 149; Greek tragic, 99; Magi 68, 79; Magi-Gnostic 64; Newtonian 70; Palaeolithic 82, 85, 89, 93; Platonic 96, 101; resentful 93; sacrificial 89, 90–3, 101; scientific xi, 40–1, 51, 70; Sophist 55; sorcerer 38, 39; trickster

24, 55, 93, 108; Vedic 77-8, 80, 84-5, 89, 91, 93, 99-100, 101; Zande 40)
wrestling 78

Yazılıkaya sanctuary 56
Y-shape 10, 110, 115, 117, 125, 127, 128, 148, 152

Zagreus 153, 154
Zalmoxis 63
Zarathustra (Nietzsche) 78
zero xii, 10, 101, 122, 147, 170, 171
Zeus 17, 45, 51, 52, 60, 126, 129, 152
ziggurat 167, 175, 179